THE WORLD AT MY FEET

SANDIE SHAW

The World at My Feet

A Personal Adventure

HarperCollins

An Imprint of HarperCollins*Publishers*

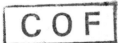
First published in Great Britain in 1991
by HarperCollins Publishers,
77–85 Fulham Palace Road,
Hammersmith, London W6 8JB

9 8 7 6 5 4 3 2 1

BRITISH LIBRARY CATALOGUING IN PUBLICATION DATA

Shaw, Sandie
The world at my feet: a personal adventure.
1. Great Britain. Pop music.
I. Title
782.42164092

ISBN 0-00-215921-X

Photoset in Linotron Bembo by
Rowland Phototypesetting Ltd,
Bury St Edmunds, Suffolk

Printed and bound in Great Britain by
HarperCollins Book Manufacturing, Glasgow

To all the people who took part in my adventure. Thank you for helping me to put my past into context, clarify my place in the present, and open up the infinite, exciting possibilities of the future.

ACKNOWLEDGEMENTS

I'd like to thank the following people: Jeremy Pascall, for starting me off; Mike Fishwick, for champagne and sympathy; Juliet Van Oss, for hanging in there; Dick Causton, for his advice; Charles and Cathy, for their patience; Grace, for her opinions; Amie and Jack, for the lighter moments; Nik, for putting up with my sleepless nights; Mum and Dad, for providing the nest.

CONTENTS

PART ONE

Best Foot Forward

Deep Throat

16TH JUNE, 1986. The first day of my first tour in Britain for twenty years.

I woke up with glorious sunshine streaming through my bedroom windows and I had a lump in my throat. Well, not so much a lump, really, more like someone had tried to throttle me in my sleep. Nerves, I thought. Psychosomatic. Or maybe I had tried to strangle myself in a dream. Whatever it was, it was there and could not be denied. With dreadful consistency, every time I swallowed, I felt it – The Lump. Dr Punt would have to be sought out once again.

Good old Dr Punt! The first time I had visited his rooms was at the beginning of my first recordings for Polydor Records a few months before. I had insisted on doing guide vocals during rehearsals so that the band could build their arrangements around my voice rather than the other way around, as I'd struggled to do all those years ago in my early recordings in the Sixties. Anyway, I'd caught a cold, and sang myself into a frenzy straining to be heard over the band. The result was hoarse vocal chords and flagging throat muscles. I was assured by my brand new business manager, Charles Negus-Fancey, that Dr Punt could save the day.

I had never had my voice treated before – there wasn't such a thing in my teens. We just sang until we croaked, and then we croaked until we dropped, and then we were carried off to bed with a bottle of cough linctus. I was always losing my voice then. Every other newspaper cutting seemed to have a picture of me ill in bed, nursing my throat, and now I was petrified that this would happen again. Feeling apprehensive, I asked Cathy, who worked with Charles, to

3

come along for my first appointment to give me moral support.

It didn't start too well. After a series of saucy Diana Dors jokes on the way about her real name having been Diana Fluck, and her local mayor getting nervous at the town hall benefit and introducing her wrongly as Diana Clunt, Cathy absent-mindedly mispronounced Dr Punt's name on the entryphone. As the receptionist opened the door she found the embarrassed Cathy collapsed in a reddened heap at my feet. At that moment she was about as much support as an over-washed panty girdle.

Now here I was again, this time with Charles, waiting to undergo the humiliation of the treatment. I think Dr Punt knows you're not faking when you come back for more.

The frayed affluence of his Chelsea address and scarcity of free appointments indicated that he must be good, otherwise he would not be doing so well out of all those stricken operatic divas, tongue-tied thespians and West End prima donnas who were said to queue desperately for his attentions. The theatrics that must have gone down in here, I thought, as I waited my turn and studied the well-paced carpet.

My first visit was still playing on my hyperactive imagination. The weird and wonderful ritual to which I had been witness had had a mystic, occult quality, with all the pent-up psychic tension of a tarot card reading. As I entered, his room had seemed dark and ominous. He sat at his desk like an ageing Merlin. First he had taken down my notes. He peered up at me over bifocals. 'You're a mezzo soprano,' he revealed. 'That's good. It makes things a lot easier. Sopranos are a devil to treat,' he added mysteriously.

He led me over to the treatment chair. I sat down meekly. My heart pounded furiously as I observed the strange silver bowls of bubbling liquid being heated over a small flame. I held tightly onto my Filofax like a talisman, my knuckles turning white. I listened with mounting terror at the strangled noises I voiced when I attempted to follow his instructions.

'Say AH!' he urged.

'URGH!' I gagged, as he held my tongue out firmly with a

piece of gauze. He peered way down my throat past my tonsils with elegant long-stemmed mirrors. I gazed spellbound at the shiny instruments resembling an alchemist's kit. Suddenly he stuck one of them up my indignant nose.

'This won't feel very nice,' he understated. Then he fed a long tube down into the dark caverns of my thorax and dropped his magic liquid formula on to my sore vocal chords.

'It's fine,' I lied, and nearly threw up all over him.

Very soon it felt as if a large apple had got stuck in my gullet.

'You'd better rest your voice for a few hours. Don't talk,' he advised.

'Fat chance with this Granny Smith jammed down my throat,' I attempted to mutter.

After punching me playfully on the cheek to demonstrate how I had been mistreating my voice, he submitted me to the final indignity . . . I was asked to bend over and expose my other cheek. He explained that the steroids injection he was about to give me would stimulate my glands to make hormones rush to the rescue wherever there was inflammation. I went home terrified that I would sprout hair on my chest. I examined myself hourly in front of the mirror.

But it worked. The next morning I sang like a bird – thankfully still a mezzo soprano and not a baritone.

Charles led me out by the arm after my second bout of treatment. The injection deadens the leg, so I was dragging it along behind me like Quasimodo as I hobbled out of the surgery. Heaven knows what Dr Punt's neighbours made of this strange procession of patients limping out of his house, clutching at their throats.

Unholy Trinity

THE SUN BEAT DOWN INSISTENTLY on our heads as Charles drove me home from Dr Punt's in his ancient but highly credible open-topped Golf. I looked up at the sky – not a cloud in sight. A good omen. It had pissed down unrelentingly throughout the three-week rehearsals.

I couldn't decide what to wear on stage at Cambridge. I had been hit by a sudden attack of indecisiveness, probably brought on by my TV appearance on 'Whistle Test' the week before. Clothes have always been a pain to me. I like wearing them as long as they don't pinch or trip me up, but I can't bear wasting time thinking about them, planning them, choosing them, shopping for them or trying them on – not a very good attitude for someone in the public eye. One of the things I enjoyed about my early retirement was being rid of the obsession with appearance that seems to go with the job.

'Steven', a song I had then just written about Morrissey, has the lines, *'You dressed me in my gladrags, you in your gladioli'*. It refers to the first time, in 1984, that he asked me to join him and the Smiths on stage, at the Hammersmith Palais. I hadn't a clue what to wear then, either. Luckily Morrissey relished the task of dressing me up. Before the performance I turned up at his flat with a huge pile of clothes and did an hour-long fashion parade in the kitchen while he scoffed tubs of vegetarian goodies from Marks & Sparks. Finally he proclaimed, 'I want you to walk on stage as if you've just walked in off the street,' and dismissed all the outfits with a theatrical wave of his teaspoon. He insisted I wore the jeans I arrived in, and a fresh Smiths tee-shirt. He lent me his belt to hold my jeans up and then took great pains over selecting a blue plastic popper-bead necklace from his bag of jewellery. Something old, something new, something borrowed, something blue . . .

Since then, I had developed my own sense of how I wanted to look as I went along. It's funny how a pop star's image evolves. It doesn't happen overnight – it's a gradual metamorphosis. One day you're stuck at home wearing the faded old tracksuit with babyfood stains down the front, the next you're in the studio feeling more comfortable in zebra-striped leggings and a biker's jacket. I wonder if Diana Ross ever worries about what to wear for the weekly supermarket run, or Cher when she drops the kid off at the nursery on the way to a production conference?

I still feel slightly schizoid about it. I had of late managed to acquire several different personae, with outfits to match, that covered all the different aspects of my life. This helped the people around me to know what I was up to at that particular moment. Sometimes I was in such a rush I didn't have time to change, or else I had so much to do I got in a muddle. Then I confused everyone by turning up at a Buddhist meeting in full stage make-up and eye-catching gear or arriving in the photographic studio in the school visiting get-up of pleated skirt and Scotch House jumper. Anyhow, everyone knows that if I've got no make-up on, haven't been to the hairdresser for a week and have forgotten to change my outfit for two days running, then I'm busy writing and they all wisely steer well clear.

For 'Whistle Test', I popped down to the shops, armed with my budding but fragile confidence in the clothes department, and selected some great miniskirts in black, white and denim, all very 'girl-next-door', or rather, 'woman-next-door'. I asked my artist friend Laurence Stevens, whose collages splattered my daughter Grace's bedsit walls, to design a polo-necked tee-shirt. I gave him some of my recent photos to work with, plus letters from Morrissey and cuttings from a series of old fan albums that my hairdresser friend Keith Wainwright had picked up in Camden market. The result was F-A-B.

Being the implacable eccentric that I am, I decided to christen the 'look' on 'Whistle Test'. This TV programme, the Eighties answer to 'Thank Your Lucky Stars', was directed by two extremely affable and efficient young women, who looked and sounded suitably trendy with their spiked hairdos and Glaswegian accents. Believing in the enlightened female consciousness of the Eighties, I donned my outfit and cast my fate to the winds. Naively, I felt safe in the knowledge that we had grown out of the Sixties habit of sex-crazed up-the-skirt shots.

I marched bravely on to the set in my polo neck, minimal skirt and fringed boots. The smoke machine belched merrily away, creating a seductive, smoky atmosphere suitable for a thoroughly modern Mrs like me. I threw myself around with my usual gay abandon, totally unaware of what the man with the hand-held camera was doing at my feet. At home I watched the show in horror as he started focusing on my feet, then my ankles, my knees, then zoomed up into the realms of my extreme embarrassment. Thank goodness I don't have cellulite!

I was shocked rigid. The youngest kids, then aged two and four, sat perplexed and silent, not sure who that funny lady was and what she had to do with Mummy.

'W-E-L-L?' asked Grace, my sixteen-year-old, accusingly.

I rushed out of the room. I didn't know who to talk to – who does a mature woman-of-the-world confide in at moments like this? I phoned my mum.

'Don't be such a prude,' she scolded. 'Me and your dad loved it!'

The next morning I was still in a state of shock. I decided to reserve my miniskirts for very special 'alternative' situations. Goodbye knees!

So here I was on this sizzling hot day in June pondering what to wear for the first date of my first tour for twenty years at a Cambridge University May Ball. As the same old panic started to grip me, I decided to make no decision at all and flung everything I had into suitcases. (Some people say I'm indecisive, but I'm not sure!) Charles and Cathy were extremely patient as they loaded my junk into the shabby Golf which was already bulging with contracts, sweetie packets, and what looked like Charles's art-student son's dirty laundry.

The journey to Cambridge was hot, sticky and rather uncomfortable for all of us. The 'iron butterflies' were already racing around my stomach. I had no idea what to expect.

Cambridge is a beautiful town teeming with intense young women balancing elegantly on bicycles, wearing Laura Ashley prints, their frizzy hair tied sexily back in buns. The river is full of intense young men in baggy trousers and slicked-back hair balancing clumsily on punts to impress these young women. They reminded me of Jonathan King's hilariously macho attempts to romance me on my visits to Cambridge with him while he was acquiring his English degree. Poor Jonathan tried in vain to convince the world that he was having an affair with me. I acted as his 'walker' at the Cromwellian Club and in return he protected me from the over ardent approaches of drunken pop musicians.

As I re-entered the gates of Trinity I had to fight back old emotions about class. I can't bear exclusivity of any kind, especially when it's me that's left out! The very nature of Oxbridge seems to encourage a feeling of superiority that it's your job, your place in life to continue tradition and run the world. I think that it's jealousy on my part. I would love to have spent my youth amongst piles of dusty old books, jotting down the odd thesis between stimulating lectures from sexy long-haired dons − a life totally impossible for someone who discovers the joys of formal learning so late in life.

Trinity College is at first overwhelming. You would need great self-assurance to measure up to the sheer magnitude of the place. History clings heavily to its muscular walls.

Brian Johnson, the tour manager, was standing sentry at the gates. He had already been nicknamed 'Nice Man' by the band for bringing unusual humanity to a job that is renowned for its ferocity in keeping unruly musicians, self-willed road crew, and egotistical stars in line and on time, and ensuring money owed is paid by reticent promoters. In other words, he allowed them to get away with murder – providing it did not affect me directly.

'Everything's fine,' he grinned, unconvincingly. I could feel his nervousness and it was reassuring to know that someone else felt the same way. It was a perfectly natural reaction – none of us knew what to expect.

We pinned on our identity badges, 'ACCESS ALL AREAS – SANDIE SHAW'. They were so pretty – little pictures of my single sleeve for 'Are You Ready To Be Heartbroken?' printed on bright pink. I think I will keep these and the matching tour itinerary for ever. I have them neatly filed away under 'Mementoes' along with the gold star from the dressing-room door at the London Palladium '66, another star from the Olympia Theatre in Paris '65, and a few old frocks circa '64 to '69. Today, these stage passes really clinched the feeling that – YES! – I was here at last, two decades on, an Eighties icon on the University Tour I'd always wanted to do.

Brian led us through a vast maze of stark, towering walls and garrison-like gates to a grassed quadrangle enclosed by ancient buildings. We entered one of the doorways and went up the time-worn stone slabs. At the top of the staircase was a scruffy, threadbare study. Posters of obscure drama productions plastered the walls. Postcards from Paris and Florence crammed full of tiny, introverted handwriting were propped on the mantelpiece. Literature burst out of the bookcases – the whole place reeked of centuries of frenzied swotting. Large lattice windows opened out on to the quadrangle and the twangs and thumps of Katrina and the Waves' sound check flooded into the room.

I settled in and did my singing exercises along to the cassette tape my singing teacher Ian Adams had made for me. The tape meant I could take him with me everywhere.

'Now I want you to sing through your nose making the sound "UNG" like a you-en-gee, going into the vowel and coming back to E,' cooed his soothing Scottish tones over the piano guide. As the tour progressed Ian would often come to mind while I was on stage, urging me to use my bum muscles for a more powerful sound. It was hard to keep a straight face.

While I did my exercises, fresh-faced youngsters tapped on the door at various intervals asking for Anthony, whose room I was borrowing. They probably wondered why Anthony was making such funny noises.

I went down to explore the grounds. I came across a group of officials briefing the security men on how to identify and keep out those frightful cads who hadn't paid a hundred guineas to get in. They were warned to look out for people faking tickets, feigning illness, climbing over walls, paddling in from the river or shinning up trees – all in their dinner jackets and ball gowns. It seems there's nothing these upstarts won't stop at to gain entry into this well-heeled, beefy-brained fortress.

Neatly kitted-out caterers flitted about organizing the booze and banquets, occasionally stopping to mop their sweaty brows with a stray napkin. The heat was by now practically unbearable. An elderly waiter reminded me that the last time I had performed at a Cambridge May Ball was twenty years ago and he had been working there then too. I closed my eyes and it all came back . . .

Prince Charles had been in the audience and I had had great fun pulling his leg during the act. Apparently it went down rather well. They said I caught his fancy, though I couldn't see for myself. I'm as blind as a bat. I had given up wearing spectacles since Leslie Purkiss had cruelly snubbed me in music class at school. The contact lenses of the time were those nasty glass things that felt like huge lumps of grit in your eye. I tried them once and cried for days. I decided that I'd rather fumble about and risk making a surprise new friend.

Things were less sophisticated twenty years ago. I had sung in the open air on the steps of Trinity with a single spotlight, a couple of knee-high speakers and my little four-piece band that sounded exactly like a little four-piece band. It was a wonder anyone heard us at all.

A downpour of rain in a later year must have precipitated the introduction of the marquee, which was quite unnecessary tonight. It was so hot that standing still proved a most exhausting task. Everyone glowed pink and trickled with perspiration.

'If only I had an electric fan on stage,' I fantasized, and bumped
into someone carrying one. Great, now there was a slight chance
that I might survive the performance.

Back in the dressing-room, everything I tried on felt sticky
and uncomfortable. After my 'Whistle Test' experience I didn't
want to wear a miniskirt, even though it would be cool – the
stage was high enough for the front-line audience to have a great
view of my privates. So I grabbed a pair of scissors and cut the
legs off my jeans right up to my bum. Hello again knees! I
threaded a CND chain through the belt loops and popped on a
Sandie Shaw tee-shirt, then I slung a denim jacket over my
shoulders. I left the trouser legs hanging from the mantelpiece
autographed 'Love to Anthony'.

The temperature and atmosphere had become almost tropical.
The bottles of Chablis were warming up and the fresh-cut
flowers drooping. The ever-ready Brian clattered up and down
the stone-flagged Gothic staircase with buckets of ice for the
wine, like Steerpike in *Gormenghast*. Cathy and Charles happily
took care of the Chablis while they busied themselves doing all
those backstage things that make an artist's life easier. I used the
ice buckets for my feet.

Outside, through the open windows, we could see the various
groups of taffeta'd and dickie-bowed graduates and undergrad-
uates queuing for strawberries and cream or a hunk of roasted
flesh from some poor dead animal being turned on a spit. All
kinds of weird and wonderful cocktails were being consumed
with carefree gusto. Security guards were still vetting a long
queue of hopefuls desperately waving their tickets whilst being
serenaded by a jolly Caribbean band.

The night was full of contrasts – the cold, rigid walls of
tradition and the hot sweaty atmosphere of the marquee; the
frontstage person uncomfortably stuffed into formal attire and
the backstage person clad sensibly in vest and jeans; the neatly
clipped tones of the Cambridge grad and the Cockney twang
and northern drawls of the road crew.

Renee, Charles's secretary, arrived in a rubber boob tube and
bottom-pinching skirt, her hair scruffed up into a frenetic blonde

mass. She stood out like Struwwelpeter in the sea of lace and frills. Later she discovered my husband Nik's mobile telephone, which she grabbed with drunken girlish delight and proceeded to phone her father, a foot doctor, in Iowa to negotiate a price for him to treat my bunions.

Nik, having made his own way there, was having an informative conversation with a stage-struck security guard, who, unaware of Nik's identity, confided what he'd like to do with me given half the chance. Nik listened sympathetically, then said, 'I did that with her last night – and she's not that good!'

I was ready to go on. The band, followed by my bare-legged self, trooped over to the back of the tent, where we hopped around nervously like newly trained gladiators awaiting our first trial of strength in the arena. I peeked through the curtain. Massive piles of speakers towered either side of the stage like sentries guarding the vast assembly of technological dreamware. A bank of monitors distinguished the boundary line between the watchers and the watched. The floor was littered with wires and leads and all manner of equipment. It was light years away from my little knee-high speakers. I wondered how the hell I was supposed to find my way on through all that foreign-looking junk. The band filed on to plug into their stacks of amplifiers, and there was even less room for me.

Suddenly I heard someone shout my name to the crowd. My head span and my stomach did flip flops but instinctively I propelled myself forward to meet the roar of welcome. I strode on to the stage. It felt more like my front room – not in the least bit strange.

For a brief second, with the torrid chords of 'Hand In Glove' jangling in my ears like giant sparkly fruit spangles, I thought, 'What on earth am I doing here? Did I let Nik know I was going out? Did I leave something for the kids to eat? Have I cancelled the milk? Did I leave the washing on?' Then, as if programmed to respond automatically to an audience, I started to sing, and I felt a power and a joy in my life that was immense and frightening. I had forgotten it existed and now it was a million times more overwhelming. What a feeling! It hit me with a surge of pure delight. A moment's panic threatened yet again. I was entering new territory here. I toyed with the idea of turning round and going home.

'Oh, what the heck,' I thought. 'There's no going back now. Might as well just lie back and enjoy it.' And I did.

Verse, Chorus, Verse, Chorus, Middle Eight and Out

THE NEXT DAY WAS SPENT AT Westside Recording Studios with producers Clive Langer and Alan Winstanley. We were making a B side to go with the release of 'Frederick', my second single for Polydor Records, with whom I had recently signed a deal to make two singles leading on to an album.

The musicians Clive and Alan had chosen for me were wonderful. They were Kevin Armstrong, a guitarist who had just finished working with David Bowie, Steve Nieve, Elvis Costello's keyboard player, Neil Conti who subsequently became Prefab Sprout's drummer, and on bass James Eller who later joined Chrissie Hynde's Pretenders. I could not believe my luck at having such a supportive and talented team. They loved all my old work and really cared about the new recordings, bringing fresh ideas with them every day. On their days off they popped in with a wife or a friend to listen to the mixes.

I sang along self-consciously doing guide vocals while they put down layer after delicious layer of guitars, drum patterns, and bass riffs. I would stay late at night while Steve Nieve invented intricate keyboard programming, taking in everything, absorbing it all in a crash course in contemporary production.

I was just beginning to get into the swing of current recording techniques. It was quite an experience recording again. The modest four-track engineer's panel of the early Sixties looked like a pre-school Lego set compared with the mass of knobs and switches on a forty-eight channel Solid State Logic desk.

Walking into the studio with its banks of twinkling lights was like boarding Starship Enterprise. Alan and Clive sat at the controls like Dr Spock and Captain Kirk waiting for me to embark on our new journey chartwards, to boldly go where no other pop star had ever been before. My first recordings back here on planet Earth in the Sixties had been so different.

It would all start in Dinely's Rehearsal Rooms with Chris Andrews, my songwriter. Chris and I had grown up around the corner from each other, nourished by the factory fumes and inspired by the smoggy atmosphere of Dagenham.

We would arrange to meet in the smallest, cheapest room. There was just enough space for him, me, and two cups of tea balanced precariously on an upright piano. He would immediately dust off the piano lid and begin to plonk away on the yellowed keys with all his latest bits of tunes and lyric ideas. We drew on our shared urban angst, purging our pain in song, laughing so much we usually spilt the tea over our notes and had to write the whole thing all over again.

I was very sure of my likes and dislikes and I directed him. 'Yes. No. Yuk. I like that bit. Not that. That's good, let's stick that bit on the first bit and rewrite the middle.' I was ruthless and totally primitive in my taste.

This gawky creative process in that grotty little room led to about forty hit singles being written for world consumption, seventeen in the UK alone, plus albums of glorious primal teenage self-expression. Chris's unhappy first marriage, my fumbling attempts at romance, our successes and our tragedies would usually lead to yet another song. We relived our lives in verse, chorus, verse, chorus, middle eight and out.

With our new songs written on tea-stained paper we then visited the arranger, Kenny Woodman. We had a quick run-through on the piano to check the key and then Chris and I imitated the noises of the instruments in the places we wanted them to go in the song. Kenny would translate our efforts into squiggly dots and dashes on fresh music sheets, while Chris and I stuck our heads out of the window to avoid choking on his pipe smoke. That done, Kenny would contact a Musicians Union booker, who 'fixed' the musicians to do the recording session.

Chris and I would then spend the night down the Bag o' Nails club, talking to all the pop musicians and stars who congregated there, listening to the black American sounds and West Indian blue beat and ska music that we loved, and ignoring the increasingly ferocious phone calls from Chris's German wife from his doomed first marriage. I often left him there, drinking himself under the table with Bill Wyman. He used to get through about three containers of Gold Spot on his way home to her, to mask the smell of the brandy he had downed to be able to face the inevitable confrontation. Occasionally I had to cover up for him. I didn't mind, Chris was my best buddy, the big brother I had always longed for.

At the appointed hour Chris and I arrived for the recording session. Everyone crowded in to the jam-packed studio. I nervously picked my way past the harp, the cor anglais, French horn and cellos, squeezed between the Hammond organ and vibes (both musical and atmospheric) and clambered noisily over the drum boxes and percussion paraphernalia to my corner behind a sound screen. I sat there silently, in purdah, in my glass box.

Kenny Woodman would flurry in with music parts piled up to his pipe which he distributed to the musicians. They all had zappy names like Vick Flick, Herby Flowers, and the Ladybirds. Then Kenny stood uncomfortably on the conductor's stand while they tuned up.

The musicians spent the afternoon alternately looking at the parts, reading copies of dirty magazines, studying the form in the racing papers, and glancing at the clock for opening time. Every so often there was a 'take'.

Everything was recorded at the same time on the four-track machine, in mono. The brass went on one track, strings on another, rhythm and backing singers on the third, and my voice on the fourth. If anyone went wrong, everyone else turned round and glared at the perpetrator or fell about laughing and we had to start all over again.

More than three takes on any one song, including my vocals which were done at the same time, was highly unusual.

'Dropping in', that is, cutting into the track to go over and redo the mistakes and iffy bits, just didn't happen. Consequently the adrenalin ran thick and fast.

An A and B side would be recorded and mixed in an afternoon. An album of twelve songs would take three. On reflection, it had a lot in common with the Dagenham production line I thought I had escaped.

The production team were Chris, Kenny, Bill Street the engineer, and myself, though only my manager's name, Eve Taylor, appeared on the label. 'You don't want people thinking you have to produce your own records!' she reasoned astutely, then took the credit herself.

In fact, because of her penchant for hysterical tantrums, usually brought on by one of my trendier musical ideas that did not fit into the budget, we usually locked her out of the studio until we were finished. She would enter the control room regally to listen to the final mix with relief and delight. As time went by Eve forgave me for not being Shirley Bassey and became one of my biggest fans, and I grew to depend on her emotionally more and more.

To be fair, Eve's motives, though misconceived, were well-intentioned. She only wanted to hang on to as much money as she could – for both of us; but I would rather have made good records with it, and anyway we didn't have time for Eve's hysteria – we had hits to make.

TIME = MONEY

At the age of seventeen I learnt this lesson the hard way. I quickly perfected the art of choosing material, recording, mixing and delivering a master in the minimum amount of time for the minimum amount of money.

No one seemed to care whether I knew the songs or sang in tune, as long as my voice was captured on record. As far as they were concerned, the end product was just wonderful. On the up-side it enabled me to be spontaneous – a rare gift now in these days of perfectly packaged, precisely programmed excuses for pop culture. However, I feel that I could have really developed as an artist given the time and money that is lavished on today's successful artists. Still, if I had reached my peak then, there would be no point in my singing now, would there?

I saw Kenny Woodman, my old arranger, again a few years ago. We rerecorded 'Always Something There To Remind Me' for the soundtrack of the film *Letter to Brezhnev*.

I asked him a question that had been nagging at me for years, 'Ken, you know when I thought I was singing funny and I asked you if I was flat and you said "No"? Well, I've been listening to those records again recently and I'm definitely singing flat in places.'

'No no, Sandie, you never ever sang flat,' he reassured me. Then, after a tug on his pipe, he added, '*Sharp* maybe . . . but never flat!'

I was dumbfounded.

'We thought, why mess with the mechanics of genius! So we kept it in,' he laughed.

He had a point. Nowadays, when you have so many ways of perfecting and changing the original vocal or visual performance, the danger is that you also take away the unique qualities, the character of a performer. I am singing my life, not a computer sample that can be thrown on the vinyl junk heap. I don't give a toss if that's considered old-fashioned!

Two Time Lords ruled over my recording world then. One was Eve Taylor, who controlled the Purse Strings. Although we co-financed the recordings, it was she who knew how to do those mysterious things like pay bills, write invoices, haggle over prices, and – the ultimate mystery – write cheques. I never wrote a cheque before my first marriage at twenty-one. Although I was earning fortunes I just had pocket money and a clothes allowance. Eve opened up accounts for me everywhere – that was all I needed. I just walked into shops, ordered things, and the bills were somehow paid.

The other Time Lord was the Musicians' Union booker, who, like the White Rabbit in *Alice in Wonderland*, was obsessed with time, and not in the least bit interested in music. He hung around the studio, his eyes glued to the clock. As soon as the hand passed the three-hour session period, a curious gleam illuminated his face and my heart would sink.

Now it was Time To Negotiate and White Rabbit was in his element. Time-and-a-half rates were in order to complete the track. At that point Evie Purse Strings, turning up at the end of the session expecting to hear the final mix, would intervene. Recording stopped. We had to use what we had in the can. White Rabbit slunk out of the studio without his carrots, and the musicians packed up their instruments, dirty books and racing results and adjourned to the pub with Kenny.

Early habits die hard. To this day, like one of Pavlov's dogs, my reaction to a red light is quite extraordinary. The adrenalin rushes round my body and the excitement of knowing that NOW is the most important time of my life rules everything. Whenever I see a traffic light turn to red I feel an uncontrollable urge to break into song.

The seductive sparkling lights of Clive and Alan's high-tech recording desk had enticed me back to the microphone. It was not easy. I was nervous and apprehensive about the results. I felt awkward and inexperienced in these new surroundings. Everybody kept looking at me as if I knew all the answers, expecting me to act like the superstar they imagined me to be. I think I threw everyone by arriving by tube at the beginning of each session instead of turning up in a limo at the end.

However, everything went smoothly. The music spread over the tracks like butter. It was really cooking. Soon it was time for the icing on the cake – my vocal track. All the musicians stayed behind to listen. I was frazzled with fear. The voice of a girl of seventeen would obviously be different from mine. What would my voice sound like now? Had I picked the right key? Would they expect me to be perfect first time? Would they like what they heard? What was I doing here anyway? Was I kidding myself to think that I had anything of relevance to offer to the world? Was I too old for this game? Should I roll over and make room for someone new? What the hell was I trying to prove? Was this really fun? I felt like a total novice. I asked if I could take a break and do my evening Buddhist practice of *gongyo*. Clive cleared the studio and Alan gave me some atmospheric lighting to help me on my way. They tiptoed out in a reverent hush.

I knelt alone on the bare wooden floor at the foot of the mike stand, next to the drum kit, and recited the two key chapters of the Buddhist teaching called the *Lotus Sutra* and chanted '*Nam-myoho-renge-kyo*'. I continued chanting until all my questions were answered satisfactorily and my confidence started flooding back.

When I returned to the control room it was empty except for Clive. 'I'm just sending out for a drink. I don't suppose you indulge – with all that stuff you've been doing?' he said nervously.

To his surprise and mine, I heard myself saying, 'I really fancy a big vodka and tonic.' I hadn't had one in years. I knocked it back, returned to the studio and just sang till he told me to stop.

When I walked into the control room Clive and Alan were beaming.

'Well fancy that,' muttered Clive to Alan. 'One drink and three takes and we've got it. A drink always does the trick. I never thought she'd be like everyone else.'

From that moment our relationship changed. We stopped being over-awed producers and paranoid pop star and began to relax with each other. While I was not quite 'one of the boys', I was no longer 'one of the girls'. I even started writing songs with Clive, notably 'Steven (You Don't Eat Meat)'.

The chemistry was absolutely right. It was clear to all of us that we were on to something special. In that first set of sessions we recorded three stunning songs, 'Are You Ready To Be Heartbroken?', 'Frederick', and 'Steven', and started on an amazing treatment of 'A Girl Called Johnny'. It would have made perfect sense to carry on and make a sensational debut album, but at this point Polydor, in line with their contractual rights, wanted to stop and put out a first single to test the market reaction.

My original misgivings about the contract being based around a singles structure proved to be valid. Deep down I knew that as soon as I got into the studio it would just snowball, and that to make my work purposeful, to do justice to myself artistically, I would naturally come up with something more substantial than the factory-farmed singles of the past.

I really should have trusted myself more but in those first tentative steps I had not developed enough confidence to go all the way. I was devastated when Polydor called a halt to the recording.

Yes!!!

THE SECOND AND THIRD DATES on the University Tour were Newcastle and Liverpool. There was a marked difference between the privileged corridors of Cambridge and the struggling institutions of the Northern cities. This was poignantly illustrated by the contrast between the information communicated by the common rooms and toilets of the three universities. While Cambridge posters sedately announced debates and forthcoming dramatic events, with not even a roll of loo paper littering the pristine toilets, the walls of Newcastle and Liverpool were ablaze with news of protest marches against apartheid and Clause Twenty Eight, and their toilet doors were scrawled with Rape Crisis numbers and feminist slogans. As Cambridge studiously preserved the status quo, Newcastle and Liverpool merrily undermined it.

We were met by the entertainment reps of the Students' Union, Jona, a black beauty, and his assistant, a handsome blond. They were noticeably excited by my visit, and kept falling over each other on the way to the dressing-room in their efforts to please. They made such a fuss of me.

At this point I was still finding all this hero worship a little embarrassing. These new young fans I was collecting had only ever known me as some huge untouchable symbol of the past, who had suddenly blessed them with a 'second coming'. I knew myself as the intensely private person I loved to be, wandering around the London underground and local chip shops, the backside hanging out of my trousers, with the wonderful freedom that anonymity brings. If anybody recognized me I didn't notice and I didn't care. When people challenged me, 'Are you who we think you are?', I would deny all knowledge of myself.

23

Of course I knew I could not go on for ever like this, that sooner or later I would have to come to terms with my past and thereby open up my future, but I did not want to give up my liberty – being famous no longer held any fascination for me. It can destroy the soul. Becoming addicted to it suffocates creative and personal freedom.

In the previous five years, since the beginning of the Eighties, I had had a couple of serious attempts at overcoming this dilemma about being famous, but was thwarted each time (or saved, depending on how you look at it!) by the births of my daughter Amie and son Jack.

The first opportunity that presented itself came in 1982 in the shape of a band called Heaven 17. I met them at a garden party in Oxford given by Virgin Records, when Nik Powell, whom I later married, was still its boss along with Richard Branson. I had not had a record out for around a decade. Nik asked me if he could introduce the band to me as they were planning an adventurous new album using different guest artists to sing old songs that they would rearrange electronically.

At that time computerized music was the new saviour of the record industry, although I was not aware of this; I had stopped listening to music during the Seventies, along with millions of others of my generation who deserted the record stores in their hordes. Luckily I had brought along a young friend, Lee, who was really into the stuff and he urged me to have a go. A lot of good fortune comes my way from listening to and respecting young people's opinions, so I accepted the challenge.

We did a beautiful recording of the Bacharach/David song, 'Anyone Who Had A Heart'. It was a wholly new experience for me. Instead of singing with musicians I sang along to machines, no longer in a key or a tempo but in a machine code number. Without the restrictions of unions I was able to do lashings of overdubbing and tracking harmonies. Although I was only a guest on Heaven 17's album, I loved the way I sounded and began to get a dangerous taste for it.

When the album, *Music Of Quality And Distinction*, came out

I was stunned with the reaction from the radio and press. I had no idea that people were still so fond of me or how much they admired my past work. I had always taken myself for granted.

Suddenly, it seemed that everyone I came into contact with turned out to be fans – dee-jays, journalists, directors, producers, cameramen and make-up artists. People from the world I had not been any part of, indeed had actively avoided for over ten years, were very much in awe of me and treated my contribution to their life in terms of music and, I suppose, well . . . British culture (how embarrassing!), with great respect and warmth. Gradually I began to look at myself again with a little more enthusiasm. But my self-confidence was still very fragile, and being on public view was very difficult for me to sustain for more than a few days at a time. Being comfortable with fame does not happen overnight.

By self-confidence I don't mean bravado – I have no trouble being a dare-devil, but that's all front, a fake. What I'm talking about is that deep inner conviction in yourself, in life, that is totally unshakable by any outside event – good or bad. I knew I needed to develop this to come through unscathed the second time around. Any fool can get up and sing. It takes a really wise person to give and receive something of value through the experience.

Around the same time, as a result of *Music Of Quality And Distinction*, Virgin, who released the album, offered me a recording contract, which I was thinking about. I also met Chrissie Hynde of the Pretenders.

I had heard that she was a great admirer. I couldn't believe it. She was new, and was making great records; I couldn't understand what she could possibly see in me.

Mutually intrigued by each other we eventually spoke by telephone. She was on tour. Almost as soon as I put the phone down she rang me back. Would I consider joining the Pretenders on stage for their London concert in two days' time?

I looked down and realized that my nose was peeking out of my shell. I quickly yanked it back in again. 'Oh no. Thank you but no . . . I haven't been on stage in years . . . besides, I have a cold.'

Two days later Chrissie rang again. 'Has your cold cleared up? We're here, at the theatre, all set up for a sound check. We're only round the corner. Just come and have a listen,' she coaxed.

My cold hadn't cleared up, it was Christmas Eve and it was snowing, but I turned up at the Dominion Theatre in Tottenham Court Road half an hour later, swathed in woolly scarves, sucking cough sweets.

The Pretenders – Chrissie, Pete Farndon, James Honeyman-Scott, and Martin Chambers – sat me down in the empty auditorium at the front of the stalls and proceeded to play their version of one of my early songs, 'Girl Don't Come', just for me.

'How do you like it?' asked Chrissie excitedly. 'Is it in your key?'

'Well, yes, I suppose it is in my key.'

'Will you sing it with us tonight then?'

I was very flattered and moved by all their attention. To my horror tears began to well up in my eyes. I blew my nose, having the cold as my excuse. 'Yes I'd love to,' I promised.

That evening I stood in the wings waiting for my cue. This was the first rock concert I had been to since standing backstage in the Sixties to watch bands like the Who, the Stones, or the Beatles. Chrissie looked really good out there, much raunchier, much more equal than the girls of that bygone era. I began to get frightened. I sucked furiously on my throat lozenges. I must have smelt like a chemist shop.

The band came off and went on again for their encore. I was hoping they had forgotten about me. Then the stage manager called me over and Chrissie announced me to the stunned audience. 'We have a big surprise for you. Here is a lady that has been a great inspiration to us all!' I looked around to see if there was any other lady standing in the wings, and then she called my name.

I walked on stage to join them. It was a very special moment. It felt as if it was pre-destined for us all to meet together in this way, and for the first real communication between Chrissie and me to be sung and not spoken. I am for ever indebted to her and the band for dragging me out of my shell. Shortly after that James died of drink and drug abuse and then Pete died of a heroin overdose. Both deaths were accidents. It was a sharp reminder to me of the heavy lows that accompany the terrific highs of stardom.

Chrissie and I discovered we were neighbours, so we often visited each other after this. While rummaging through a box of old press material that my ex-manager Eve Taylor had recently dropped off, my daughter Grace spotted a really funny old photo-card of me smiling sweetly on one side, and mean and moody on the other. As a joke she had put this photo on the mantelpiece, daily displaying the appropriate side to go with my frame of mind.

As soon as Chrissie walked in shortly after Grace had started this, she made a beeline for the photo. I was concerned that she might think I surrounded myself with nostalgic knick-knacks, wallowing in my past like some ageing movie queen, but she was so excited by it that when asked I gave it to her as a memento.

Chrissie and I have a lot in common: we are both brutally honest and I think a little daunting to the faint-hearted. We became great friends. She has a pure and generous heart, and her professional enthusiasm was a great boost to my self-esteem, although I don't think she was aware how much I was struggling then with my self-confidence. In a stray interview at the time with *Melody Maker*, I lost my bottle during the meeting and actually offered the journalist a fiver not to print the article.

Chrissie and I had an immediate rapport. We even found out that we were pregnant at the same time, she by Ray Davies and me by Nik Powell.

My pregnancy instantly solved the problem of whether or not I should sign to Virgin and start recording again. The energy and self-absorbed single-mindedness required to launch a new career in the precarious music business is totally at odds with the hormones rushing round a pregnant woman's body telling her to calm down and build a secure nest for her fledgling. One really has to fight the urge to run round to Mothercare for a wholesome, flowery maternity tent to wear.

On a less romantic note, my usual bouts of morning sickness make it difficult to sing without throwing up. Traditionally, record company men are very nervous about real women who do things like having babies. They are much more comfortable dealing with sex objects.

Chrissie and I spent the next nine months swapping baby tips and gynaecological jokes, marvelling at how two such skinny boyish bodies could swell to such huge womanly proportions. Every time I saw her careering round the corner on the way to a monthly check-up I thought, 'Wow! I'm not *that* big am I?' and I'm sure she thought the same about me.

The next opportunity arrived soon after the birth of Amie. A gush of gorgeous fan letters started arriving at my door. The first, in child-like scrawl, read:

Post House Hotel. London Hampstead. August 8th 1983

Dear Sandie,

We could never begin to emphasize the endless joy we would feel if you would care to listen to our song with a view to possibly covering it.

Obviously the song was written with you in mind. It is an absolute fact that your influence more than any other permeates all our music. Without doubt we are incurable Sandie Shaw fans. Studying all your material, as we do day and night, we felt that your future musical direction must avoid the overt icky momism trap that most of your 60s contemporaries seized.

We have strong ideas about the musical backing which should accompany your version of 'I Don't Owe You Anything'. It should be upbeat and immediate; after all, the audience you left behind was a youthful one – the audience you must seize now must also be youthful. Ken Woodman's arrangement on such as 'Keep In Touch' or 'You've Not

Changed' could easily be an electric guitar. But let's leave the past behind, good as it was. We feel that your future needs an injection of high spirit and vengeance. Should you dislike 'I Don't Owe You Anything' we can supply others with variation. You must surely realize that your name is sufficiently on the lips of young people to demand interest in new, vital product. We would be honoured to provide material for consideration. The Sandie Shaw legend cannot be over yet – there is more to be done!

    Love forever,

      Morrissey (Wordsmith/voice)

      Johnny (multi-instrumentalist/composer)

      THE SMITHS

It was delivered by Nik one weekend when he joined me as usual at our seaside cottage. It was a welcome break from the industrious insanity of his burgeoning new film production company, Palace Pictures. He came tumbling in the door, film scripts piled up to his chin, with more wedged under his arm and bulging out of his shoulder bag. He held a package clenched between his teeth which he dropped at my feet. 'I was having a drink with Geoff Travis from Rough Trade Records and he asked me to do him a favour and pass on some fan mail to you.'

I picked up the sodden package from the carpet along with a nappy, assorted toys and a copy of *Woman's Own*, and tidied it away behind a cushion, where it stayed for a week or so. I came across it one rainy day when Amie was taking her nap. Inside was a cassette and the letter.

At the beginning of the year I had decided to say 'yes' to everything that came my way instead of running in the opposite direction. So one evening a few months later, I joined the Smiths at Matrix, a cheap and cheerful studio, and discovered the intense joy of singing with human beings who loved playing and who respected me, and consequently did not have one eye on the clock and their nose in a dirty magazine.

The drummer and bass player, Mike Joyce and Andy Rourke, are a formidable rhythm team, and the diminutive Johnny Marr, who has a giant talent, plays the guitar with fire and lucidity and total commitment. When we worked together on tracks like 'Jeane' I felt his life open completely to mine. It was inspirational.

Between takes I was bombarded with questions about my records, my work, the Sixties, myself . . . I was taken aback by their detailed knowledge; things I had forgotten or hadn't considered important they treated as major issues. These young men, the Smiths, were unashamedly fans.

By the end of the Sixties, things had distorted to the point where, for many bands, fans were just for bonking and music was just for providing the money to support their hedonistic lifestyles. Even today there is a tendency to treat fans merely as marketing targets for meticulously planned selling campaigns.

Unusually, the Smiths had a great deal of respect for their fans. Their attitude was like a breath of fresh air. Spending more time with them I realized a lot about the unique relationship between an artist and his or her fans; how we develop as one, how completely interdependent we are, the perfect fusion that can be achieved.

The Smiths were masters of this art. They and their fans were mutually created. The Smiths were a band that was truly for the people and of the people. This is why they were totally independent of the record industry merry-go-round. The only way they could be destroyed was from within – just like the youth culture of the Sixties! No wonder I felt at home with them.

Together we completed three triumphant tracks –'Hand In Glove', 'I Don't Owe You Anything', and 'Jeane'.

Rough Trade Records issued 'Hand In Glove' as a single. It went leaping into the charts and – even more exciting – topped the Indie singles. On 'Top of the Pops' I wore stilettos and the Smiths played barefoot.

Quite by surprise I felt that I was teetering on the brink of a personal and professional breakthrough. Rough Trade and the Smiths spoke of doing an album. I was thrilled to bits.

A few weeks later, I met Morrissey to tell him the news.

'You're pregnant?' he repeated incredulously. 'Aren't you brave!'

Once again, overcoming my fear of going into public ownership was shelved while I added to my family. The one difference was the big dollop of record royalties I received from Rough Trade for the single. At last I could afford a nanny to help me with the kids. This was definitely a great change for the better.

I bumped into Chrissie again and she was having another baby too, this time by her new husband, Jim Kerr from Simple Minds. I was so happy to see her so much in love.

I sat patiently through my pregnancy plotting and planning while knitting romper suits and changing nappies. To keep my mind occupied I started writing children's stories. It was all very cuddly and maternal, but deep down I was desperate to zip back into my jeans again. Some days I wondered if my waistline and I had parted company for ever.

After Jack was born in 1985 I decided I wouldn't wait for another opportunity to present itself – I would make the opportunity myself. I asked Charles Negus-Fancey, whom I had met through Chris Andrews, my Sixties songwriter, to be my business manager. Then I signed to Polydor Records.

My waist reappeared courtesy of the tricycle which I acquired to ride around London. Bus and taxi drivers leaned out of their windows and shouted, 'Wotcher Sandie! Making any more records?'

'Nah. Not any more,' I lied, denying myself once more.

As Polydor had now decided to put out 'Are You Ready To Be Heartbroken?' and 'Frederick' as singles and call a halt to my recording for a while, I had no album to promote on the University Tour I had set my heart on doing. Not to take advantage of a self-financing headlining tour seemed to me a ludicrous waste of a marketing opportunity on their part. As there was no shortage of demand for me to do live dates, I decided to go ahead anyway without Polydor's help. I did not want to be held back. I was anxious to go out and meet all my newly aquired fans. I wanted to see what they looked like and how they responded.

However, Polydor's lack of involvement did pose a bit of a problem regarding material. Nowadays an act would use this opportunity to present the new songs on their latest album. I decided that this would have to be an introductory performance to bring everybody up-to-date and fuse the past with the present in such a way that would make it timeless.

It was really working. At Newcastle University the exuberance was catching. It was great fun to see all those young faces bouncing around and singing along to both new and old songs. The boys got a bit boisterous and there was quite a lot of slapping and tickling going on amongst the crowds amassed at the front. I was not quite sure how to take their lustful looks – they were a bit young. Some brave girls draped themselves coquettishly around the stage front, but it was mostly boys.

By the time I finished the act it was all a bit frenzied. A huge crowd of lads decided that they definitely wanted more and broke through security to get to the dressing-rooms. They surged down the corridors squirting fire extinguishers at anyone in their path.

Jona and the blond ran to my room in a panic. They were shocked when I told them not to worry, that I would see them all, one by one, providing they calmed down. After all, I'd come on tour to meet my new fans.

Sanctify Yourself

AFTER THOSE HEADY, SWEATY CONCERTS at Newcastle and Liverpool a certain kind of brashness set in. Guitars were being wielded with an infinitely more manic strut. I began to really look forward to rolling about on my back in front of the amplifiers. I found it boring singing vertically all the time, so I took to the floor, sitting, kneeling, crouching, lying in a series of poses inspired by Antonioni's *Blow Up*.

I discovered the sublime sensation of feeling the bass throbbing through the floor boards up into my body, and of course there was the added bonus that I could relax and get my breath back – it takes an awful lot of puff to pant a pop song. I became more and more at home in my 'front room' with all those insistent, enthusiastic young 'house guests'.

The girls applauded, screamed, stuck little notes to the windscreen, adding 'My mum loves you too'. The boys pinched my shoes, and if given half a chance scrambled up on stage to shower me with affection. It's a bit daunting to have someone advancing on you unannounced, their lips puckered in impending passion. My only defence is to flash one of my 'How Dare You!' looks. This usually stops people in their tracks.

In the past, these Medusa glares have always proved to be far more effective protection than any bouncer's muscle, not counting the time at a song festival in Venice in the late Sixties when a crowd of Latin lovers encircled me backstage so that I could not do my Medusa on all of them at once. One cheeky lad behind me had had the audacity to indulge in the Italian national sport of bum appreciation. I span round furiously and punched him on the nose. He fell to the ground in a confused heap. Mistakenly I had hit the wrong boy. He must have been under the impression that this was the English way of reciprocating appreciation.

Through the years that Medusa look had not lost any of its potency, and all but the most ardent young men settled for a hug and a sedate peck on the cheek.

The band's backstage pulling power (some things never change!) and my box office pulling power had been confirmed. I was so happy that I threw myself into the tour with unbridled enthusiasm. It's a much more original approach to mid-life crisis than taking a toy boy lover! This was all great stuff to tell my grandchildren, I thought, imagining them clustered around my knees and climbing on to my lap as I creaked back and forth in my rocking chair, my old leather biking jacket slung carelessly around my shoulders like a shawl.

The sun had continued to grin down on us approvingly. We were blessed and protected by all the gods. The morning we left Liverpool for Edinburgh, Charles left for London, and a red-bearded Celt who worked for Polydor Records 'up North' accompanied Cathy and me onward and upward across the Pennines over the border.

I was looking forward to Scotland. Having lived there in the countryside around Stirling for a year or so at the end of the Seventies when I was emerging from my 'Dark Ages', I had acquired many friends from the local university and Buddhist fraternity.

During the rehearsals for this tour I had had a stimulating interview with an intelligent young man from *The List* magazine, a Scottish *Time Out*. I was impressed by his diagnosis of the personal dilemma I was struggling to overcome. He called it 'Emotional Agoraphobia'. Having a name for it immediately made me feel a lot happier. It made it easier to identify and isolate, easier to attack: a devil I knew.

So far I had studiously avoided any interviews with some of the tabloid press, based on the premise that I don't want to appear willingly in a newspaper that I wouldn't want to eat my chips from. On the other hand, I really do enjoy interviews with the current fresh-faced 'alternative' journalists working for a minority readership. Put together, these publications reach a formidable number of young people.

I feel safe being honest and open with these journalists. A lot of them become friends. The interviews are always fun and they often have some original observations they want to try out on me – for the seal of approval from an old hand at life maybe . . . (groan). They have a knack of making me feel crumblingly ancient and uniquely contemporary at the same time.

The further north we travelled the more clouds we acquired. When we arrived in Edinburgh the sky was riddled with grey thoughts completely hiding the sun, and it began to drizzle depressingly. The gods seemed to have forsaken us entirely. I took these omens as a warning of unspecified horrors to come.

I knew from the onset of the tour, even before anything was planned, that this moment was due. Nothing great and positive was ever achieved without a good kick back from life's abundant store of negativity. In fact it is the tug and pull, the friction of these two energies, positive and negative, that creates the spark of ignition, gives us lift-off. The bigger the obstacle, the better the outcome. I had a sneaky feeling Edinburgh was the venue where I was to start to do battle with my worst fears.

In the past I had been no stranger to winning battles, but I had not really learnt the knack of winning on my own terms. I suppose years of winning publicly and losing privately had been one of the causes of this 'Emotional Agoraphobia'. You could never imagine the supreme effort it was taking for me on this tour to go over old ground with a fresh untainted-by-experience approach, and publicly too. It was like jumping into a raging fire, believing that it won't hurt this time while remembering how much it burned before. Why on earth had I decided to do the tour? I could be sitting safely at home watching Bobby in 'Dallas'.

It's hard to explain what it does to the soul continually to win the battles that society encourages you to win, to be a 'good girl', but to lose the war within you to be yourself. It gradually chips away at your self-esteem; the world outside may admire you but inside you are a mass of deep, red-hot, tender wounds that never have time to heal before the next trauma reopens them. It is a very schizophrenic existence. You are never quite sure who you are, whose reality you are experiencing. It results in a paralysing fear of challenging any of the things that really matter to you in life, of exposing yourself to a painful but potentially rewarding experience.

One wound I remember vividly. How I got involved in the first place I really can't fathom. It was like the inexorable climax to a horror movie in which I unwittingly starred.

It started with Eve Taylor announcing grandly in 1967 that she had pulled off this amazing coup. For one moment I thought she had got herself invited to a tea party at the Palace. But no, she assured me it was far more incredible than that. The BBC were begging me to sing the UK entry in the Eurovision Song Contest!

Visions of hairy-legged Scotsmen warbling jolly ditties while their kilts swung to and fro in the glen, and dotty duos trilling birdie songs came to mind.

'The Eurovision WHAT?!' I exploded. 'You've got to be joking.' I plunged my head back into *FAB* magazine and decided to ignore her temporary (I hoped) madness.

From then on there was a gradual build-up of pressure, starting with casual Euro-droppings into the conversation and working up to full-scale screaming matches.

'The BBC want to update the contest's image,' Eve punched ineffectually into the air.

'Not by ruining mine,' I dodged to the left.

'There's an audience of millions, including the Iron Curtain countries.' An attempted uppercut.

I bobbed away. 'You mean all those people seeing me make a fool of myself. No thanks!'

Then a swift jab at my cheek. 'This will really help your career. You'll get a TV series. You can't go on making records for ever.'

'Why not? There's nothing else I want to do – anyway I'm good at it,' I slammed back.

'But you've got to show you have *real* talent,' she thumped.

Then her killer hook, 'Anyone can make hit records,' (she must be joking) 'but you have to be an ALL ROUND ENTER-TAINER!'

I swayed at the impact. 'Oh God,' I thought, 'is this what she has planned for me?' Endless pink chiffon sequinned frocks swam before my eyes. I was taking quite a beating but I refused to go down.

Then came the final pummelling. 'By the way, your last record isn't doing too well.' And one below the belt. 'I just hope we can keep the divorce scandal you're involved with out of the news – you're not still seeing that bastard are you?'

I was floored. But still I managed to crawl back on to my feet. 'I'd rather be loveless and destitute than do your bidding,' I proclaimed defiantly, with the pure naivety of an incurable reader of romantic novels. (As I'm not an incurable reader of romantic novels, I actually said something more earthy than that.)

I was still a bit wobbly on my feet. The telephone rang in the outer office signalling the end of the round.

'It's the BBC!' Eve's secretary called through excitedly.

I stumbled back to my corner in an Earls Court bedsit to freshen up for the next round. What was I, an international megastar, doing in an Earls Court bedsit? Good question.

This was part of Eve's master plan to keep me away from the aforementioned divorce scandal boyfriend. For a few quid a week I rented the tiny maid's room next to the laundry room at the back of her friend B's mansion flat, where they could keep an eye on me. They didn't realize that I used to slip out of the window and climb over the coal bunker to escape for the odd illicit rendezvous at the local Wimpy. I would turn up for my date looking and feeling like Cinders.

Later that night, after I'd cried myself through umpteen boxes of tissues, Adam Faith, my discoverer (makes me feel like a continent), called me. This was an unusual event.

''Ow are ya luv?' he purred sympathetically. 'She bin puttin' ya froo it? Look, do ya'self a favah – do it, get it ovah an' done wiv', 'ave anuvah big 'it. Ya nevah know – could be a great song. Get Chris Andrews ta wroite one. Ya can't lose. Eevah way ya win,' he refereed skilfully.

This was definitely outside Queensbury rules.

'Go on, say you'll do it, an' shut 'er up,' he coaxed.

I was grateful for a real friend. He seemed to have no other interest but my happiness. I threw in the towel.

'OK. Tell her I'll do it.'

It wasn't until many years later that Eve, on one of her 'Adam's a shit' campaigns, told me that the man who discovered me had not only been taking a percentage of all my earnings, but also had an interest in the publishing on most of my songs. On reflection this was a reasonable business arrangement, but I wish I had known about it at the time. Dear Adam. He may never have been a great singer, but he was always a fine businessman.

The first batch of songs was selected by a panel of men who, to me, at nineteen years of age, seemed as old as the Ark. They narrowed the songs down to six. I had to sing these one by one, live, on a Rolf Harris TV series, so that the great British public could vote which one would represent them in the contest in Vienna.

When I was announced to sing the last song in the series, the studio audience applauded so loudly that I couldn't hear the intro. I stopped it midway and started again. This song was called 'Puppet On A String'. I hated it from the very first oompah to the final bang on the big bass drum.

Even in those days, before the phrase 'chauvinist pig' had been coined, I was instinctively repelled by its sexist drivel and cuckoo-clock tune. The writers were men, the panel of judges were men, all white faced and stiff collared. Was this how they wanted women to behave – like stupid puppets? I dismissed the song as a joke. It had no chance of being selected, it was so awful.

You cannot imagine what it did to my nervous system when Eve announced that the TV viewers had chosen 'Puppet'. It had failed to register with me that anybody staying in regularly on a Saturday night to watch 'The Rolf Harris Show', as entertaining as it might be, would hardly be in tune with current popular taste in music or social trends.

I did think of running away, changing my name and living on a desert island. I also thought I might put on a wig and assume a completely new identity as Dusty Springfield's kid sister. But in the end I determined philosophically to lie back, grit my teeth, close my eyes and think of le Royaume-Uni. So off to Vienna I went with my pink chiffon sequinned frock.

We had not managed to contain the divorce scandal and Eve had been having huge rows with the BBC and people from 'The Rolf Harris Show' who she claimed wanted to drop me rather than be associated with my damaged public profile. I still do not know whether this was true or was another of Eve's paranoid ramblings, but the mention of it certainly had an effect on my confidence.

However, the BBC, having read the mail they had received for me (much to Eve's chagrin), did seem to think that public opinion had turned against me. So much so that they insisted that I secretly tape the final set of songs in a 'closed' studio to save me from the risk of an ugly confrontation with a live studio audience or the press.

Consequently the atmosphere in our little BEA plane bound for Vienna was so heavy it was a wonder we took off. It was packed with TV execs, record bosses, music publishers, the song writers, promotors, press, musicians, Rolf Harris and his entourage, and me. I was accompanied by Eve, Adam Faith and his wife, Kenny Woodman, and my mum and dad. Then there was Vera Lynn with her husband from the Music Publishers Association, one of the groups responsible for selecting the songs. Her presence added to the wartime flavour of the flight.

Vienna is not exactly the most fun place in the world for a teenager to be unless you are into waltzes, spas, or cream cakes. It also helps if you are over forty – so most of the British party were fine. The whole town was abuzz with my arrival; this took the BBC completely by surprise as they had not fully appreciated that I was already a huge star in Europe. I was continually chased by the press and I was exhausted.

Nevertheless, on the evening before the Song Contest, Eve decided that I should have a night on the town with Adam, his wife and my mum and dad. This was quite contrary to my natural inclination, which was to roll up in a tight nervous ball in my hotel room. I would have preferred to spend the night throwing up rather than being dragged out.

We ended up in a sedate Viennese *Bierkeller* with the oompah music that 'Puppet' had familiarized me with farting away in the background, while everybody tapped their feet in careful appreciation so as not to crease their *Lederhosen*.

I shrank out of sight into a dark corner only to be confronted by a barrage of flash bulbs prearranged by Eve. I shrank further and further into the darkness. Eve's Schiaparelli Pink talons plunged in after me, pulling me back into the glare of the lights.

'Jump up on the table and dance,' she hissed in my ear, 'then they'll get their pictures and go away.'

'No I won't,' I protested.

'Yes you will,' she persisted.

'I won't!'

'If you don't, I'm leaving and I won't ever speak to you again.'

'What a relief,' I thought, wistfully retreating into my shell.

And then she upped and went, dutifully followed by Adam and his wife and the host of photographers.

On the night of the Eurovision Song Contest my parents and I found ourselves completely alone. Heaven knows what contagious disease Eve had told the rest of the British party I had caught but not a soul came near me. Mum and Dad hugged me and wished me luck and went off to find their seats in the auditorium.

I sat down in the dressing-room to put my make-up on. I had the heavy feeling that if I lost, no one would ever speak to me again. The family audience would not forgive and forget the divorce scandal, and the record buyers would not forgive and forget my singing such a rubbishy song. As I put on my pink chiffon sequinned dress I decided I would win like no one had ever won before. Then *I* could choose who *I* wanted to talk to.

After the performance the votes were collected from all the different countries. Backstage, on camera, I was so worried that I would lose that I could not bring myself to look at the score, although on stage I knew I had won before I even opened my mouth. When the result was announced, even I was staggered at the number of points I received. I had so many they ran off the scoreboard. It was and still is the most spectacular win in the history of the Eurovision Song Contest.

I took the winner's award back to my dressing-room which was invaded by every Tom, Dirk, and Henri. Eve's head popped out of nowhere round the door, and as if nothing had happened between us she kissed me ravenously on the cheek, and told me I was invited to a big celebration in my honour.

I took one of the bottles of champagne that were piling up on the dressing table, and with what little honour I had left, went over to the party, had my picture taken with the previous year's winner, Udo Jurgens, who was milking it for all he was worth, and went straight back to my hotel.

I'd left my room keys in the concert hall, and not knowing how to uncork my champagne bottle, I fell asleep exhausted on the floor outside my hotel room, stone cold sober, while the rest of Europe fêted me.

I have since seen a film of my performance. I seem so full of youthful confidence and joy, I positively shine. It looks like I must have known I had something special that no number of stupid songs or silly frocks could disguise. It was all mine and nobody could take it away from me. I can also see a hint of something else – inside I was crushed by the hard facts of life I was learning at such a delicate age.

The grey Edinburgh sky frowned dourly down. The clouds sprayed on us unceremoniously. Grey road, grey buildings, grey hair, grey thoughts.

Not one Sandie Shaw poster was to be seen livening up a smelly doorway or derelict site. It was all frightfully staid. My heart began to sink.

We arrived at a grim building which housed the local radio

station – too late to do the planned interview. A middle-aged man in a grey tweed suit trotted out to greet me in the back of the car, where I had removed my specs and was busy painting my eyes on.

He was the dee-jay. Something about him reminded me of those tired-looking TV execs in charge of 'family entertainment' that this university tour had enabled me so gleefully to leave behind in Vienna. The conversation reeked of 'They Don't Write Songs Like They Did In The Sixties' speak. This is all terribly reassuring if you're over the hill, but as I'm still only half-way up my little mountain I found it a shade disconcerting. Rather than interrupt the scheduled local agricultural report, we agreed to do the interview over the phone at the hotel.

The hotel, save for the fussy net curtains, looked very similar to the radio station, the kind of place that made you yearn to be bombarded by your adorable screaming brood at home. Instead, we were greeted by three chattering biddies, all twinsets and tight lips. They gave us a minimal welcome, peeking over wire-rimmed spectacles with the pained and patient disdain of long-suffering Highlanders being overrun by yet another horde of rowdy Sassenachs.

'You'll need a key if you're back after eleven,' one tartan-skirted lovely warned sternly. We trembled in our Chelsea boots.

A crowd of American tourists piled into the foyer clutching their shortbread and Aran knits. Upstairs in my room I sat on the ice-cold satin eiderdown, waiting for the make-your-own-tea kit to brew. In the radio interview, for the first time, the dreaded Euro-questions emerged.

'Didn't it feel great when you won, Sandie?' the elderly dee-jay asked excitedly, recalling his own fond memory.

I stared out of the window at the falling rain.

'Well, frankly, no, but . . .'

That was not what he wanted to hear. What he wanted was boom-bang-oompah-chirpy-cheep-cheep. I was being asked to act out of character again. His questions hit me like wadges of stale haggis.

Unaccountably my sense of self-esteem began to trickle away. 'Is the real me so uninteresting?' I thought. I was tempted to crawl under the bed and count the carpet fluff.

When I arrived at the gig my stomach was knotted and tied in enough ways to confuse the most efficient scout master. The little notice board outside displayed the only Sandie Shaw poster in town, sized down to a meagre ten-by-eight inches – you could barely see my credentials. It gave a good indication of the amount of work the promoter had done for the show.

I entered with apprehension. The heavy oak doors creaked forebodingly. The sight that greeted me finally clarified that curious clause in entertainment contracts –' . . . if artist is prevented from appearing by riots, strikes, war, floods, fire . . . and other Acts of God'! I had been booked to appear in a converted Presbyterian chapel.

Wooden pews encircled the altar which was now a stage. A huge organ towered majestically over the congregation of tour roadies. Our disconcerted Welsh sound man had erected his own altar of sound equipment, and was twiddling irreverently with his knobs, vying for power with acoustics that were meant for the solemn hymns of a church choir, not my act, geared as it was toward the taste of raucous college students.

The disconsolate band shuffled around on the stage in embarrassment, repeating the ritual twangs, thumps and 'one, two's of the sound check so meekly that they were guaranteed to inherit the earth.

As I stood watching, grim-faced, in the aisle, a nervous hush came over the gathering. I wanted to cry. I rushed straight out the back to the vestry to the nearest telephone.

'Charles, I'm not going on.'

'Fine. It'll only cost you a few thousand pounds.'

'I can't face it. I thought I'd left all this in the past. It's Songs of Praise Golden Oldie time,' I whimpered.

'Then come home. They obviously don't realize that times have changed and don't know how to promote you to your new audience. It's a mistake. You should have played Glasgow where all the kids are. They probably can't sell tickets and are hoping you'll cancel so they don't have to pay. But . . .' like a red rag to a bull, 'why let them get away with it?'

'But how shall I *be*? I can't be what they want me to be.'

'Then *be* yourself. You never know, they might even like it . . . then again they might not! It's up to you.'

I marched back into the church like a Sally Army officer and informed the troops that the show would not only go on exactly as we had always done, but it would also be the best one of the tour.

Backstage, as I passed the dressing-room of the support band, I heard the lead singer sobbing hysterically. 'All I wanted was a big audience to sing to.'

'Don't we all,' I thought. A performer's worst nightmare is having no audience. Whatever the circumstances, success or failure, the ego always takes it personally. I wondered if anyone at all would turn up.

In the quiet of my dressing-room I religiously prepared myself for the performance, systematically cleansing and making-up my face like a priestess preparing for midsummer solstice.

When I was a child I loved to sing so much that on Sunday I attended all the services at the local Baptist church one after the other with my schoolfriend Janet Llewellyn, and then I would go with my other schoolfriend Kathy Murphy to Catholic mass.

I really only went for the singing, but I also loved the wild mysticism in parts of the Bible. My favourite was the Book of Revelations, full of intense images so enticing for the pubescent mind. I can still quote from it verbatim. After the *Oxford Dictionary*, Lewis Carroll's *Through the Looking Glass*, and my illustrated *Encyclopaedia of the World*, it was my favourite book.

Along with Janet and Kathy I passed my Religious Knowledge GCE with flying colours. I also toyed with the idea of getting baptized, as was the custom at the Baptist church I attended. I was thrilled by the thought of the ritual.

Janet actually decided to go through with it. I'll never forget the wonder of seeing the floor of the church open to reveal a vast swimming pool. The minister, in his flowing robes, descended from the pulpit and strode into the water. He beckoned to Janet, who was wearing a long white gown, to join him. As she went solemnly down the steps her dress rose up and swam around her ample thighs in the most carnal fashion.

As she was plagued with puppy fat, the minister found it rather a heavy task holding her weight and dousing her in the water. He wobbled under the strain and dipped her in further than he had intended. Janet came up gasping for air and I collapsed in a fit of giggles.

Then I witnessed a miraculous transformation. Janet had entered the water a girl. She emerged – as if out of a Bounty Bar ad, eyes glowing, sodden gown clinging voluptuously to every curve and dimple – a woman! I wasn't ready for that.

I have never yet come across a singer without the religious impulse, if not in the overt way of Cliff Richard, Tina Turner, Cat Stevens, or even the High Priestess of Soul, Aretha Franklin, then in the distorted sense of worshipping and extolling the virtues of money, sex, drugs or cars. Some agree with their audience and idolize themselves. Morrissey thinks God looks like James Dean and his wife looks like Joan Simms. This is walking on dangerous water . . .

I think there is some deep karmic connection between singers and religion. For one thing singing, historically, has always been used in spiritual praise of the divine. In the West it is only in recent times, with the advent of popular commercial music, that music has generally become associated more with romance and sex. For another, singers have an intuitive understanding of the principle that all human beings need an object of worship. That's why they feel such a great need to claim that function for themselves!

I myself don't want to be an icon particularly. I've already been there and got the tee-shirt. I believe that my job as a singer is to use my sensitivity to its fullest extent, to be really open and aware, to appreciate the richness and diversity of life and convey this in my work, in order to inspire people and help them feel good to be alive. I want the listener and onlooker to know that everything they see in me is in themselves, not separate or different, but universal, and that if they think I'm great it's because they are great, because life is great. A star is someone who embodies the hopes, dreams and desires of their fans. What we see in them is a reflection of ourselves. I have to admit, though, it's rather nice to be adored – even from afar!

I couldn't have felt further away from being adorable than when standing waiting backstage in the chapel to go on. I remembered what it felt like to descend into the pit, to live in that dark, airless basement, to be traumatized by pain, to be paralysed by fear.

Twelve years before, in 1978, at the beginning of my Buddhist practice, after Jeff my husband had finally left and I was living alone with my daughter Grace, I had begun my emergence from my 'Dark Ages'. Gradually I was gaining the courage to step out into the light. I was taking emotional risks, exposing myself to life, understanding and overcoming the pain and the fear that had become such an integral part of my existence and which I thought was how all things were and always would be.

Sometimes life kept hitting me so hard that I would crawl around on all fours unable to stand up. For days I hid under the smoked glass table top, curled up foetus-like. Grace, who was then only eight or nine years old, would pass meals to me, coaxing me outside. Sometimes she would literally force my mouth open and shut to chant '*Nam-myoho-renge-kyo*'.

I'll never have enough time to thank her for all her love and care. We developed a bond that no one else has been able to touch. When I had my children Amie and Jack a few years later it was she who supported me and held my hand throughout their births. There are things I have shared with Grace that I could not share with anyone else in the world. Sometimes I love her so much that I think I'm going to explode. I hadn't gone through all that to retreat now.

The band started up with a heavy thump worthy of a Mississippi bible basher. The congregation amounted to maybe fifty in all, seated reverently in the pews – little kids and their mums, a few grandads, the odd punk and a couple of Smith lookalikes: a family audience.

I performed with evangelical fervour, without sacrificing an inch of my integrity. My message, based on the principle of revealing your own true self, was delivered with uncompromising zeal.

By the final note I emerged from the stage as a born-again singer. It was an organic, self-inspired renaissance. It was great fun. It stunned me. It stunned the audience. They loved it, every sweet precious one of them. Scotland the Brave!

East of Eden

THE HEATWAVE RETURNED the next day and Manchester, usually enshrouded by rain, beckoned warmly. The cosy red brick walls welcomed us to its comely barmaid's bosom. Those steamy hot streets rekindled good memories.

In the Sixties, 'Top of the Pops' was filmed and 'Coronation Street' was rehearsed in the same studio, tucked away in Manchester's backstreet suburbia. In the dressing-rooms we often came across a discarded 'Coronation Street' script and read out the parts in broad Mancunian accents, searching out clues to how the next week's storyline would go.

Manchester vied with Liverpool not only over football teams but also over pop groups. It was the spawning ground for bands like the Hollies, Herman's Hermits, the Mindbenders, and Freddie and the Dreamers.

In the Smiths it now had a new home-grown talent. The audience tonight would undoubtedly be full of Smiths fans. I had continued my idiosyncratic involvement with the band ever since that fateful summer day when I received their first letter, followed by a flow of written intimacies from Morrissey.

I had never heard of the Smiths then and at that stage nor had the rest of the world – with the exception of a handful of Mancunians. If the communication had not come through Nik via Geoff it would have been easy to dismiss them as cranks – which I did for a few days.

Then my curiosity got the better of me and I listened to the cassette – a frontroom demo, with Morrissey whining tunefully in his as yet undeveloped but inimitable style, and Johnny Marr twanging soulfully away in like manner. Although the song did not strike an instant chord, I was intrigued. They displayed such

48

front. I thought the least I could do was write and thank them for their interest.

I called Geoff, who pleaded on their behalf with the dexterity of a legal advocate, 'Morrissey would die to meet you.'

At that point I was unaware of Morrissey's amusing penchant for melodrama and that Geoff was talking literally. Deeply embarrassed I dismissed his impassioned pleas. I passed sentence, 'No, I'm sorry, Geoff. I don't really think so.'

'You don't have to sing their songs – just meet him,' he badgered. We adjourned so that I could deliberate.

The next day Geoff introduced fresh evidence in the post: reams of indie press coverage, and another notelette from young Steven Morrissey. All this eagerness was very touching. I called Geoff again.

'Yes. I'll meet him, but no promises of involvement. He is on probation,' I warned.

'A reprieve!' cried Geoff joyously. 'You'll never regret this.' (I wonder if *he* ever did!)

The following day a hysterical story broke in the *Sun* saying that the Smiths were releasing songs based on iffy subject matter: 'Reel Around The Fountain' was supposed to be about child molesting or something, and another, 'Suffer Little Children', to be about the Moors Murders. I rang Geoff to cancel. 'If this is true,' I said firmly (which was unlikely as it was in the *Sun*, but marginally possible), 'then I can't have a pervert in my home with my kids.'

'It's not true. They've twisted everything, I promise.' Geoff read me the lyrics. They certainly were not the usual moonlight and roses stuff but they were OK if a little obscure. 'Look, I'll come with him to chaperone,' he offered.

Still not fully convinced of the purpose of the meeting, but trusting Geoff, I uncancelled the appointment.

I was running a bit late on the day. Fearing I might look like the harassed mother that I was, I decided to don full make-up and lie glamorously in the bath afterwards to get that fresh dewy look that Bianca Jagger recommended in the *Woman's Own* article.

I was putting the final touches to my lipstick when Amie had a tantrum because she wanted some too. I had just managed to calm her down by swapping it for some lip salve when two over-anxious young men arrived on my doorstep. I opened the door, resplendent in full make-up – still wearing my pyjamas.

Geoff shuffled nervously. Morrissey looked transfixed. It was excruciating. I asked them in, trying to act as if I normally entertained young men in the afternoon in my nightwear. Morrissey continued to stare helplessly, so Geoff took him by the arm and guided him forward.

Sensing my uneasiness, Amie clung to me like a limpet, so I had to drag her along with me, attached to my pyjama leg. She then hid behind the sofa where I sat, and Geoff and Morrissey placed themselves either side of me in a pair of matching Victorian armchairs.

I scrutinized Morrissey. He didn't look like a child molester to me. Amie seemed to feel otherwise, and again I began to question my wisdom in meeting him. All my worst nightmares vied with the sweet angelic vision seated before me. As soon as he managed to mobilize his mouth and speak, all my fears subsided. He was the perfect gentleman – a real little charmer – old-fashioned even.

Like nervous fledglings his hands fluttered in the air to accompany his words. In his gentle Northern accent he proffered bunches of flowery compliments – all presented in a down-to-earth Mancunian manner. This perfect paradox dumbfounded me.

It occurred to me that he would look just as incongruously at home in an episode of 'Coronation Street'. I could picture him in the Rovers Return seated between Minnie Caldwell and Ena Sharples in the snug, supping his lemonade shandy through a straw, and doing nowt else but enjoying a right good chinwag. Later when Pat Phoenix, who played Elsie Tanner the barmaid, died, Morrissey was distraught with grief and attended her funeral along with thousands of others.

I just couldn't make him out. I didn't know whether to take him seriously or not. He was the antithesis of a modern-day would-be pop idol, more Quentin Crisp than Elvis Presley. Whatever he was, I always recognize a twin soul when I meet one, and I knew he had recognized me too.

I showed them to the door and to my amazement heard myself arranging to meet him again. 'I must be certifiable,' I thought afterwards. Somehow this charming man, Morrissey, reminded me of my meeting with my first Prince Charming, Adam Faith, in 1963 when I was sweet sixteen . . .

I had run off the stage of the Hammersmith Commodore theatre after only one number during my first ever professional performance and had hidden behind the curtains. I could not go back on. Everything was going round. I felt sick and the rum and blackcurrant Auntie Jen had given me for Dutch courage was wearing off. I ran straight into the arms of a clutch of good-looking pop musicians called the Hollies and the Roulettes who were standing in the wings watching my big-time singing debut. It was a far cry from the Ilford Palais where I had come second in a talent contest just a few weeks before.

I had entered the contest urged on by my school mates Janet Llewellyn and Kathy Murphy, and in an effort to get the boys' attention so maybe one would ask me to dance. I was a mod. I had just grown out my crop and was wearing my hair in a back-combed bob with a 'black tulip' rinse that Kathy had put on.

Kathy always did my hair. Once, while on a camping holiday, she had back-combed and lacquered my hair so high that it stuck out of the tent at night. In the morning the dew made it congeal like a well-licked stick of candyfloss. I refused to take up Kathy's offer to cut it off. It took all day to painfully brush it out.

For the Ilford Palais Talent Contest, Janet had made my pencil skirt, worn just below the knee and with a fashionable kick-pleat at the back. I had had my ears pierced and wore the silver crosses that were *de rigueur* in the mod scene. Even though I was tall and as lanky as a beanpole I thought I looked ace, but nobody had asked me to dance all evening and I was tired of dancing with Janet or Kathy.

Although I only won second place the trendier part of the audience really loved me and shouted their approval. When I came offstage, both Janet and Kathy had found dance partners and still no one approached me, except a red-haired lad who said his uncle was a showbusiness promoter up in town.

Well, my mum had warned me about boys with tall stories like this, but I gave him a neighbour's phone number just in case it was true. Then a spotty but nice boy called Clive asked me to dance and took me home in his battered Ford Prefect. All in all quite a successful night. The most I had expected was a lift home on a Lambretta.

The phone call came from the red-haired boy's 'uncle' up in town. He was REAL. It was the music publisher Terry Oates. Jimmy Henny from Radio Luxembourg was with him. Would I come up to London to do an audition?

'What's an audition?' I queried nervously.

'We want to hear you sing.'

I went alone. I don't think they had ever seen anyone like me before – I could tell by the stunned look on their faces as they took in my mod outfit. Without the guitars and audience, I couldn't sing for them. I stood there feeling a tall, gawky fool.

'Don't worry,' they assured me. 'We'll arrange for you to try things out with a local band, Tony Rivers and the Castaways, and we'll see then.'

I rehearsed two numbers in the front room of a semi-detached house in Ilford with the band. The reports must have been good because Messrs Oates and Henny asked me if I wanted to sing in a charity concert in a big theatre in Hammersmith along with the Hollies, and Adam Faith and the Roulettes.

DID I? To tell the truth, some of me did but a lot of me didn't. It all seemed a bit too big-time to me. But Aunt Jen said she would come with me, then Mum and Dad joined, then more aunts and uncles, Nan and Grandad, and my cousins – until pretty well all the family had booked a seat to support me.

I wore a short, white, empire-line frock for the show with a dangly jet brooch, pink sling-backs, my hair piled high and my fringe hanging low over my eyes.

I'd been backstage twice before. The first time had been at the Romford Odeon when the newly recording Beatles were playing on a Roy Orbison tour. The week before their show I had sung for nothing at the Saturday morning pictures so that the cinema manager who, like nearly every grown-up at that time, had never heard of the Beatles, would let me in the stage door to meet them.

On the night, Janet Llewellyn and I stood in the wings watching the show. As Paul went on he kissed my cheek and said, 'This one's for you, la.'

I couldn't have cared less. John was the only man for me, but he completely ignored me. I couldn't understand it. When he came close I could feel my whole being shudder with anticipation. Surely he felt it too?

Later, in the dressing-room, Ringo tried to put his hands up Janet's blouse, and we both marched out indignantly. It's a good job he didn't try that on with me or he would have discovered the cotton wool padding in my otherwise empty bra.

The second time I went backstage was when the Beatles, having since become national heroes, appeared at the Albert Hall. I rang and said I was John's long-lost cousin Sandra, and he only came to the phone didn't he? His delicious Liverpool drawl curled down the receiver and tingled around in my ear.

He couldn't remember me from Romford, but would I come backstage and jog his memory? I borrowed next week's pocket money from Mum and rushed up there, where he appeared from behind the crash barriers of Entrance C. He signed my autograph book with lots of love and lashings of kisses and asked me to come back later, nudge, nudge, wink, wink . . .

This sordid arrangement was not the romantic liaison I had envisaged, so I decided to miss my chance to make the earth move with John, and went home all misty eyed, tenderly clutching his autograph.

It wasn't till a year later, when we met professionally on the set of 'Shindig', the American TV show, that I finally realized that the fantasy was all on my side (shared with a million other girls too!) and that he would never leave Cynthia and marry me.

Meanwhile, backstage at Hammersmith, the Hollies and the Roulettes were very impressed. Behind the stage curtain I span from one set of arms to another as they hugged and congratulated me. Then Adam Faith's guitarist, Russ Ballard, suggested I go with him to Adam's dressing-room. 'He must hear you sing,' he said as he dragged me unwillingly along the corridor.

When I met this big star for the first time, I was shocked rigid. He was so tiny that even in his Cuban heels and platform soles he still barely scraped my shoulder. But he was charming – a gentleman even, in his Cockney way.

'Go on, gel. Give it a go.' He encouraged me to sing to Russ's guitar accompaniment. I sang 'Everybody Loves A Lover'.

'Great!' he cried out and popped his head around the adjoining door. 'Come on in 'ere, Eve. Get a load of this. This gel's got talent!' he shouted.

Eve Taylor, his manager, entered the room, accompanied by John Bloom, the washing machine millionaire. Eve was an attractive, tiny blonde in her early forties, resembling Ruth Ellis. She tugged on a cigarette and tapped her foot impatiently.

Eve nodded to Adam and I started nervously to sing again. Eve listened to one line, glared at me, then at Adam, whispered something in his ear, then turned on her teetering high heels and tapped briskly out.

Adam was visibly ruffled by Eve. It seemed I was banished from the Garden of Eden for the moment. Adam reached up and patted my shoulder. 'Don't worry, luv. I'll fix it for ya. You're gonna be a star,' he pronounced.

Pretty soon I was having publicity shots taken with my 'discoverer', Adam Faith. We stood on steps, he on the higher one and me on the lower, or we sat. I crouched over and bent my knees for the close-ups. He showed me all the tricks to disguise our difference in height. Adam was an old hand and tried to ease me out of my awkwardness.

'Come on, cock. Watch the birdie!' he coaxed. Adam only ever got mad at me once, during a break in the photo session when I stuck my chip in his egg yolk without asking. He went berserk – and shouted that only he could do that, it was his special treat. I did not mean to steal his thunder, either with his egg or later on when my career rocketed and his did a nosedive. It just happened that way.

Now Morrissey, my new-wave Prince Charming, six foot tall in his socks, picked me up for another photo session to promote our budding musical collaboration. His letters had been constant and wonderful; warm, tender, funny, intimate, always supportive, but I still did not know him too well. In the back of the taxi I could feel his eyes on me, examining the minutiae of my appearance. I was a bit fazed.

'I'm such a mess,' I excused myself. 'I didn't have time to put any make-up on.'

'You don't need any make-up, you look great. I love your glasses,' he replied adoringly. It was at that moment that I gave in. I decided I would believe that he loved me and enjoy it.

In the same photographic studio, Chrissie Hynde was just finishing up in front of the camera with the Pretenders.

'You can borrow my Polyfilla,' she yelled across at me helpfully, as I sat down at the make-up mirror. I don't think Morrissey took to her brand of humour. I felt awkward, and puzzled that two such good influences on my life should not get on.

I squeezed self-consciously into a tight black minidress that the stylist gave me for the photo. I was still about half a stone overweight after having Amie. Morrissey dressed up in an ill-fitting second-hand dinner jacket and bow-tie. We were placed side by side under the lights in front of the camera. I wasn't quite sure what to do with myself, but the photographer wanted me to gaze haughtily into the distance – which I did, while Morrissey knelt at my feet, using his popper beads as a rosary, and studiously worshipped me. I couldn't take it seriously, but everyone else did!

Two years later, on the tour, at the Hacienda Club in Manchester, I continually thought about Morrissey while on stage. I laid into 'Steven (You Don't Eat Meat)', the song I had written with him in mind, and followed it with 'I Don't Owe You Anything', the song he had written with me in mind. Then finally I sang 'Hand In Glove' and 'Jeane', while our mutual Mancunian fans went potty. Why he hadn't shown up to watch I will never know – maybe he wanted to give me my space, but I was hurt and angry. His words rang in my head . . .

'Let us dance barefoot in the snow until all of St Petersburg is aflame with jealousy . . . Ever and ever, Morrissey.'

Butter Fingers

MANY MOONS AGO, during my second Italian tour, in Palermo, the capital of Sicily, I managed to upset the Mafia. They thought that if they offered enough money I would be tempted to do anything. My mind, unfortunately, does not work that way. I wish it did; I would even go as far as surgery to have this character trait corrected – forget the facelift, let's go for the lobotomy!

The Italian agent had booked me at a Sicilian club, and the owner of another club was so jealous he wanted me to sing at his place too. I, on the other hand, fancied the night off.

The second club owner was deeply upset when I refused his generous offer, particularly since, anticipating my acceptance, he had fly-postered the whole town. As he had made no prior booking arrangements with me I knew he had no claim on my services. I was wrong. In England this may be so, but in Palermo I was drastically out of touch with local custom.

The next morning, when the band and I returned from the beach, all bright and sunny in our swimming togs, we found our hotel surrounded by local police. They had been sent by the club owner. I was encircled and jostled off to my apartment. As they were pushing me past my secretary, Jenny, I managed to whisper that she should secretly make her way to the window outside my bedroom.

In my room, with Italian fervour, the police turned out my cupboards and suitcases. When my belongings were all emptied on to the floor they began to select what they considered to be the most valuable items. I knew what was most valuable to me – our passports. I had tucked them into the bottom of my skimpy bikini. It took quite an effort to back out of the lounge into the bedroom without causing myself a gynaecological injury but, risking a slight drop in the future population figures, I made my way to the window.

I threw the passports down to Jenny who was crouching in the bushes below. This was her first week working with me, and as I watched her grab them and scramble away on all fours, I thought it would be the last. Fortunately she decided she liked the danger and intrigue and stayed for many more years of adventures.

When I returned to the lounge the police chief was waltzing round the room with one of my stage minidresses flung over his uniform, singing 'E Ti Avro', the Italian version of 'Girl Don't Come', in an astonishing basso profundo. The other officers had taken their boots off and were dancing barefoot, whilst providing the counter-tenors on the choruses. When their bizarre operetta came to an end I applauded with gusto. Then, to my horror, they left, taking with them my entire earnings and all my belongings.

I stood in the doorway in my itsy-bitsy bikini, wondering what to do. Strangely, all the telephone lines from the hotel were jammed. Jenny and the band assembled on my verandah and we took stock of the situation. The police had not managed to find our transport or our vanload of instruments. We had our passports, swimming costumes and suncream, and a concert to play that night which would give us some cash to buy food, clothes, and some SOS phone calls to England. The only way was forward.

That night, to the delight of the audience, we performed in our swimwear. This went down a treat. After the show, as I was being paid, Jenny noticed some suspicious-looking characters edging their way menacingly backstage.

I had a West Indian trumpet player who was always complaining about having to sleep inside on a bed. I decided to take him at his word and told him he could sleep on the beach that night. I wrapped the wages in a polythene bag and gave it to him for safe-keeping. I stood aside as my dressing-room and later my hotel room were searched by the heavies, and couldn't resist screaming with laughter as they left empty-handed.

The trumpet player buried the money in the sand and slept on it. The next morning he returned it to me, saying he had never had such a good night's sleep. We repeated the same plan, successfully hoodwinking the hoodlums, for the next three dates.

Meanwhile, back home, Eve Taylor went potty when she found out what was going on. She called the Foreign Office and my lawyer, and then she and he flew to Italy to meet up with an official from the British Embassy – to rescue me.

The trio caught up with us on the Isle of Ischia. The hotel was very nice – lots of flowers and bowls of fruit. We were given interconnecting suites. The hotel staff were also very nice but regretted that the police guard would have to stay at our doors. Eve was furious. She stormed out of her room to deliver one of her famous mouthfuls and found herself staring down the barrel of a gun held by a uniformed gentleman. Unaccustomedly cowed, she slunk back into the room.

While she howled uncontrollably the lawyer and the Embassy official retired next door to deliberate. I ordered a pot of tea and began packing my money into the familiar polythene bag. Eve finally calmed down and the men returned solemn-faced.

'Well? Do you have any ideas? What's the plan?' I asked.

They both shook their heads gravely, the way experts do. Then our man from the Embassy walked over to the balcony and peered down into the beautiful gardens below.

'There's just one thing that might work,' he suggested.

We all breathed a sigh of relief.

'Well, tell us,' snapped Eve.

'We..e..e..ell,' he hummed and hahed. 'I notice we all have twin beds with two sheets on each.'

The lawyer and I looked at him quizzically. It was an odd subject to bring up.

'Yes, yes, I know,' agreed Eve. 'But what's the use of home comforts when you don't have your freedom?' She started bawling again.

'We..e..e..ell, I'd like to suggest that if we tied all the sheets together and hung them from the balcony, I'm sure they would reach the ground. Then at least we could escape.'

We stood in stunned silence. Maybe the Embassy had sent us someone trained in espionage instead of diplomacy.

Then he started to laugh. 'OK, I suppose we had better go back and negotiate some more.'

I don't know what agreement they finally drew up to secure my release from custody, but to this day all my belongings from the tour are gathering dust in a courthouse in Palermo . . . unless of course the local police chief is using my stage clothes for his amateur operatic productions.

In the late Sixties I always did these tours on my own, without Eve. I acted as tour manager, wardrobe mistress, interpreter, banker, wages clerk, and shoulder to cry on. Eve, on the other hand, sat in the cosy luxury of her plush West End office, nursing one of her headaches, while sending me off to play in all the world's political hotspots. She had no idea about things like wars and revolution; her knowledge of social unrest stopped at the Harrods sale. Eve's only criterion for accepting a booking on my behalf was the profit margin involved. After all, she reasoned, *someone* had to be in it for the money!

After quite a few similar international incidents I began to put in a few of my own criteria, like half the fee paid into my bank in England before I set one bare foot on foreign soil, and the balance, in cash, before I placed the two of them on stage. This at least minimized the risk of financial, philosophical or cultural discrepancies.

On one occasion Eve booked me in Greece. It sounded nice, lots of sun and ouzo, but the week before I left the government was overthrown by the military junta, and unknown to me the army had taken over my contract. Although Eve must have known (to be fair she would not have considered it important enough to mention to me), I did not find out until I peeped through the curtains before the show and saw row after row of uniforms glittering with military insignia.

A smiling mustachioed face appeared around the curtain. 'Are you ready to go on, Mees Shaw?'

'Well, there is a small matter of business to settle first,' I said.

'Ah, yes? And what ees that?' He continued grinning amicably.

'Where's the balance of my fee?'

His smile disappeared and a look of sheer terror overshadowed his sunny face. 'Shhh . . . don't you realize eesa great honour to sing for dee generals?'

I assured him as gently as I could that my honour did not depend on local political power, that I considered myself to be a citizen of the world, that my manager, Eve, would be happy for me to sing for anyone providing they paid my fee, and that although I did not completely share her philosophy on life, a deal was a deal and I was sure the new regime would be only too happy to be gentlemanly about it.

Ten minutes later, after the generals had had a whip round, we were still well below the fee. We all waited patiently, the audience out front and the band and I backstage, while a party of military personnel took off in a jeep to acquire the balance. An hour later than scheduled I went on stage, leaving an officer's hat piled high with drachmas sitting on my make-up table.

In 1970 the Shah of Iran asked me to sing for him at his palace. His sister, who fancied herself as the cultural caretaker of the State, also wanted me to do some extra, free, outdoor concerts 'for the people'. Eve negotiated a fee for the Shah's show, and though four months pregnant with Grace, off I went.

I did the open-air public concerts at night. The audience, consisting mostly of young kids, huddled all round and on the stage, rolling big fat joints just as we would crack open a bag of pop corn at the pictures. They seemed to have abundant supplies as they were tugging on individual spliffs rather than indulging in that peculiar Western habit of passing a single, measly, soggy specimen around. As the pungent smoke drifted persuasively across the stage it became increasingly difficult for me to finish each song without bursting into fits of giggles. I don't think this was the cultural exchange the Shah had in mind.

By day, while I waited for the Shah's royal command, Jenny and I explored the kasbahs and backstreet hookah parlours, chaperoned by the twenty-stone, six-and-a-half-foot-tall French Moroccan agent. The few women we saw scurrying past in the shadows were swathed in swirling dark robes and veils, shielded from the stark glare of the sun and the men. We were dressed quite unsuitably, imprisoned in our skin-tight Mr Freedom tee-shirts against which my bulging tummy strained. In the evening we were entertained with exotic belly dancing and offered Middle Eastern delicacies like sheep's nasty bits and goat's naughty bits, which, as vegetarians, we fortunately had to refuse.

After a week the novelty began to wear off and I began to nag the agent to do the Shah's show. Each time it was cancelled due to pressing State business. We were looked after pleasantly enough in the hotel, but on arrival they had taken our passports and plane tickets 'for our own security', so we were virtually prisoners at the Shah's whim. To appease me I was offered an antique Persian rug, a diamond, and an emerald, all of which I refused – I just wanted to go home. The French Moroccan haggled with me on behalf of the Shah as he had previously haggled on my behalf with the merchants in the bazaars. Eventually, after all else had failed and I had become frightened for our safety, I played my final card . . .

When the French Moroccan came to visit our hotel suite with fresh goodies to tempt me to stay, Jenny opened the door in pretended panic and dragged him horror-stricken to the next room where I had collapsed on the floor faking imminent childbirth, writhing and howling, clutching my stomach like a crazed dervish dancer. I flew home full-bellied but empty-handed. This heralded a downturn in fortune for me.

Things were so much simpler as a child. Every Thursday evening my mum and dad sat across the table from each other, their pooled wages arranged in neat piles earmarked for the weekly bills. While they assembled these piles and pushed them back and forth, I played in the back garden with our dog, Prince, until I was called in to collect my five shillings' pocket money.

Once, while in the middle of this ritual, my parents were called to the front door. Prince, impatient for his dinner, slipped inside, placed his paws on the table and gobbled up the money. For the next three days my mum followed the bewildered dog round the garden, poking his pooh with a stick until she had retrieved every penny.

My first wage packet from Ford's Motor Company in Dagenham was seven pounds, fifteen shillings and eleven pence. A handsome sum in those days. I did not do much to earn it. I spent most of my working hours in the sick bay with real or simulated period cramps. I found the smoggy early mornings on the bus down to the works the most depressing journey imaginable. I could not wait to leave.

Shortly before this I had been accepted for a foundation course at an art college. My mum was so thrilled. She came along for my interview, during which I was told that I would be studying for about five years. This seemed an extraordinarily long time to someone just turned sixteen. When we arrived home I informed her that I would not be going to art college because it interfered with my plans to become a singing star. As I had never mentioned these plans before, they came as a bit of a surprise.

'A singing star? You? You must be joking! You mean you've been taking those singing spots at the local dance hall seriously? But Sandra you're so shy! What are you going to do when everyone looks at you? . . . and what are you going to do for money until then? . . . don't think you're going to sit on your backside round here waiting for stardom to come walking through the front door, young lady . . . you'll have to get a job . . . you'll have to pay your own way . . . and how do I know that you're any good? I've only seen you doing impressions!'

That much was true. I was infamous for my wicked take-offs. My first effort was when I was ten years old, to break the tedium of my form teacher's lessons. Behind his back, for the benefit of the kids on my row of desks, I impersonated Beryl Reid. To my surprise they all fell about laughing.

Turning to face the source of laughter, the teacher asked me to come out in front of the blackboard, stand on a chair next to him and repeat the entertainment for the whole class. Trustingly I pulled off my two silver signet rings, threaded them on to hair clips and hung them from my ears again. I stood on the chair and in a broad Brummie accent said, 'Me noim's Mawline. D'ya loik me earrinks?'

Everybody broke into fits of laughter and I felt the first sweet swell of success. Without warning the teacher delivered a stinging slap on the backs of my knees. The shock and shame numbed my senses momentarily, but my legs soon began to smart painfully as I made my way back to my desk. Holding back the sharp tears of humiliation, I shrank back into my shell. With my first bitter-sweet taste of fame I learnt that not everyone is able to enjoy your success.

At Ford's I limited my lampooning to caricatures of work-mates and bosses drawn on the cards I was supposed to punch holes in. I sat at my idle punch card machine sketching away dreamily, wishing for the day to end. I must have stretched everyone's patience to the limit.

My first monthly salary cheque was a delight. I went rushing home to Mum to ask her how to cash it into real money. Then I gave her some towards my keep and took the rest to Ilford shopping centre to buy a coat. I could not afford the one I fancied, a fashionable brown tweed swagger with a *real* fur collar. So I borrowed some from Mum and saved for weeks to pay her back. It was worth it. When I tried the coat on and posed shamelessly like Christine Keeler in front of the changing-room mirror, I felt like a million dollars.

A year later, when I received my first record royalty cheque, I went on a shopping spree at Harrods. I could not decide between the silver fox, the Russian lynx or the pink mink fun fur, so I bought the lot. I don't know which purchase gave me more pleasure. I realize that this was ideologically unsound, particularly for someone who is now so resolutely against cruelty to animals, but what do you expect from an unenlightened young *nouvelle riche*?'

When I came of age, Eve presented me with a large sum of

money she had secretly invested on my behalf. A month later, when I married Jeff Banks, my parents presented me with some more of my money that they also had been saving for me. Altogether it was enough to buy a large period town house in Knightsbridge and a big country estate in the home counties.

However, instead of becoming a rich landowner, I paid a deposit on a house in Blackheath to live in with Jeff. Obviously I could have afforded to buy it myself outright, but it was important to Jeff, then an unknown struggling fashion designer, to pay his own way and share the repayments. I admired his independence.

After we were married, much to Eve's anxiety, Jeff recommended that his lawyer and accountant were better than the ones I shared with her. I was not happy with the financial control Eve had over me and as I did not know a balance sheet from a binding agreement, and was not interested either, I was relieved to pass the responsibility to Jeff. My business was transferred to his lawyer, and my accounts, along with the money my parents had given me, were sent to his accountant.

I loved the house in Blackheath. It was a massive, double-fronted Victorian villa, with a garden that went on for ever, filled with huge, ageing mulberry, fig, chestnut and may trees, and an orchard with row upon row of gnarled fruit trees that blossomed with such abundant splendour in the spring that it made my heart leap. In the summer we ate strawberries and cream in the long grass and in the autumn I picked the fruit and conkers and painted, standing my easel in the doorway of the gazebo. In the winter, I could lie in bed and watch a pair of robins playing in the berry bushes outside the bay window. I ran blissfully about barefoot in my hippy frocks, keeping house, trying new vegetarian recipes which Jeff, as a strict carnivore, regularly threw out of the French windows in disgust, and buying and restoring furniture and ornaments from the Greenwich antique shops. The house seemed always to be bathed in brilliant streams of sunlight, or cradled in crisp newfallen snow – even the thunderstorms did not pose a threat as I nestled cosily on the window seat, listening to Joni Mitchell and watching the rain drip languidly from the leaves. Yes, I was rich, in more ways than one.

I spent the money Eve had given me, a fortune big enough to set you up for life in those pre-inflationary days, on modernizing this beautiful house, and with Jeff's designing flair we turned it into four equally beautiful flats. It was much too big for just us. We shared the house with my roadie/assistant Jenny and her boyfriend, two of Jeff's young staff, and some songwriter friends in the basement flat.

I saw less and less of Jeff. He had left the two partners with whom he had started Clobber, a trendy boutique in Blackheath village. The runaway success of the Sandie Shaw range of clothes that we collaborated on had enabled them to move to a smart West End showroom from which they sold their designs internationally. When they split up Jeff set up his own business, the International Clothing Company. It was not strictly his business; on paper it was mine too, but I always thought of it as his because I had nothing to do with the running of it. The reason I became a director was that the sum of my money which had been given to one of Jeff's accountants had gone missing. Jeff, feeling responsible for the mess although he had nothing to do with it, tried to put matters straight by making me a director and shareholder of his new venture. The money turned up magically as a loan in the new company. I was so impressed to be called a 'Director' and be a 'Shareholder' that although I had absolutely no idea what this meant, I was happy with the arrangement.

The lawyer wanted me to sign some bits of paper personally guaranteeing a factoring agreement the company needed. It was not until twenty years later when I read a book written by my friend, Debbie Moore, called *When a Woman Means Business*, that I fully understood what factoring was; I was so naive and ignorant. But I was very flattered to be of use. I passionately believed in Jeff and his talent, and as he was my husband I trusted his judgement implicity. He was my hero and could do no wrong. In retrospect I wish I had had the wisdom to show my love and loyalty to Jeff in a more valuable way, but I do not regret the feeling of wanting to support him with all I had. I signed everything I was asked to, just as our lawyer advised, not giving it a second thought. I was having a baby, and I was so happy.

Although we were married, Jeff liked the idea of my being financially independent. It meant I was never a responsibility or a burden to him, and he could concentrate all his efforts on himself, establishing his career and building his own fortune. I was able to buy all my own things, like clothes, especially the ones from the company – he insisted I was seen to pay for these to set an example to the staff so that they would not be tempted to pinch any for themselves (though in practice this never worked!). I even paid my maternity bills and bought new-born Grace's first pram and most of her baby things. Jeff was always very generous to his employees and workmates; he helped them with loans and mortgages – even so, a few took money and goods without bothering to ask.

Once, on a rare holiday, in Kenya, at Christmas-time, our co-director had a primal trauma. Dressed up like Jesus he deserted the party and went off in search of his Self. Unfortunately his new identity did not include his wife and children whom he left behind with us. Thinking it was just temporary insanity incurred by too much sun, jungle juice and his over-dependency on marijuana, we chased him cross-country, over rivers and hot dusty plains, in our jeep. Eventually we caught up with him in Mombassa. He felt no remorse; on the contrary, he felt a great sense of release, had never been happier and was not coming home. In spite of his leaving us in deep manure, Jeff was legally bound to hand over large sums of money for his shares on his resignation from the company. This put the business under considerable pressure. Well, at least it was good entertainment.

As Jeff's business got busier and he ran round in circles like a mad dog trying to catch his own tail, he had less and less time for me and little Grace - or for himself for that matter. He was obsessed with his clothing design and manufacturing business, driven by the idea of proving himself, to me, to the world. I just wanted him to spend some time with us as a family.

The perfectly tailored Jeff Banks shirt became a famous and treasured item in many womens' wardrobes. When following me up the stairs, instead of admiring the pert swell of my backside he sized up the cut of the trousers, and grabbed me on the landing not in uncontrollable passion but to re-calculate the 'rise' measurement between the legs. I have always been in awe of Jeff's manic capacity for work.

One day I received a phone call from Jeff telling me that he had just been to an auction and bought a pig farm.

'What with?' I asked.

Something called a bridging loan, he told me. He wanted the family to live in pastoral splendour in Buckinghamshire and was going to do it up just as we had done up Blackheath.

'Where will you find the time?'

'After work,' he replied.

'But you are always at work.'

'Where's your sense of enterprise?' he scolded.

Eventually stark reality hit us in the face. We had to sell Blackheath to pay off the loan for the farm, which lay empty and deserted waiting for Jeff's attentions. He acquired a new loan to pay for the damage caused by vandalism and fly-tipping on the property, which now looked more like a bomb-site than the peaceful retreat we had envisaged. Then we had to sell the farm to pay off the new loan, Jeff's overdraft and some housekeeping bills. We were destitute.

Jeff's unfortunate neglect of our family affairs was the result of his mammoth struggle to keep his business from going under during the Seventies slump. Sadly, he lost the fight. Unable to recover from a fire destroying most of the stock, the company was declared bankrupt and we were faced with thousands and thousands of pounds' worth of debts. Being old-fashioned working class people we thought we ought to pay them back.

Just before this, I had, for a laugh, visited a fortune teller in Oxford Street. As she laid out the cards on the table her look of animated interest turned first to puzzlement, then to a frown and finally her face became markedly expressionless as if she was trying deliberately to withhold some information she had divined from the cards. I pressed her to tell me what she had seen. She reluctantly replied, 'I see paper, business agreements, legal contracts and endless financial hardship.'

'When does it finish?' I asked, a terrible dread gnawing away in the pit of my stomach.

'I can't see,' she answered and got up from the table. The reading was over.

We had nothing. We were homeless. My first thought was to secure a roof over Grace's head. For only a fraction of its worth I cashed in an investment that would have made me a virtual millionairess in my thirties when it matured. I asked another of our accountants, who was holding some money for me in his client account, to release it to me. He then mysteriously disappeared, along with these savings. It was becoming a nasty habit.

Jeff furiously ransacked the accountant's house, chased him round a golf course and finally caught up with him on his gin palace of a boat. The mortgage he took out on the boat did not raise the full amount that was missing, but it was enough, with the investment money, for me to buy a little cottage and some land in Ireland for Grace and me, with a good bit over to live on for a few years.

I was tired of picking up tabs and repaying debts, and I wanted to try life on my own for a while, to live simply in ways that I could understand, to see if I could survive without any more financial 'help'. I wanted to have a go at being independent. Jeff managed to convince me that it was not possible for me to do this alone and that I needed him to make Ireland work. This was not difficult for me to believe as by this time I was clean out of self-esteem as well as money.

So my little cottage fantasy, coloured by Jeff's wonderfully flamboyant brush, became a great big mansion that took ages to make habitable and, with all the debts, ate up all my savings and all the earnings we could muster. During this time we lived in caravans parked in the grounds, with Jeff's mum and dad.

Jeff and I commuted back to London, frantically trying to earn money, where we stayed in his parents' tiny two-up two-down terrace in Chislehurst.

My deep-seated habit of parting company with my possessions continued. I had taken my last remaining fur coat from the Harrods spree, the lynx, to be cleaned. Jeff was bringing it back to Chislehurst on the train, the burgundy-coloured Bentley and matching Mini now having gone. On the journey home he fell asleep with exhaustion and missed his station. When he woke up suddenly, he jumped off the train leaving my coat on the seat. With Tolstoyan pathos the doomed Russian lynx went riding off into the distance never to be seen again. I bet some British Rail cleaning lady is still wearing it for Sunday-best outings.

Some weeks later, while working abroad, I was paid thousands of pounds in cash. I was very relieved to get this as we needed it really badly to pay an overdue bill. Not having time to get it to the bank before the plane left for Ireland, I hid it in my suitcase for safety, planning to deposit it on my arrival.

I was so tired by the journey that when I reached the caravan I went straight to bed without unpacking. Jeff was joining me the following morning. During the night I had a nightmare that the money had been stolen and woke up in a terrible panic. I scrambled under the bed for the suitcase to reassure myself. I opened the case. It was empty. I shut it and I opened it again. The money still was not there. I repeated this again and again. Surely I would wake up soon? Finally, I accepted that the nightmare was reality. I never knew where the money went, or how it went (in customs? in transit?), only that it took with it the remains of my grasp of the logical world.

The shock finally hit me. Every value system I had based my life on had crumbled away. The world that was once warm and welcoming was now dark and threatening. I had been brought up with a working-class sense of awe and respect for professional people, yet I had witnessed some of them acting without any sense of morality, completely abusing the trust I put in them. Quite unfairly, I had built Jeff up to be a paragon of virtue, a superman, my hero, and I was devastated to find out that he was only human after all, with all the frailty that goes with the condition. Cruelly I blamed him for everything. I was unable to take any responsibility for what had happened to me, and this made me feel powerless to effect any change in my situation. I lived in a permanent state of panic, terrified that at any moment, from any direction, another terrible surprise would jump out and hit me. I was just not socially or spiritually equipped to cope with the horror of it. At some moments, mercifully, my emotions would cut out; at others I was taken over by a savage sense of outrage – '*Why* is this happening to *me!*' For months I was so depressed I could not get up; I stayed semi-conscious by taking regular half-doses of Mogadon.

Poor Jeff, who was on the verge of his own personal madness, did his best to break through to me with his indefatigable sense of humour. One night he came back to the terraced house in Chislehurst unaccustomedly early, running up the stairs with a big sack over his shoulder like Father Christmas. He threw it on the bed as I lay there in a drugged stupor and emptied out the contents all over me. It rained gaudy costume jewellery and fake diamonds, all from a fashion shoot - sparkling necklaces, rings, and tiaras.

'It's only pretend,' he laughed, 'but just imagine that it's real and it will cheer you up!'

When Jeff and I finally parted in the summer of 1978, I was penniless.

The next stop on the University Tour was Warwick. The students were fresh-faced and well organized and the event was H-U-G-E. So was the big wad of cash I was given after my performance. This is a rare occurrence nowadays – we are usually paid by cheque, plus VAT. Knowing that the nostalgic feel and smell of the notes would really turn me on, Charles and Cathy left me alone in my dressing-room with my memories and the cash before it went into the safety deposit.

In a Bacchanalian orgy I tossed the readies in the air and let them flutter sensuously all over my body. I wallowed in the delicious aroma. I lay in the fivers, rolled in the tenners, fanned my face with the twenty-pound notes, curled my toes in the fifties and hundreds in abandon. When all my energy was spent, I gathered the loot and arranged it into neat, tall piles all over the floor just like my parents' housekeeping. Then I asked Cathy and Charles to come back in. Like some well-fingered groupie the dosh was carried out.

Please Help the Cause Against Loneliness

'WELCOME BACK SANDIE' screamed the walls of Leicester Polytechnic. They were emblazoned with giant posters and pictures of me and signs and messages to me. A windowless cubby hole behind the stage was called the dressing-room, and as this was the only facility the band and I were all crammed in together.

It was great to have the bass player, Chris Bostock back again. The night before at Jesus College, Oxford he had to be replaced because he had been beaten up in Liverpool by the hotel's club bouncers. His face had blown up to the size of a football, and sported the colours of both Liverpool and Everton. We had tried rubbing haemorrhoid cream on the bruises as I had heard all the ageing Hollywood stars did for the temporary removal of wrinkles and blemishes, but it didn't work. The other casualties were the road crew's dirty socks and pants. They had been stolen from the equipment van in the Liverpudlian car park while we were on stage – a perfectly normal occurrence, the student union secretary informed us. The unlucky burglar must have had a very poor sense of smell, and the fence who opened the bag probably got a nasty shock.

I managed to find a space to sit in the Leicester dressing-room. Mark E. Nevin, my guitarist and musical director, located the cans of beer while Rob Marche re-strung his Rickenbacker. Chris horsed around with the drummer, Sean McCluskey, and Rocky Holman the keyboard player did his impression of Stan Laurel. Unused to sharing a room, and feeling choked and claustrophobic with the smoking and backstage banter, I went for a look out front. I sat in the empty hall, watching all the

73

sound technicians, roadies and lighting crew rushing abo
trying to make everything perfect for me. I was slightly emba
rassed and slightly excited by all the fuss.

That evening Cathy and Charles were with another of the
artists, Deon Estus, who was playing with George Michael f
the final Wham! performance at Wembley. I was beginning
miss Cathy and Charles. With them around, the tour was mo
like an extended social occasion – I felt safe and cared for. Tod:
I felt a bit lost and alone, and an old, long-forgotten memo
started nagging at the back of my mind. I could not shake
off, it just kept growing bigger and bigger. In an effort to p
myself out of it I left the hall and went for a walk along t
waterfront. Then it took over completely – a sense of she
loneliness. I wrapped my arms around myself and tried to cudd
it away . . .

The time I was remembering was just before an earnest
requested guest appearance with the Smiths in Manchester
few years before. I wandered aimlessly round the backsta
corridors until Morrissey invited me into the band's dressin
room to help him pick a shirt for his performance. The atmo
phere was tense with the kind of well-rehearsed, famili
antagonisms present in all groups. I felt more and more u
comfortable, like an intruder. So . . . left out, yes that's it – li
sitting on the edge of the playground, watching the other ki
play their stupid games, feeling . . . left out. I just went ar
hid in a cupboard and sobbed my heart out. It complete
threw Morrissey who, as usual, had enough problems of h
own to contend with. He stood outside trying to convin
me that everything was all right and that everyone real
wanted me to be there. Unable to calm me down he le
me to my own devices. I chanted for a full hour before t
feeling lifted.

Gill Smith, my PR lady and minder-companion for the da
was quite unnerved by the close proximity of the Smiths ar
my unusual behaviour, and spent the whole time engrossed
Simone de Beauvoir's book *She Came to Stay*. This was probab
the most sensible thing to do, given the histrionics of t

occasion. Everyone looked relieved when I eventually emerged, smiling, from my dressing-room.

I strolled on stage in the middle of their set without introduction, as planned, in front of thousands of rampant, adoring Smiths fanatics. Morrissey slipped back into the shadows and left me standing in the spotlight. At first all went silent. Then, as recognition vied with disbelief, the screaming and shouting started up again. I stared at the audience and then back at Johnny Marr for what seemed like a lifetime, trying to get my bearings.

I leant over and whispered in Johnny's ear, 'I want to go home. They don't want me, they want you.' He stared at me stunned. He knew Morrissey was a nutter but he had never had to cope with the likes of me. He was impatient to play. 'Come on Sandie,' he encouraged, 'can't you hear them? THEY want you, WE want you – just SING!' So I did – and with a rush and a push the land was ours . . .

In Leicester, Brian, my tour manager was trying his best. He joined me at the waterside and suggested he book me into a nearby hotel so that I could prepare for the Leicester show in privacy. Dear Brian, young, intense, gaunt and gangly, forever sensitive but unboundingly manly in a caring and supportive way. He had been a fan for most of his tender years. At our first meeting he was stricken with nerves and shook so much that the café table wobbled and spilt the coffee everywhere. I had taken one look at this trembling bag of bones, who for some reason was making the most excruciating effort to meet me and become part of my life, and decided that the only thing I could do was teach him to practise Buddhism; then at least he would be able to stop shaking for long enough to get his own life together.

At that time, Brian was working for an outfit who managed Samson, a heavy metal band with the daunting distinction of a masked drummer who played in a cage whilst chained to his drumkit. Firstly Brian became my friend and confidante, and now, when I needed someone I could really trust on my first University Tour, he was the tour manager. It was perfect.

The hotel room's neutral and efficient luxury reminded me

of all the thousands of others I had stayed in as a teenager. Aft
the 'divorce scandal' when I was nineteen, Eve threatened
make me a ward of court (we did not 'come of age' un
twenty-one in those days), unless my dad chaperoned an
travelled with me. Although I love my dad, I don't think I
was the most natural choice of company for an energet
teenager hungry to experience her youth. I had been attracte
to the music business because it freed me from the constrain
of my background but, cowed by the ignorant, vicious com
ments of the divorce judge and consequent press coverage,
accepted Eve's conditions.

Although my dad was characteristically shy at first, tourin
certainly brought him out of his shell. We went everywher
together – to France, on the Johnny Halliday tour, where a
the hard-nosed, long-haired French roadies and musicians calle
him *'le daddy'* and were on their best behaviour when he wa
around; to Australia, where the hotel managers thought w
were husband and wife as we shared the same name and h
looked so amazingly young (as he still does); and to Ne
Zealand, where I got so bored one night that in an act of rebellio
I set light to the hairy legs of the Pretty Things' manager whi
he was asleep and started off the fire alarm.

Then, while filming a television special in Hamburg, th
magnificent Jimi Hendrix made eyes at me all through th
rehearsals. He perched dangerously near the edge of the stag
balancing on his skinny stork-like legs like an exotic bird
paradise in crushed velvet plumage. I loved his red bandana an
hippy American drawl. As he lunged at his guitar he reeked
excitement, and when he fell to his knees and plunged his teet
into its belly of strings he became one huge, hungry, electrifie
howl. I watched transfixed. I ached to drown in his Purple Haz
This spelt trouble to my dad who kept moving me around th
studio out of view. Jimi, however, out-manoeuvred my da
and had a note passed to me, making a secret rendezvous afte
the show.

Later that night, back at the hotel, I pretended to go to be
early. I dressed to go out and then put my pyjamas on top s

that when Dad came in to say goodnight I looked the picture of innocence. Just as I was about to leave he came in again with a telephone message and I rushed into the bathroom and pretended to clean my teeth while I put the pyjamas back on. He must have suspected something because he kept popping back to check me out. Each time I repeated the performance in the bathroom. By the time I got away I had gone through almost a complete tube of toothpaste, my teeth sparkled and I reeked of peppermint. Jimi didn't seem to notice. He took me to a daringly dingy nightclub with loud, dirty music, where I was showered with champagne and red roses . . . It was certainly worth the effort. (Sorry Dad!)

After that first taste of independence – at long last I had felt part of what was going on, a part of my own generation again – I knew it was only a matter of time before my dad slipped quietly back into his own life. He had also enjoyed his taste of being independent and wanted to do his own thing too. My mum, who all that time had helped me by running my fan club, was so pleased to have Dad back home again full-time. They moved away from Dagenham to the country where they started a successful boarding kennels business.

When I was a baby and we were all still living with my grandparents, I was dressed up daily in my best and put outside in the fresh air, propped up in a pram. I can still see the colour and feel the texture of my blanket and smell the aroma of the privets after the rain. I waited desperately for a neighbour to pass by and take notice of me. As I grew older I longed for a brother or a sister like my cousins or schoolmates had. I don't think my parents ever realized the existence or depth of my loneliness. I regularly ran away from home to my Uncle John or my Auntie Doll with some minor complaint about my poor mum that I had built up to monumental proportions. I loved to be around my cousins' busy families. While my mum diligently worked as a clerk in Ever Ready's offices or at the Royal London Insurance Company, not only to keep her brain active but also to supplement the family income so that we were able to afford our lovely new house opposite the park on the outskirts of the Dagenham housing estates, *their* mums stayed at home as housewives in the council houses. When I arrived on one of my cousins' doorsteps it was buzzing with activity, not empty and quiet like my place. But in many ways I came to enjoy my isolation, going for long solitary walks in the park. I played for hours upon end with only my imagination for company in the bushes and by the brook that ran through the dairy farm next door or in the woods of the old folks' home opposite, examining spiders' webs, and searching for cuckoo spit or priest-in-the-pulpit.

By the time I was in my teens I was best friends with Kathy Murphy from school. Kathy's prolific Irish Catholic family was in complete contrast to my own. I often went past my bus stop and accompanied her home after school. Her family did incredible things. Her mum loved to sit in the kitchen with kids scattered all over her, telling wonderful stories and singing songs with lots of strange noises which sounded even better when she took her teeth out. On dark winter nights we huddled together for warmth, the windows glistening with condensation, and listened intently as she told our fortunes. When she was out of the room we played with a Ouija board. The children ate things that I was not allowed and some things that I had never heard of. Once on the way home I watched in wide-eyed wonder and horror while Kathy tucked hungrily into a pig's trotter.

Kathy had so many brothers and sisters that they all shared beds and rooms; some even slept in the lounge. I really envied her all that company. On the other hand, when I started singing and was away from home, Kathy loved to stay at my house with my parents, craving the peace, quiet and privacy of my big empty bed in my big empty room.

While we were still at school, Kathy and I had two other friends, Marlene and her cousin Sheila. We all went dancing together every week. It was the highlight of my life, a chance for me to shine. I loved music, I was a good dancer and sometimes I got up to sing with the band. Once, at a time when everybody had managed to acquire boyfriends except me, they turned to me after a private, huddled conversation and announced that they would not be going to the dance hall that night, and that the reason I was so upset was because I was just using them for someone to go out with – and I was not really their friend. The event was insignificant and common enough but the surprise and intensity of the pain left a long-lasting impression on me. Humiliation always hurts more when you are not expecting it.

Since becoming famous I had never really had a best girl-friend. Linda, my hairdresser, followed my father as travelling companion after a brief and spectacularly unsuccessful spell with a retired comedian Eve had hired. I did not find him very funny. Eve had given him strict instructions to keep me out of mischief which he followed somewhat over-enthusiastically in order to please her and keep his job. On his first and last week away with me his imagination ran riot if he did not know where I was every moment of the day, and especially the night. This culminated in an hysterical outburst of tears and abuse on a Liverpool railway platform when he discovered that Mike McGear had sneaked me out to meet and stay with his parents, the McCartneys, overnight. He carried on as if Mike had taken me to an orgy. Eve decided that a desk job was better for his nerves.

At Eve's invitation, Linda left her job as a hairdresser at the Regent Palace Hotel and joined me and the band for a European tour. I recall spending most of the time trying to find her doctors to prescribe pessaries for a yeast infection she wanted to get rid of before her wedding, and a dentist to put back the front tooth that had fallen out while playing rather over-boisterously with the band in the sea. She refused to come ashore without her tooth. By a miracle I managed to retrieve it from its burial in the sand, four foot under the water.

Although our lives were very different, it was great to have another female around. I was intrigued by all her intimate girl-talk, having spent my late teens with men and older women. Unfortunately, by the time I began to understand what she was talking about, her yeast infection had cleared up and she left to get married.

Eve replaced Linda with a friend of her secretary, a prim Jewish girl who had never set foot outside Golders Green . . . but she could drive! I had just had a beautiful new Lotus Elan delivered. I could not drive, so it crouched in latent potency in the driveway. When I asked if she wanted to use my car she nodded enthusiastically, thinking I meant the Mini, but the sight of the bulging, silver hot-rod ogling her eagerly with its sleeked-back headlights was a shock. To her credit she gave it a try, sneaking gingerly behind the wheel. You could hear the engine's obvious disappointment as she crawled slowly along the road in sheer terror at its power. The rest of her short ride with me was pretty much in the same vein.

By this time I had met Jeff, and knowing how lonely I was for company I could relate to, he suggested his friend, a model called Debbie Moore, to be my roadie.

Debbie had been a beautiful and successful model since she was sixteen, but after suffering an emotional trauma when her husband unexpectedly left her, she developed an illness that made her blow up to eleven stone or shrivel down to seven stone in an erratic and extraordinary manner. Her modelling career had come to a dramatic halt. She had to sell all her clothes either to pay the bills or because they just did not fit any more.

On the road, Debbie's every action was a perfect study in thrift, self-discipline and economy of effort, from the way she neatly sat or used her time between shows to carefully darn a hole in one of her two cashmere sweaters, her strict diet of steak and salad regardless of the goodies on the menu, to the matter-of-fact way she left the room after meals to inject herself with a huge syringeful of medication. She had few belongings, but each one was sleek, streamlined and efficient. She never lacked class. We were fascinated by each other.

Debbie observed my every move, taking mental notes on my professional behaviour and presentation. She watched like a hawk as I performed my backstage metamorphosis from a messy-minded girl-next-door to an international superstar, whether I was singing to three people in a struggling Greek restaurant or three thousand in a posh nightclub. I'm glad somebody noticed and appreciated the tremendous effort it took. Almost fifteen years later, Debbie's dance studio company, Pineapple, was quoted on the stock exchange, the City gents took her to their heaving, pin-striped chests, and she was voted Business Woman of the Year.

Then came Jenny.

Jenny was the archetypal hippy. She believed in peace and harmony and she really did love everybody – all the heavy, straight, breadheaded, small-minded, thick-skinned, cynical types that congregate in the music business, and with whom she had absolutely nothing in common. Whoever they were, whatever they did, Jenny always managed to find in them some redeeming characteristic. Yet she never budged from her own hippy values; she just bowled them over with her love and light. She was truly subversive in her own gentle way. I was absolutely mesmerized by her.

Eve did not like Jenny. Her mere presence undermined the balance of power that Eve had spent so much time and effort creating. Jenny seeped into and freed my soul like pure fresh spring water and as I began to realize the validity of my own dreams and aspirations, the power politics between Eve and me started shifting dangerously. Eventually, through Jenny's sheer persistence, even Eve succumbed.

Much to Jeff's disdain, Jenny taught me to be a healthy vegetarian. Having talked through the ethics with her, I finally took the plunge on a trip to Argentina, whose economy is built on the meat of cows. Every mealtime I was assaulted by waiters offering massive beefsteaks. It was really gross. Jenny and I would tuck into a welcome bowl of salad before sneaking out of the hotel to explore the backstreets and discover the real Argentina.

Before Jenny worked with me she had been a photographic assistant for Lord Snowdon and Hans Feurer. Her last assignment had been to assist at a Marlene Dietrich session, where the Blue Angel herself had also been captivated by Jenny's free spirit and had offered her a job. Luckily she stayed to share her unique view of the world with me. I always envied Jenny's natural, uninhibited goodness. I loved her so much. She was my one true friend in all the madness that pervaded my life.

I do not know what caused it, what it was about, or why we had our argument. I suspect it was my possessiveness. Jenny left to go and live out her Bohemian lifestyle in Ireland.

Many years later, in 1979, I received a letter from a gaol on the Spanish–Morrocan border. It read, 'Another fine mess I've gotten myself into . . . Mucho Amor, Jenny.' In a crazy bid to help her boyfriend in Ireland by earning some 'easy' money to buy a new horse, she had been caught by customs smuggling thirty-three kilos of hashish under her car from Morocco. In her hippy trusting way she had taken full responsibility so that her friend, her accomplice, could go free. Jenny thought she would get about two years, but both she and I were devastated when she was sentenced to eight.

By this time I had been a Nichiren Shoshu Buddhist for about eighteen months. The only practical way I could answer Jenny's plea for help was to teach her to practise too so that she could discover why she had ended up in such a horrific situation, change her karma, and gain something from the experience. I had always wanted to pay Jenny back for the tremendous effect she had had on my life but it was bizarre that it should happen in this way.

We poured our hearts out in hundreds of letters to each other throughout her stay in Spain. My life felt tied to hers in some unseen, mystic way. Her every mood touched me and I tried desperately to respond in an encouraging and positive way. My knowledge of Buddhist practice was minimal at that time and Jenny stretched me to the limit with her endless stream of questions.

Together we fought her fate and her negativity, and she shared with me her experiences with her colourful Mediterranean inmates, the Spanish judicial system and her personal heartbreaks. Some days I was in floods of tears because I felt so inadequate. I pored over my study books and went for constant guidance so that I could write to her exactly what she needed to know.

But most of the time Jenny's open, childlike search for the truth was a constant inspiration to me.

One day Jenny wrote, 'Chanting "*Nam-myoho-renge-kyo*" is the best thing that ever happened to me – better than Lebanese gold, Pakistani black, and Thai temple bells!' Then I knew we were winning. Never in my wildest dreams had I thought that someone like Jenny would ever trust me so completely, and it was a wonderful responsibility.

Because of her good humour and abilities as a cook, Jenny was given charge of the prison kitchen. When she was eventually released early, after all manner of special concessions and having served only three years of her sentence, we were all treated to the most amazing vegetarian paellas, Spanish omelettes, and exotic sun-kissed delights.

In Jenny I had found a real and honest friend. As I thought about her in that anonymous Leicester hotel room I held the warm feeling to me and hugged it close.

When I was very little I often ran into my parents' room in the middle of the night, scared of being left out. My heart sank with disappointment when I was escorted firmly back to my own bed. I am fascinated by the triangular politics of a single-child family. I often watch unnoticed the jolly threesome on trains, or beaches, in restaurants, in the park, having grown-up or childish fun all together, the jealousies and passions all con-tained within the neat, tiny unit. There is simply no one else to turn to when things go wrong. The grievance is either accepted and absorbed by the trio or nursed silently, alone. It's always two against one; it's difficult to achieve parity, easy to feel left out. Even with my first playmates the triadic power structure continued, either with my two girl cousins Carol and June, or with June and her brother Terry, or with my friends Maureen and Linda, two sisters who lived opposite. It now continued with Cathy and Charles. I felt like an abandoned child.

Brian picked me up from the hotel after I had finished my evening *gongyo* and swept me past all the obstacles to the side of the stage. It was sweltering under the spotlight; the audience, pressed body to body, was welded by the heat into one pulsating, sweating, cheering, buoyant mass of effervescent juvenescence. Their enthusiasm spilt over on to the stage where I was well protected by well-built young men stripped to their tiny tanned hips, biceps glistening with perspiration. Beer cans were exploded and sprayed over the crowd to cool down the frenzy. Pretty girls, close-shorn heads cupped in hands propped on the stage front, gazed dreamily, beaming up sunny crimson smiles. I certainly did not feel left out. I was an independent adult, no longer a child, and I was with dear old friends.

Mother of Three

WE DECIDED TO CAPTURE the last show of the tour at the Town and Country Club in London on video – a relatively new medium for me. At every date there had been a pile of presentation tapes of suggested directors, sent by Polygram, the music video company. The work struck me as being professional, slick and glossy and quite devoid of character or originality. I loathe that aspect of Eighties culture, all packaging and no substance. I wanted a director who would enjoy filming a passionate, spontaneous and unpredictable performance which would be dangerous too – I always have the feeling that somehow I might not survive the whole song, might not complete the set; that I might not emerge the same person at the end. It's like being on the edge of death and the brink of new life at the same time.

When I was seventeen I worked with the innovative pop director Jack Good on a Beatles special (ooooh John!) for the American TV show 'Shindig'. On my arrival at the rehearsal room in some dusty London suburb, Jack broke everyone for lunch. He sat down with me and a cup of tea and got me chatting about myself. I usually played my cards pretty close to my chest, but somehow I opened up to him, confided all my love life to him. When I got to the heartbreak bit I started sobbing uncontrollably. Jack jumped up from his seat and switched the record player on, and my song, 'Always Something There To Remind Me', came blaring out.

'That's it! Keep that! That's the feeling I want – now we can start rehearsing!' he shouted excitedly. After three run-throughs I was completely cried out. Jack was over the moon. I have been 'method singing' ever since.

I finally chose an Irish director, Ken O'Neil, for the Town and Country video, which was to be called 'Sandie Shaw – LIVE in London'. The Irish appreciate eccentricity like no other race. I had worked with him before on my very first TV appearance with the Smiths in 1984 on a programme called 'Ear Say'.

At that time I had not completed my reincarnation from Sixties Dolly Bird to Eighties Pop Icon. I had turned up at the studio straight from the kitchen, still in my work clothes, having left a wash on. When the glorious strains of 'Hand In Glove' came tumbling out of the speakers like a Monday washload, I quite forgot where I was. Frothing at the mike, I swirled around the highly amused Johnny, Mike and Andy of the Smiths, bubbling over with uncontainable joy into millions of TV sets. On transmission my embarrassment was intense. I thought I looked like a demented housewife in a washing powder commercial. I suppose those who aspire to fame must learn to endure minor humiliations!

This peculiar performance was followed by an old excerpt from 'Ready Steady Go', an adolescent me singing 'Girl Don't Come', swishing a shimmering curtain of hair across my face like a houri's veil, then being interviewed by Keith Fordyce. I spoke in a strange little Dagenham-girl voice, uttering total inanities with a sensual sophistication certainly not acquired in this lifetime. My daughter Grace does a wicked impersonation of this interview.

In the studio, Morrissey and I had watched these clips from our interviewees' seats, he in rapt adoration and me in squirming discomfort. As the presenter turned to me with a question, I could not stop thinking, 'Am I still talking rubbish after all these years?' and even more disturbing, 'Am I still sexy?'

That vision of me as a young girl is firmly locked into older people's minds and, not having had the opportunity to see me mature gradually over the years because of my disappearance from public view, they expect me to look and be the same as their memory of me. I was uniquely lucky to have a new, young audience now who allowed me the freedom to develop naturally

...r successes and our tragedies would usually lead to yet another song. Chris Andrews, my song writer,
Adam Faith, my 'discoverer', at Dinely's Rehearsal Rooms. (REX FEATURES)

...oah way ya win.' Returning 'triumphant' from Vienna. (EXPRESS NEWSPAPERS)

'*Without doubt we are incurable Sand*
Shaw fans,' wrote Morrissey and J
Marr. (EXPRESS NEWSPAPERS)

'*THEY want you. WE wa*
just SING!' *So I did - and*
rush and a push the land w
(PAUL SLATTERY)

I decided I would believe that he loved me. Steven Morrissey. (PETER ASHWORTH)

We went everywhere to[...]
roadies and musicians c[...]
'le daddy'. The hand[...]
one next to me.

. . . my mum followed the
bewildered dog round the ga[...]
poking his pooh with a stick[...]
Prince with my dad.

*There are things I have shared with
Grace that I could not share
with anyone else in the world.* At 8.

*. the kind of place that made you yearn to be
nbarded by your adorable screaming brood at home.*
nie and Jack, at 5 and 3. (SUE MILLMOORE)

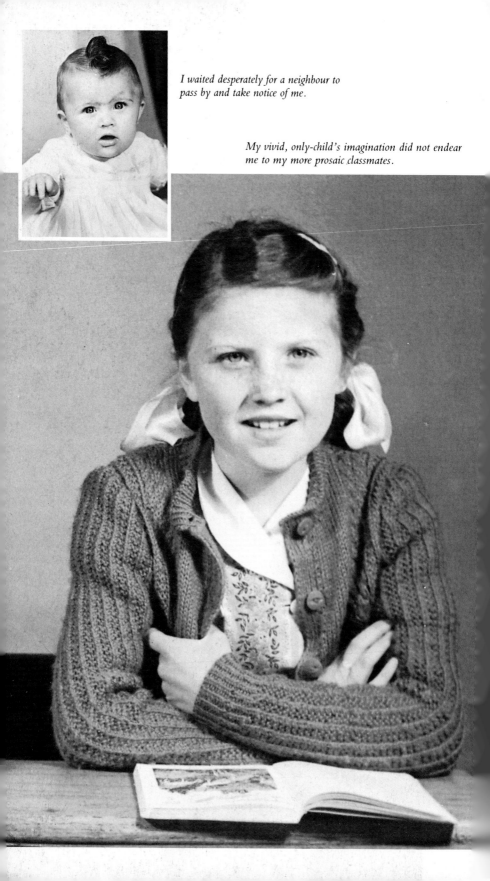

I waited desperately for a neighbour to pass by and take notice of me.

My vivid, only-child's imagination did not endear me to my more prosaic classmates.

*I clung to him for comfort as if he were my teddy bear.
Jeff and me in 1967.* (GORDON MOORE)

*I am often suspicious of couples whose marriages
break up 'amicably'. 1970.*
(TERRY O'NEILL)

*Our daughter Grace is the tangible reminder
of the more creative results of our relationship.
Jeff, me and Grace in 1986.*
(REX FEATURES)

'You were wonderful, Mummy,' she whispered emotionally. She was so relieved, because she actually approved of me. Teenaged Grace, at the time of the tou

. . . cheekbones thrust instinctively up to the spotlight, I stood at the centre of my universe. On stage at the Town & Country Club. (DENIS W. LEWIS)

an artist, with all the advantages but none of the restraints of the past. As I am fairly well preserved, everyone says in amazement, 'You haven't changed a bit!' Well, I have. I and the camera know that.

The camera has always loved me. I spent most of my early years with it focused passionately on my face. Would it still love me on video?

I made my first pop video in 1982. It was for the single 'Anyone Who Had A Heart', taken from the album '*Music Of Quality And Distinction*', in which the band Heaven 17 had asked various artists to join them in covering their favourite old songs. As I had been out of circulation for ages, and was not sure at all whether I wanted to get back into it, my confidence was extremely shaky, so the director, Steve Barron, and his sister Siobhan, the producer, were very gentle with me. They found me an American make-up girl called Paula Owen who was so supportive and made me look so incredibly beautiful with her big box of magic tricks, that in order to thank her I began to tell her how to practise Buddhism.

My attitude to make-up artists has not always been so positive. They always had very definite ideas about how I should look, none of which corresponded to my own. In Germany they covered me in pancake; in France they were so subtle I looked anaemic; the BBC refused to black my eyes; in Spain they gave me red lips; and in Italy they stuck my eyelids back with false eyelash glue to make my eyes look as huge as Sophia Loren's. It's a pity they could do nothing about my chest! Eventually, I always did my make-up myself. Just before the University tour, when I had made my second video for the latest single, 'Are You Ready To Be Heartbroken?', I received a priceless tip from the South African make-up artist. He advised me that if instead of wearing a base the same tone as the skin you wear it a few shades darker, then the lighting man can really blast on the light. On camera the skin reverts to its normal colour and all the blemishes and nasty, saggy, wrinkly bits are supposed to disappear miraculously! And it works – up to a point. After that you are at the mercy of your genetic and spiritual make-up. I

would not advise this for casual daywear unless you want
walk around holding a spotlight to your face to make you lo
normal.

Personally, although I would like to look good, I don't rea
feel the urge to fight the ageing process too obsessively. The
is something so sad and undignified about the battle. It's sucl
burden having always to look the same for your public un
you turn into a pathetic caricature of your former self. I do
share the awful modern fear of maturity, of mortality, of deat
I know I'll be re-born with a new young body. Maybe I'll t
big tits and blond hair next lifetime, just for a change! Till th
I am still firmly committed to growing old disgracefully.

Some of the people at Polydor did not have the same sen
of fun. On release of the 'Are You Ready To Be Heartbroke
single, I was booked to plug it on 'Wogan'. It was very stran
to go back to the same TV theatre at Shepherd's Bush where
sang all those Eurovision entries on 'The Rolf Harris Show
While I was sitting in the canteen telling my new musicians
about it, the fire alarm went off and everyone rushed out of t
theatre and tumbled into the alleyway outside the stage doc
Terry Wogan huddled in the doorway with an aide, while
signed autograph books, cigarette packets and five-pound not
for the surprised fans waiting there. Terry did not recogni
me.

'Who *is* that?' he asked his friend.

Maybe I did not look like a star any more.

False alarm over, we returned to our dressing-rooms. D
spondently I tried on all my outfits in front of the mirror. No
of them inspired me. I did not feel star-like. In desperati
I gave Jeff Banks a call. He is always great at last-minu
transformations. He sent over a brilliant black coat that s
aciously swung and clung to my legs and slipped slinkily off t
shoulder. I teamed this up with tight black jeans and sneaker
Perfect!

On set, the beautiful jangly guitars of my latest song, casca
ing in crystal fountains around the studio, was a million lig
years away from the farting oompahs of 'Puppet On A String

I was so happy I thought I would burst. I swirled the coat around. It slid down my back. I twirled it in the air and threw it over the cameraman's head. I sank to the floor and finished the song lying upside down across the stairs in a cruciform.

Everyone thought it was great fun.

Jeff rang me to get the coat back.

'Can't I have it?' I pleaded.

'Sorry Sand'. I designed it for Bob Dylan. If he finds out what you did with it he'll go bananas!'

Later, Dylan decided the coat did not flatter his tummy too much so I was able to buy the wonderful garment from Jeff.

A few days after the 'Wogan' appearance Charles was summoned to Polydor's promotion department and given a rucking for allowing me to 'blow it' with my performance. For others it went down as a highly amusing piece of TV memorabilia. I sometimes wonder why some people go into show business. They would be better off working in a bank.

'Ready Steady Go' was always completely chaotic. That was its charm. Like millions of others of my generation, I watched the show religiously every Friday evening as I got ready to go out dancing with my boyfriend (the one with the Ford Prefect from the Palais). The music pounded in tumultuous waves round his front room and a whole sea of teenage consciousness moved as one as each young viewer turned on and tuned in to programmed anarchy, while their parents looked on in bewildered fascination. With each song the excitement mounted. I lashed on my eyeliner more feverishly and my boyfriend's sister backcombed her bob higher and higher until she was at least five inches taller and it stood out like a platform at the back. By the time the titles rolled the show to an ecstatic climax we were bopping around the sofa and ready to go . . . 5 – 4 – 3 – 2 – 1 !!!!

When I made my debut on the show it was like stepping off the bus straight on to the set, it was such a familiar part of my life. I made friends immediately with the presenters Cathy McGowan and Michael Aldred, Patrick Kerr and the dancers, and all the production crew. We all went out together to dance halls, talent spotting for trendy dressers and good movers to give audience tickets to. One of the production assistants, Paul Raven, now known as Gary Glitter, was just desperate to be a star. Gary loved to stand in for the bands and singers for the afternoon camera rehearsal while they had fun backstage. One evening his dream came true . . .

There was always a shortage of space behind the scenes and the girl singers were often all put in the same dressing-room. On one such programme, which was going out live, I was so busy nattering to Cathy that I missed my cue. I zoomed into the dressing-room and started rummaging around myopically in Dusty's (who was also as blind as a bat), Cilla's, and Lulu's clothes trying to find my outfit. Suddenly I heard my record over the Tannoy system. In a panic I grabbed Dusty's dress and rushed into the studio. There, in front of the camera, was Gary Glitter, barefoot and radiant, wiggling his bum and miming to 'Long Live Love'.

The day before the Town and Country video was filmed I felt like an alien in my own home. The kids' usual requests – a glass of milk, telly on please, tie my shoelaces, where's my Carebear? – all fell on deaf ears. I was a nervous wreck and I wanted to concentrate a hundred per cent on feeding my worries and paranoia. Instead of inflicting my raw nerves on my family, I moved out and checked into a hotel overnight. There I could indulge my headache, stomach upset and sore throat in peace.

It was sweltering in the nineties and really uncomfortable. Grace came over for dinner in my room but it was too hot to eat. I spent the night alone in strict celibacy, like a boxer preparing for the big fight, with only my migraine for company.

The next day, the Town and Country was bursting with lighting, sound and camera technicians in a flurry of activity with all the accompanying equipment. I edged nervously past the mobile studios blocking the alleyway up to the stage door, then trod carefully over the mounds of wires and cables woven across the stage. I looked around at all the people and equipment and thought, 'All this for *me!*' It was a heady feeling.

I greeted the band, and then I introduced myself to everyone and found out their names and their jobs. I made particular friends with the chief sound engineer, the lighting director, the cameramen, in particular the one with the hand-held equipment (I learn fast), and then the make-up girl, the kitchen and door staff, and of course the director. These were all key people. I needed their support, so I wanted them to be aware of mine for them. Unless we were all working together harmoniously I could not give it my best shot. I was determined that *everyone* would enjoy the evening.

We did a brief sound check. This tour had taught me very quickly that you can't get the right sound without an audience to soak it up, so the purpose of the run-through was really for the engineer to check everything was working, to find out the various idiosyncratic sound problems of the room, and for the musicians to warm up and refamiliarize themselves with the material and with each other after a break from playing. One of the guitars sounded decidedly unhappy. We carefully nursed it back to life and patched it up with some tin foil.

The lighting rigs were set up and the lighting plot was loosely pre-planned, leaving plenty of room for spontaneous creative expression from the team. Long, mid and close-up shots from various angles were covered by the cameras. The rest was up to the performance – and the edit.

Then, without a second to catch my breath, Cathy whisked me off to be made up and Charles went out front of house to chivvy everyone along and take care of the audience already arriving in sweaty anticipation on this sexy, hot, summer night.

Suddenly I was on stage. I greeted the crowd in song, cheek-bones thrust instinctively up to the spotlight, where I stood at the centre of my universe. It was steamy hot, physically and mentally exhausting as I stretched myself to the limit, but I felt nothing but exhilaration and the trickle of fresh perspiration down my neck, my back, my arms, my legs . . .

I finished the show. They wanted more. I changed into some dry clothes, brushed my hair, offered my face to the make-up girl to patch up, came back on stage and did another song. They wanted more. I did another and bid adieu. They still wanted more. I traipsed on stage yet again, exhausted, riding on the energy of the audience. As I went back and forth, I glimpsed in passing the eyes of the backstage technicians, the stage manager, the boy on the camera cable, the monitor crew, the musicians – they were all as elated as I was with our success. I felt no separation between on and off stage, it was as if everything was on view, and in fact it was, on camera – it followed me everywhere.

When I came off stage I fell on to the dressing-room floor, absolutely drained. I put my feet up on a chair and took deep breaths to calm down. At this point Grace arrived in the doorway, having just witnessed for the first time this latest incarnation of her mother as a pop star. She took one look at me lying there and burst into tears.

Grace is a fearless critic of artistic merit. Seeing her reaction I panicked, anticipating an early second retirement.

'She hates my work! I've embarrassed her! I'll have to wear a bag over my head at Sainsbury's!'

On the other hand, Grace, who had never seen my backstage antics before either, had thought from my heavy breathing that I was on the verge of expiring with all the strain! She knelt down at my side.

'You were wonderful, Mummy,' she whispered emotionally, copiously piling on the praise. She was so relieved, firstly because she actually approved of me, and secondly because of my instant revival from the edge of 'death' when these first longed-for compliments came tumbling out of her mouth. We linked arms and went up to the party Polydor Records had laid on for us all.

A few days later Charles and I went to the editing-room to look at the footage. As I walked in I was confronted by a wall of screens, each carrying different images of me singing, jumping and rolling around the stage. It was fascinating. The mistakes were the best thing. We kept them all in, even when the camera followed me, unplanned, backstage. It gave a real sense of shared fun. I didn't look half bad either; my love affair with the camera rekindled the second time around. Ken O'Neil sat in the director's chair watching the film, chuckling like a lunatic leprechaun, and exclaiming in his Irish brogue, 'Fancy that! A mother of three!'

Marriage Rites and Wrongs

THREE DAYS AFTER the Town and Country show, my business managers, Cathy Riddell and Charles Negus-Fancey, finally decided to tie the knot. The lead-up had been agonizing.

Charles and I had lots of philosophical discussions in the car, between record company meetings. I shared with him my thoughts on marriage – which was not easy. I was seriously biased. My life seemed to be an endless search for the elusive perfection of monogamy whilst simultaneously retaining a free spirit. This is difficult to achieve but not impossible – I hope!

I'm quite experienced at getting married now. My first wedding to Jeff Banks in 1968 was a very spontaneous affair. We were like a pair of kids playing at grown-ups' games. There was no doubt that we loved each other passionately, maybe a little too passionately for our own good. In the hard and loveless adult world of my success I clung to him for comfort as if he were my teddy bear.

Our marriage was the gesture of a couple of rebellious children determined to make it on our own. It took us fourteen long, painful, glorious years to grow up, to find out that life was not a game, that every cause has an effect – some exhilarating, some disastrous. I discovered the responsibility and wisdom that go with power; that to be in control of your life, to drive your own car, you cannot suddenly leave the wheel when a dodgy bit comes up in the road. Creative living takes guts.

I also learnt that a husband and wife can divorce each other in court but they cannot divorce themselves from the formative effect they have had on each other's lives. I would certainly not be the same person today were it not for my relationship with

Jeff. As I quite like myself now and I love the way my life has turned out I can only feel gratitude to him for all the trials and tribulations in our marriage that have enabled me to evolve in this way. I have not always felt like this.

I am often suspicious of couples whose marriages break up 'amicably', those that find it a doddle staying 'the best of friends'. It indicates a level of emotional depth in the relationship that would be quite inadequate for people like Jeff and me. Our break-up was as explosive as the marriage, albeit on a slow fuse. We made one hell of a fuss, kicking and screaming for years. From time to time we still do. As highly creative, impassioned people, overcoming the other side of the same nature, our destructive tendency, has always been a struggle for each of us.

When such volatile emotions as both Jeff and I are capable of are unleashed, one becomes blinded by the sparks. Oh the ego involved! The uncontrollable desire to WIN, to bend the other person into submission to your will. More and more I refused to submit to Jeff's idea of reality. Seething resentment acquired over aeons poured out in vile rhetoric, in white-hot hate. The feeling was so seductive it would have been really easy at these times to direct my hatred at Jeff instead of at the feelings he was bringing out in me. Imagine your life is a cup of clear water with unseen sediment at the bottom. Along comes a spoon, in this case Jeff, and stirs things up a bit. The dirt in your life then floats to the top. It's no use blaming the spoon – the spoon's function is to stir. You'd do better to clean up your own act, purify your own life.

Blaming someone else for your predicament leaves you powerless, a victim. Those awful feelings are in control. Power is the ability to change yourself. Hatred, however justified you may consider it to be, imprisons you in its hell. If you can rise above all that emotion and just concentrate on perfecting yourself, then you are free, the universe is your playground. This is one of the most important lessons I have ever learnt – all thanks to Jeff.

Our daughter Grace is the tangible reminder of the more

creative results of our relationship. To parent a child together is a profoundly rewarding thing to do, especially a child as delightful and special as Gracie. So Jeff and I must have an equally strong positive as negative karmic attachment to each other. I hope that next lifetime we find another exciting way to express this connection. Maybe I'll be his accountant! Or his boss! Then again, maybe that's where all the trouble started the last time around!

For this particular lifetime, Jeff and I chose to have a dynamic, romantic, anima/animus projection. We are both only-children from unremarkable working-class backgrounds, born with the knowledge, the insupportable fantasy, that we were made for bigger things. We met in Eve Taylor's office just after the Euroyawn, he desperate for business and me desperate for company. He put forward his proposal. I had other things in mind. I loved his cockiness and sense of fun – I still do!

Jeff wanted to exploit my reputation as a Sixties fashion symbol by designing a range of clothes with my name on the label. I frantically urged Eve to go ahead with the deal because I knew this meant I would see more of him; but to him I was very cool and aloof – 'stuck-up' he told me later.

It did not take long before we were living together in his flat in the Paragon at Blackheath. He regularly threw me out the door, followed by my clothes, from the fifth-floor window, every time he realized that once again I had wangled my way into his life. I can remember being obsessed by his ex-girlfriend who had left a pair of jodhpurs and what seemed to me to be an extremely large-cupped brassiere in the airing cupboard. I combed the flat for further clues of his preferences.

Once, just after one of his clear-outs, we were invited to a party and I had literally not a stitch to wear. Jeff had a trendy boutique called Clobber in the village. He suggested I put on my fur coat over my birthday suit; we could quietly sneak out in the car and pick up an outfit on the way.

As we approached we saw crowds of people and fire engines

surrounding the floodlit shop. Jeff screamed at the top of his voice in concert with the tyres as the car screeched to a halt. He rushed into the blazing building, leaving me in the freezing cold on the back seat. I wriggled down and hid on the floor from the local press.

Some time later he staggered back, his face blackened by the smoke and his coat bulging with the stuff that he had stashed away behind a wall in the basement. Apparently the firemen thought he had gone crazy as he clawed at the bricks with his bare hands.

I gave him a quick flash, pointing out that I still had no clothes on. 'Hang on!' he shouted, and plunged back into the flames to rescue a frock from the burning remains of his stock. By this time the firemen were convinced he was completely off his trolley and dragged him out for his own good. It was episodes like this, his constant willingness to turn disaster into high drama, that so endeared Jeff to me.

Just after my twenty-first birthday I had a minor operation. While I lay languishing in a Harley Street clinic bed, still under the influence of anaesthetic, Jeff, overcome by a wave of sympathy, surprised himself and proposed to me. Sentimentality has always been one of his most lovable but dangerous traits. At first I pretended to be still asleep. I lay there quietly. Then Jeff got the shock of his life when I double-dared him and whispered, 'Yes.'

Three days later he turned up at the hospital all winks, grins, and furtive glances. He gave me a yellow minidress with a matching mac, and a short red wig for disguise. Then we sneaked out the back door and drove to the register office at Greenwich.

I waited in the car while he found two porters to act as witnesses. Because of the intimate nature of my operation I could not walk too gracefully, and the red, curly wig, which was rather ill-fitting, kept slipping over my eyes. The registrar made an incredible effort to keep a straight face. It was all over in a jiff.

Outside, in the cold light of day, the enormity of the deed hit us. We turned to each other like a pair of naughty children realizing we were in for big trouble.

'Oh Jeff. What have we done?' I whispered.

How those porters ever guessed my identity I don't know, but the next day Eve had a call from a reporter from the *News of the World* asking for confirmation of the marriage.

Eve rang us up sobbing her heart out. 'WHY didn't you tell me!' (Because she would go through the roof, that's why!) Then a different tack, 'I'm SO happy for you!' she snuffled. 'You had better tell your mum and dad before they read about it first.'

Jeff and I broke the news to our speechless parents. We suddenly realized that, as their only children, we had done them out of their one chance of a wedding. Rather than the rest of the world find out about the marriage as a gossip item in the Sunday rags, we called a press conference and announced it to everyone.

The wedding night was a fiasco. It was also a hint of things to come. After the wedding, Jeff parked me, the invalid, in bed in our new Blackheath flat and sped off to his office. Typically, he got wrapped up in his work and forgot about the morning's proceedings and the bride waiting for him at home.

It wasn't till half-way through dinner at Alvaro's with some workmates that evening, when the waiter casually asked after me, that Jeff suddenly remembered. Alvaro rushed over with crates of champagne for the entire restaurant to celebrate. I was presented with a sozzled but happy bridegroom in the early hours of the morning, who charmed me into accepting that he was only making up for missing out on his stag night.

I met my present husband, Nik Powell, in 1981, about three years after Jeff and I had separated, but were still married. I can remember being in bed, reading an article in a Sunday supplement in the early Seventies about Nik and his partner Richard Branson. It must have been just after a tiff with Jeff, when for a time his minuses outweighed his pluses, because I distinctly recall reading the copy and looking at

Nik's photo and thinking, 'I wouldn't mind being married to HIM!'

We met through my friend Roberta. She had decided to celebrate her birthday with a hen party. She was one of the people who had continually supported me in my early days as a Buddhist, during my painful struggles to put the theory into practice and extricate myself from what I now call the 'Dark Ages'.

A raucous group of women assembled at Manna, a vegetarian restaurant in Primrose Hill, for the party. The talk was fruity, fresh and frank. Half-way through the meal and mid-way through a particularly juicy joke, Roberta's late-coming friend, Barbara, joined us, accompanied by a . . . MAN!

The laughter stopped instantly as Barbara, who ran the Town House recording studios, introduced her boss, Nik Powell. They had just finished work and he was hungry so she had asked him to come along. He shuffled about uncomfortably while we took a vote and decided he could stay.

Nik was in his element. He loves to be surrounded by women. When I found out he was involved with Virgin we had a huge argument about the record business until someone discreetly informed me of the extent of his involvement – he co-owned the Virgin Group of companies. I was rather surprised; even in those days one only heard about Richard Branson. Nik was very gracious about my criticisms, though I did not deserve it. I like a man who is not afraid of a good argument.

As I already had a long-standing relationship with a student in Scotland, I mentally filed Nik away under 'good business contact'. (It occurred to me a few weeks later while we were sharing a bath that he would have to be re-filed.)

At the Venue, a Virgin club, a couple of days after Roberta's party, I 'accidentally' bumped into Nik again. I knew somehow that he would be there. He asked me for a date seven times. Each time I said I was busy. I like a man with determination.

The next day I went away on a week-long Buddhist course

in the South of France (there's nothing quite like becoming enlightened in the sunshine!). Nik went to cool down on a skiing holiday in the Alps. I realized during my stay that Nik was – The Man In My Life. This was a little strange as I had only met him twice and had never spent any time with him alone. Nik had the same realization on a downhill run.

On my return I explained this curious revelation to my student boyfriend as gently as possible. Five minutes after he walked out of my life, Nik walked in. On our first date he proposed marriage. I like a man with daring.

However, instead of jumping straight in, this time I said I would think about it. I thought about it for around eighteen months. A month before Amie was born, I accepted Nik's offer. I like a man with stamina.

Before reaching this momentous decision there were a couple of things I had to deal with first.

1. I wanted to marry a Buddhist.
2. I was already married to a Buddhist – Jeff Banks.

In the summer Nik had serious problems with Richard. I suggested he try the Buddhist practice so that he could redirect his life with clarity. To my surprise he did! Without skipping a beat he left Virgin and set up Palace Video and Palace Pictures with a new partner, Steve Woolley. I've never seen someone move so quickly and so confidently. I was very impressed. He often invited me to sit in on his business discussions while he set up Palace's structure and I really began to admire his way of dealing with people and situations. Nik is above all honourable and disarmingly honest. One of his most attractive qualities is that he is totally devoid of that powerful primal urge that so many other successful and influential people I know are afflicted with – the desire to be famous.

In the autumn I planned to tour Australia and then go on a pilgrimage to the Head Temple, Taisekiji, at the foot of Mount Fuji in Japan. Nik wanted to join me. It was looking good. I had on a previous visit to Taisekiji promised myself that I would only marry a man who loved me enough to accompany me on my return.

On his arrival in Sydney I went right off the idea. Nik proceeded to exhibit all his tendencies that niggle me most, as if making an unconscious effort to say, 'Well? Do you love me warts and all?' I became more and more critical.

By the time we arrived in Tokyo I did not like him at all. We went to the local Daiganji Temple for Nik to have *gojukai*, the Buddhist ceremony of formal acceptance, just as I had done myself many years before. Fellow Buddhists all over the world always warmly welcome people into their homes where they practise. Making our way there through the tiny, neat suburbs, I knew this was going to be a bit of a culture shock for Nik. This experience was not the beautiful but inscrutable Japan of the tourist brochures. Nik was being thrown right into the heart of Japanese culture that normally eludes foreign visitors. I wondered how he would take it.

We were greeted outside the temple by the priest's shaven-headed, white-robed assistants who took our shoes and our introductory letter written in Japanese. They were all prepared for us.

We were taken inside where the air was filled with sweet-smelling incense and the ringing of bells. We sat alone at the back of the temple on the *tatami* mats and chanted while waiting for the priest to come and start the ceremony.

A group of local Buddhist leaders entered all dressed up in their Sunday best out of respect for Nik (who was in jeans and tee-shirt), and for the occasion they had come to witness. Nowadays this ceremony is usually conducted in a person's home country. In the UK every two years a priest visits to give *gojukai*. But as Nik, like myself three years beforehand, decided to visit the Head Temple privately, we had the ceremony in Japan. Somehow we felt at home in the foreign setting. The priest entered with a swish of robes.

'*Neek Pah-wer San!*' His huge deep voice boomed like a gong in our ears. Nik looked around the room quizzically. I nudged him in the ribs.

'He means you,' I whispered.

'What shall I do?' he hissed back.

'Just say "*Hai*" and move forward,' I guessed.

Neek Pah-wer San towered above his Japanese hosts. They all knelt down together in rows around him. From my vantage point at the back I noticed that Nik not only had odd socks on but had a hole in each big toe! I like a man with eccentricities.

Nik's Roman Catholic background and study of European history has left him with a profound suspicion of all organized religion. So that night, before we went to the Head Temple, he insisted that he had a full translation of the two key chapters of the *Lotus Sutra*, which was written in Chinese in the prayer book we use for the practice of twice daily *gongyo*. This was no mean feat. The book consists of pages and pages of Chinese characters with Western phonetics printed underneath explaining the most profound Buddhist principles, which he could not possibly understand straightaway. I was really irritated with him for being so difficult, but even so, to put his mind at rest, I accepted the challenge, staying up all night to copy out painstakingly the English translation under every Chinese character. We had to leave so early the next morning for Taisekiji that he did not have time to read it.

We took the bullet train from Shinegawa Station and arrived at Fuji Station two hours later. From here we had a thirty-minute taxi ride to the grounds of the Head Temple. We finally arrived in the Sho-Hondo where the most sacred object of worship for Buddhists, the Dai-Gohonzon, is enshrined. All the other visitors reverently chanted their prayers for world peace. Neek Pah-Wer San also chanted – counting the bums on the seats and calculating the overheads. I figured that we all come to our understanding of life from different directions; the important thing for us was that we had arrived here at the same point, together. Anyway, I like a man who appreciates the true value of money!

The next big hurdle was talking Jeff into agreeing to a divorce. He was a most reluctant divorcee. Periodically, over the years, I had asked him. Every time he would go into one of his screaming tirades and I would back off to wait for him to be more ready to face it.

One night, out of the blue, Jeff rang me in tears. He was calling from a cinema foyer, where he had just taken Grace to see the movie *Kramer versus Kramer*. He was deeply moved.

'Do you still want a divorce?' As I have mentioned, sentimentality is one of Jeff's most lovable but dangerous traits. Once again I double-dared and said, 'Yes.'

We weren't playing games any more.

The divorce papers were sent straightaway for Jeff to sign. Months passed by. He had become engrossed in his work and forgotten about me waiting patiently to become a 'former spouse'. Or had he? It was not until I rang to tell him I was pregnant with Nik's child that he finally put pen to paper. Characteristically, he charmed me into accepting that it had just slipped his mind.

I went to the divorce courts to formalize the custody arrangements for Grace, accompanied by my mum. No arrangements was made for Grace's maintenance as I was so worried that Jeff would change his mind about the divorce. Quite frankly I would have been happy to agree to anything just to be able to walk away a 'free woman'. But not for long . . .

My wedding dress was HUGE. So was I! Nik and I were having a Buddhist wedding ceremony at the centre in Richmond. For my witness I chose Kazuo Fuji, my friend and Buddhist mentor, and for his witness Nik had chosen his new partner, Steve Woolley.

Steve was taken aside by Richard Causton, the chairman of Nichiren Shoshu of the United Kingdom, to explain what would happen and what he had to do. Anxious to put him at his ease, Mr Causton asked Steve if he was familiar with any Buddhist teachings. Steve, unusually immaculately dressed, flicked his pony tail over his shoulder pads and assured him, 'It's OK. Nowadays Buddhism is considered very kosher!'

The room inside the Richmond Centre is quite small, so Nik

and I invited twenty-five guests each, mostly family, and a few friends, including his ex-partner Richard, and my ex-manager Eve. They all happily left their shoes at the door and filed in barefoot. My daughter Grace and Roberta's daughter Corrina acted as *sake* girls.

Their job was to offer three bowls of *sake* to Nik and me in turn, each successive bowl getting bigger to symbolize our lives as we continued to share and grow with each other. Unknown to me they had had special instructions not to put too much *sake* in the bowls as it was deceptively intoxicating on an empty stomach.

I love *sake*. As the first two bowls were passed between Nik and me to drink from, I beckoned to Corrina and Grace to pour more in. They both dutifully ignored me. When Grace offered the third bowl she eyed me mischievously and almost emptied the lot in. I greedily guzzled it down.

Afterwards we took family photos of all the guests. It looked very funny, everyone posing in their smart wedding outfits with no shoes on. But at last my mum and dad got the wedding they had missed out on first time around.

Later we had a huge party. Thousands of people came, some close friends, some I didn't know from Adam. To this day I still meet new people who say they were at our wedding reception.

My mum, Rosie, decided to really celebrate the occasion. So did Nik's mother, Jane. From outside the ladies' loos I could hear my new mother-in-law's posh pukka tones mingling with my mum's jingling Bow Bell vowels, singing and cracking jokes. I peeped inside and watched them joyfully passing a bottle of champagne back and forth.

Nik and I both invited our 'exs'. Jeff declined. Meryl, Nik's former wife, came with her new husband. We had never met before. Without introduction, I was chatting casually to her, commenting on the 'do', gossiping about Nik, when she innocently asked, 'So what are *you* doing here? Are you family?'

'Me? Oh I'm just the hostess,' I countered and moved off to have a giggle.

After the reception we made our way home accompanied by some friends with cars loaded with wedding presents. As we started to unload the rain bucketed down, drenching the wrapping paper and gift tags, making their writing completely illegible. We will never know who gave what.

For some reason we were given a surfeit of whisky decanters and tea sets – maybe they thought we looked like heavy drinkers. Friends had kept ringing before the wedding asking what presents we would like. I just wanted them to be there and enjoy themselves. It had not occurred to me that they might want to give us something. Non-plussed, I suggested things like teaspoons and tea cloths.

It was not until Nik and I went to the wedding of Jeff and his present wife, Sue, that I realized the *done* thing was to have a wedding list. I marvelled at the beautiful but highly expensive items requested from The Conran Shop and John Lewis. Nik and I managed to scrape enough together to get them four crystal glasses from the list, hoping that other friends would make up the set.

A few weeks after our Buddhist wedding Nik and I booked a civil ceremony at the local registrar's office. This had, as in my first marriage to Jeff, certain elements of pure farce . . .

The Producer, The Secretary, Her Boss, and His Wife.

I turned up at Westminster Town Hall on time and waited for Nik. He was late. I went to the telephone booth to ring his office and remind him of his appointment with me. His secretary, who was to be one of the witnesses, did not answer as she was trying to locate Steve Woolley whom Nik had asked to be the other witness. Nik was out at a business meeting. While I was on the phone the secretary arrived and, seeing no one in the corridor, went outside to meet Steve and Nik at the front door as planned.

Nik arrived first. His secretary told him I was not yet there. Panicking, they went to the phone to ring me at home. Meanwhile I had gone back to wait in the corridor. Steve arrived late at the front door. Seeing no one to meet him he presumed he had missed the whole thing and went back to the studio.

I went to try to get Nik on the phone again and bumped into him and his secretary on the way. We called Steve on his mobile phone. He was already half-way to Shepperton Film Studios. I rang my friend Dini Glynwood, who lived just opposite the Town Hall. She was still in bed.

'Can you do us a huge favour and witness our wedding?'

'Sure, I'd love to. When is it?'

'NOW!'

Ten minutes later, bleary-eyed, she joined us and we all breathed a sigh of relief. The registrar asked for the licence fee for the wedding – up front – in cash. Nik pulled out his trouser pockets and produced two pounds. He looked at me. I shook my head. I hadn't a bean on me. The secretary had left the petty cash at the office, and our friend Dini was still trying to wake up.

The registrar suggested we cancel that appointment and let him get on with his next job, a delightful couple and their three noisy children from Lisson Grove. Meanwhile Nik could go out and find a cash machine.

Nik sprinted off and eventually returned, puffing and dishevelled, with the money. We did all the 'Do you take this woman . . .' stuff but when Nik went to sign the marriage certificate he found his pen had leaked inside his pocket and the ink on his fingers ruined the document. The registrar had to write it all out again.

At last the long-suffering registrar congratulated us. Unaware that we were already married, he must have expected Nik to kiss the bride. Instead Nik, who has a habit of calling everyone 'darling' because he always forgets names, patted me on my heavily pregnant tummy, then turned to his secretary and whispered urgently, 'Come on, darling. Let's get back to work!'

And now Charles and Cathy had just got married. I attended their wedding reception atop the Roof Gardens with some of their other clients like Chris Andrews, Deon Estus and Willy

Russell and all their old and new friends and family. Cathy looked stunning in her sexy wedding dress, puritanically laced up to the neck at the front and decadently plunging to her bum cleavage at the back. Charles, in his baggy Willi Wear togs, beamed like he'd just won a major lawsuit.

As they departed for their honeymoon, I went home to prepare for the Gay Pride concert.

Wouldn't It Be Luverly

I HAD HAD A PROBLEM with the timing of my first Gay Pride appearance as the festival date clashed with Grace's Parents' Day at Bedales School. Which one to go to? I chose to attend Gay Pride.

At the outset I had not wanted Grace to go away to what I then considered to be a posh boarding school and neither, at the time, had she. Jeff, however, was adamant. After much soul-searching from myself and many tears from Grace that tripped down her pretty freckled cheeks and caused me anguish for years to come, I agreed. Gradually, after a few years or so, Grace began to appreciate the school. I was relieved when the tearful midnight phone calls begging me to come and take her home stopped.

Fortunately, Bedales was the best possible option. It is a beautiful place set in acres of rich, green, swelling countryside. It has an open-minded, strong liberal tradition and is not the least bit 'hoity toity' or class conscious: perfect for Grace.

It is the antithesis of my old school in Dagenham, the Robert Clack Technical College, built to accommodate the brainy ones, those siphoned off from the surge of post-war babies for specialist education through the eleven-plus exams. The spanking-new school building squatted self-consciously on the edge of the huge sprawling housing estate overlooking the Civic Centre.

If we worked hard and got at least five 'O' levels we could look forward to an office job in the local Ford's factory which loomed ominously over the rows of neat brick houses and blocks of flats. Or we could join the hordes of Essex commuters as City office girls, lining the platforms all the way to Fenchurch Street. The dole was unheard of: there were plenty of jobs, but

I knew they were not right for me. I spent all my school days dreaming and scheming about jumping off the endless production line stretching inevitably before me.

Art college seemed an alternative, I was good at art – or was I? My confidence was undermined when my teacher criticized my penchant for painting dark outlines round my figures – surely I didn't 'see' that? Yes! With my new glasses I could see *everything*! Did I really want to end up illustrating teen magazines? Yes! Oh yes! Anything but the factory whistle! It's lucky for Matisse that he was not a pupil in my art class or he might have ended up paintspraying Ford Prefects. At one point I was so desperate to get away that I even contemplated joining the army. My parents must have thought I'd flipped. What would Sandra come up with next?

My hungry imagination lay starved of any stimulating nourishment save for the dreary images of buxom, mink-bikini'd Hollywood starlets and quiffed American dreamboats, packaged and served safely alongside their pale British counterparts in editions of *Photoplay* or *Reveille*, or presented with tailored elegance by Brian Matthews and David Jacobs on 'Easy Beat' and 'Juke Box Jury'. But then a few more palatable morsels began to appear, dropped like crumbs from the vast table of life. I devoured everything I could lay my hands on in a desperate effort to appease the hunger – Christine Keeler in the *Sunday Pictorial*, Julie Christie on telly in 'A For Andromeda', Rita Tushingham in 'Taste of Honey'. On Sundays I eagerly awaited Fluff Freeman's radio chart rundown on 'Pick of the Pops' and then . . . John, Paul, George, and Ringo. Oh the hair! Oh the clothes! 'Love Me Dooooo!!!' Oh yeh, yeh, yeh! And though the hair was a little too short and the clothes were a little too slick, it was fine until Mick Jagger's fat surly lips appeared, sneering over Keith Richard's horny guitar riff, 'Come ON!'

'I'm coming! Wait for me!' I daydreamed ravenously at my maths desk. I decided, while Mr Osborn droned on endlessly about percentages (with hindsight maybe I should have listened, I could have saved myself a few million), that I would definitely be a model, an actress, or a singer – I did not care which – but somehow a star – and very famous.

My report read, as usual, 'Sandra must learn to concentrate.' But I was concentrating hard. I knew there was something else out there; I could not accept that my life began and ended like a car assembled on the production line – this surely could not be IT! I yearned for wild, exotic dishes full of intriguing ingredients, not the meat and two veg dollopped out at school dinners; but what I started out looking for and what I eventually found were two different things, a bit like Christopher Columbus, convinced that the world was round, setting sail westwards to get to China and India and bumping into America instead.

At Grace's school, on a clear day, you can spot the famous mums and dads huddling appreciatively round the stage for the latest drama production or engrossed in animated conversation with their offspring. I once watched John Cleese on an Open Day striding gawkily around the chemistry lab with an anxious teacher discreetly in tow ensuring he did not knock over any experiments.

That particular year Jeff and I arrived late together and missed the lunch. I was starving. So while he and Grace went on a term's work inspection, I sat on the floor in a hidden corner of the quad stuffing myself with tea and cakes. I kept my head down, hoping I would not be missed.

A pair of dirty sneakers moved into my line of vision. My eyes travelled up the jeans, over the bulge, past the skinny, tee-shirted torso and the hand extended in greeting, to the familiar luscious lips.

'Hello Sandie. Remember me?' asked Mick Jagger.

A telegram arrived at our house in Dagenham. I had never seen one before. Mum and Dad passed it backwards and forwards to each other in awe. Finally they handed it to me.

'It's for you, Sandra,' they said incredulously.

Life had certainly begun to move since I had met Adam and Eve a few months before. Adam had a girlfriend, Deidre

McSharry, who was fashion editor of the *Daily Express*, a newspaper I had first seen on Eve's desk a few weeks before. On that day I had been sitting on the floor in her office in Regent Street drawing dress designs on typing paper while she haggled over contracts on the phone. Ever since we had met, Eve had moaned continually about my 'shlocky frocks' and had even lent me twenty pounds to buy some 'nice dresses from Dickins & Jones' for my first publicity shots. So I was rather surprised when she looked over at my work and announced, 'I want three of those to give to Deidre.'

The *Express* had my designs made up. A few days later I sat in a brightly lit photographic studio with a top fashion photographer, Michael Williams. He peered at me closely, carefully scrutinizing every inch of my face. He waved a light metre across my cheekbones, nodding and umming his approval. My three dress designs hung crisply on a rail waiting for me to model them.

I was just sixteen. I had recently been to Vidal Sassoon to have my hair bobbed and wore hardly any make-up. Lit like a dream, I was totally unaware of my visual impact. The lanky body, endlessly long legs and boney, square-jawed face that had made me feel so clumsy and ugly compared with the curvaceous *Photoplay* and *Reveille* pin-ups were suddenly transformed into streamlined assets under the loving stare of the camera lens.

Michael drooled over the prints. He asked me back to the studio again to take more photos. Sandra Paul and Pauline Stone, two of the top fashion models of the time, were just finishing a session. One of them stayed and helped me with my make-up.

Michael then drove me to Virginia Water in Surrey where he unloaded all his camera equipment and started clicking away at me draped around trees, plunging into cold lakes and running barefoot in the forest. This was my first modelling assignment – for a cheese advertising campaign. It was absolutely exhausting. I quickly crossed 'model' off my list of things to be.

Michael was so excited with the results that he called in Jocelyn Stevens, editor of the *Express*, who printed the shots of me in my designs immediately. Then he invited Willie Landels, art editor of *Queen* magazine, to take a look.

People like Willy were a new experience for me. He wafted into the studio in a cloud of perfume, sporting a large fedora hat and cane. He had a curious way of pursing his lips and spoke with a funny foreign-sounding accent, punctuated with lots of 'dahlings' and squeals of delight as he looked through the prints. He thought I was 'epsolootly maaahvelous!' and printed a close-up of my face on the front cover of *Queen*. It was quite unnerving to see myself peering out from all the bookstalls when I came up from Dagenham to visit Eve's office.

I don't think I ever fully realized how beautiful I was at that time in my life. It is only now when I look back at the photos that the full impact hits me. I think part of that beauty was the joy and surprise of its discovery. It opened up a whole new world for me.

Michael, Jocelyn and Willy were great publicists; they told everybody about me. Eventually word got to a gentleman called Quentin Crewe, a writer, who among other things did food pieces for the *Evening Standard*. He was inspired to whisk me away from Dagenham and out to an exclusive London restaurant to do a real Pygmalion job on me. At last my appetite for wild exotic dishes could be indulged.

I was picked up in a shiny limousine. The uniformed chauffeur jumped out smartly and swung open the door. It was so huge inside I could almost stand up. Quentin sat in the opposite corner smoking through a cigarette holder. I liked him immediately. He was vivacious and sophisticated, but without a trace of bigotry or prejudice of any kind. His desire was to have the pleasure of showing me what the big wide world had to offer.

Our arrival at the Mirabelle restaurant in Mayfair caused great excitement. Quentin's aristocratic credentials and taste for good food were well respected. The doormen rushed to our assistance and helped me out of the limousine with a great flourishing and tipping of their hats. I waited for Quentin's chauffeur to assemble the wheelchair and lift him into it. Then, with the liveried chauffeur pushing Quentin on one side and the *maître d'* on the other, we were ushered like royalty from the lift to the dining room. I had never eaten out formally before, unless you include the canteen at the holiday camp in Shewburyness.

The restaurant was packed with sober-faced gentlemen in pin-striped suits. I wore a short scarlet polo-neck sweater-dress. Heads turned in our direction and our arrival was acknowledged by an atmospheric silence as we entered, and a sharp rise in conversational hum as we sat down. Impeccably kitted-out waiters kept bowing and fussing around us, moving things about and asking me lots of questions. I was confused. Quentin answered on my behalf, reassuring me, 'They are just trying to make you comfortable.'

The table was covered with a vast array of silver cutlery, enough strange-shaped knives, forks and spoons to feed an army, so many sparkling china plates that my mum would have had a fit about all the washing up, and enough glasses to open up a pub: longstemmed, rounded, tubular, tuliped, big ones, small ones, some as big as yer 'ead . . . which one to drink from? eat from? eat with? My head swam round with the choices laid out before me. The *maître d'* draped a napkin across my lap and gave us a menu each – in French. My heart sank.

'I am an expert at this,' said Quentin diplomatically. 'I'll help you choose.' We selected lobster quenelles in a seafood sauce, followed by veal cooked in cream accompanied by spinach. Then he patiently explained to me what a lobster was, that veal was meat and that spinach was a vegetable.

'All these years I had thought that spinach was working-class food!' he exclaimed.

'Do vegetables have class systems too?' I asked.

'Why no!' he laughed.

The waiter waited expectantly. He took our order then fiddled and fussed with the knives, forks, plates and glasses, shifting them hither and thither. Quentin showed me what to eat with what, what to drink with what and where to eat or drink it from. It occurred to me that posh people must spend an awful lot of time at the table. At home in Dagenham I used to wiggle and squirm with impatience when my nan came to

Sunday tea. I would scoff my food down, eager to get back to my records and books, while my mum threw me disapproving looks. Then I had to wait for what seemed like an eternity while my nan chewed endlessly and silently on her meal. I was not allowed to talk at the table or leave it until everyone had finished. We only ever drank alcohol at parties.

Quentin smiled across at me and offered me my very first taste of wine. I chattered away, the grapes loosening my tongue. It was a novelty to discover the social possibilities of eating out. We had a great time, he playing Higgins to my Eliza Dolittle.

I think he was already a little innocently in love with me, the waiters too. After a few glasses of claret the sober-faced gentlemen in their pin-striped suits also began to cast overtly appreciative glances my way. The seductive clink of the crystal glasses and sparkle of the chandeliers reflected the amorous glint in their eyes. It felt so wonderful to be admired. The table linen began to bob and sway pleasurably. Across the Atlantic Ocean I sailed, a New Age Columbus in search of my dream. Suddenly I sighted land. From the crow's-nest I espied what looked distinctly like the Statue of Liberty, freedom, on the horizon. 'What happens next?' I wondered.

The telegram, which was from Quentin, read, ' PLEASE COME TO A PARTY TONIGHT AND MEET PRINCESS MARGARET.'

Mum of course went hysterical. Dad went to make her a cup of tea to calm her down. Later, we found him in the kitchen, staring into space with the kettle forgotten, boiled to the last drop. I, on the other hand, took it all in my gauche stride. I was getting used to the unusual happening now.

'I'll give Quentin a ring and see if I have to wear anything special – like a tiara!' I joked.

'You might take a pair of white gloves,' Mum added knowledgeably. 'You're not allowed to touch her hands, Sandra.'

When I rang Quentin, he asked me how my singing was going. I explained that my first record, 'As Long As You're Happy Baby', had not been a hit but that it had succeeded in getting me 'in' with the 'in crowd'. Everybody at 'Ready Steady

Go' loved me, and my next record, 'Always Something There To Remind Me', would definitely be a huge hit.

'You've been on "Ready Steady Go?"' he asked, greatly impressed. 'That sounds great fun. Would you like to bring one of your long-haired friends with you?'

I rang Michael Aldred, who co-presented the show with Cathy McGowan. Mum had met him and approved of him. His hair wasn't very long, but he was growing it!

'Great!' Michael replied to my invitation. 'I'll bring along Mick Jagger.'

'Oh Christ! He had better behave himself,' I warned.

If Mum and Dad ever found out they would go nuts. The Rolling Stones had succeeded in completely alienating the entire older generation with press stories of mouthing off at old ladies and peeing on garage attendants. You know how parental paranoia distorts everything out of proportion. Anyway, Mick certainly had long hair.

I arrived at Quentin's Belgravia home ahead of Michael and Mick. The crescent was beautiful: a curve of massive white houses dappled with the evening sunlight that peeped through tall tremulous trees, trees that were just dripping with lush greenery. I wore a black floral printed Biba dress.

I was greeted at the door by a butler who led me across a deep pile Chinese carpet to the hostess, Quentin's wife. She eyed me up and down with the expression of someone identifying the remains of a run-over cat. She didn't seem to like me but Quentin did, so I sat at his feet while he introduced me with pride to all the bright sparks – from Ken Tynan to Bamber Gascoigne – assembled round him.

Instead of the usual blare of pop records, Bernard Levin sat side by side with Princess Margaret at the piano playing old show tunes. I was introduced to her and had to call her 'Ma'am'.

At this pregnant point in the proceedings there was a loud kerfuffle in the doorway. All heads turned. Michael and Mick stood at the entrance, swaying from side to side, trying to hold each other up and giggling uncontrollably.

'I'm afraid we've been a bit naughty,' spluttered Michael, and toppled into the room after Mick.

I propped them up against the piano. Bernard and 'Ma'am' ignored them and continued to play while Mick tried unsuccessfully to sing along. His face was going a peculiar shade of green. He lurched across the keyboards towards her Royal Ma'amness, that huge mouth hanging open alarmingly. Michael and I just about managed to catch him in time and drag him out of the room. We took him to the boys' room where he threw up for about half an hour.

Twenty years later, huddled in the corner of the quad stuffing my face with cream buns, I stared up at Mick Jagger's familiar face once more. Parents' Day at Bedales was the most unlikely setting I would have envisaged for re-meeting this former hell-raiser.

'How are you?' Mick asked politely.

'I think if I eat one more donut I'll be sick.' I smiled. 'Want one?'

Mick declined. 'So that's how he manages to keep his figure,' I thought.

'No thanks. Wanna share a hamper of champagne and goodies on the lawn?' he offered. 'I understand your daughter Grace is at this school.'

'Yes, she knows your daughter Karis,' I volunteered. Then, to my horror, we had a sensible parental discussion about our well-behaved, studious children.

The following term Grace and Karis shared a dorm. Both having irresponsible, irrepressible, irritatingly irreverent parents, they had a lot in common . . .

Mother's Pride

THIS YEAR TO ROUND OFF the first leg of the tour we all played hooky from Parents' Day to go to Gay Pride. The show was open air and it poured all day long. After the heatwave all through my tour, this was a bit disappointing.

Charles and Cathy had gone off for their honeymoon in a romantic Norman castle, so I was accompanied by Charles's son, Miles Negus-Fancey, an up-and-coming artist.

He arrived at my place with yet another change of hair colour, the result of spilling paint while attempting his latest masterpiece. He looked like a cross between Billy Idol and Rainbowbrite. Renee, still in her provisional materialization as Charles's secretary, came too, her blond hair piled high like a stick of candyfloss. Miles is always getting beaten up by idiots who can't tell the difference between an art student and a pet shop boy. No one would dare lay a finger on Renee's wild Amazonian proportions.

We drove round and round Kennington Park trying to find the entrance to the show. Eventually I espied a couple of men walking hand in hand and knew we were on the right track. We followed them. Progress was slow as they kept stopping every few yards to deepen their relationship.

Inside the park, groups of men huddled together under the trees, to keep dry – I think. Some had travelled from as far as Scotland. Coach loads of men and women had made the pilgrimage, but the heavy rain had managed to thin out their numbers drastically by the evening. Those that stayed stayed because they really wanted to see the show, so I determined to give them my best.

The organizers cleared out a park warden's hut for my

dressing-room and turned the gas fires on full, and an assortment of girls piled in to keep me company. I was assigned two lovely butch ladies to keep guard. They were having a whale of a time, all dressed up in their security uniforms. One took me into the corner and displayed her tattoo, a heart inscribed with 'I love Rosie'.

'So do I!' I said. 'That's my mum's name.'

In the late Seventies I had once taken my parents for a quiet lunch by the Serpentine. On our way back we had got caught up in one of the first Gay Pride marches in Hyde Park. My dad was a bit taken aback, but Mum thought it was great fun. They had never seen anything like it in Dagenham. She was so enthralled that we had to drag her away.

I wondered what my mum would make of this big woman showing me her whip. She had on a leather dress slashed to her tummy button and matching military headgear. I was mesmerized by her deep husky voice and her conversation liberally peppered with references to the genitalia of both sexes, and certain other zones that I had never considered erogenous before. She had a curious attitude towards her own body, a kind of disassociation from it, and played with her tits as if they were a set of juggler's balls. But I knew she was just trying to be funny and entertaining and she was only there because she loved me. So I gave her a kiss on the cheek and promised to dedicate a song to her. One of the security girls gave me a nudge and a wink and said, 'Isn't he a scream!'

'*He?*' I queried.

'Lola La La La Lola . . .' she sang, doubled up, laughing at me.

I don't mind what sex someone chooses to be as long as it makes them and their friends happy.

I took the precaution of asking everyone to leave while I changed – except Renee, whom I was sure about. They all moaned their disappointment but respectfully withdrew. I wore my old leather biking jacket and a tight black leotard that clung to every rise and fall from my neck to my ankles, with 'Boy' emblazoned all over it – just to keep everyone guessing!

The Communards had already been on stage and were followed by Tom Robinson. It was still pouring with rain, so Renee and I made our way over to the stage area snuggled tightly under one umbrella. Groups of girls screamed with delight as we ran past, obviously getting the wrong idea. Miles was also doing a roaring trade, selling Sandie Shaw tee-shirts to lovestruck young men who could not tell the difference between an art student and a trolly dolly. My heart went out to the wet, bedraggled audience. Here I was under the protection of a marquee, and there they were knee-deep in mud. Half-way through the act, at the risk of getting electrocuted, I kicked off my shoes and ran out from under cover to dance and sing in the rain with them. I sang the Lady With The Whip her song, and the audience were as turned on by me as I was by them.

The next week I was interviewed by Kris Kirk, music journalist and notorious writer of books like *Men in Frocks*. He asked me whether I was aware that I continually changed the gender in some songs, and why I sang other songs in their original gender, like a folk singer, staying true to the text. For instance, I had started singing my old hit, 'I'll Stop At Nothing', the way I had first heard it, written for Adam Faith –

> See that girl who just walked by
> Well she's the one my heart's set on . . .
> I'll stop at nothing
> Until I get the girl I love.

He also mentioned 'Jeane' written by Morrissey/Marr, a song about living with a woman. I remember once asking Johnny who it was about. He replied, 'Morrissey's mum probably!' Quite naturally I sang it word for word as written – that was how it was presented to me, and the song seemed perfect as it was.

This was unheard of in the Sixties. In those days I would have had to change the sex of the lyrics. I remember once being in the ludicrous situation of having to change the title of a Cat Stevens song I recorded from 'Father And Son' to 'Mother And

Daughter'. He created such a fuss. Ironically, it would not make any difference to him now, since as a devout Muslim he has disowned his old compositions as being too frivolous.

In the context of today's exciting sexual politics, to change a song's gender, just for it to appear 'normal', would be as foolish as painting a moustache on Brigitte Bardot – unless of course that was how she chose to be. I suppose I covered that subject in my act with one song 'A Girl Called Johnny'; although the song was written about Patti Smith, for me it has always been about radical change of all kinds.

I was a bit thrown by Kris's question as it was an angle that had never occurred to me. I said I would ring him back after giving it some thought. The gender-bending thing had happened unconsciously; it just gradually crept into my work as I began responding to another generation of audience. Maybe I was aware that my young fans were made up of all shades of persuasion and I wanted to relate to all of them, sing all of their dreams. Certainly the lines separating gender are much less defined nowadays, the role playing less stereotyped. Obviously their mothers' faults! So all that bra burning had been worth it! Young people now are generally more sensitive and aware of humanitarian issues; although the press is full of football thugs, for the most part the people I come across are a caring lot. It seems to me that the feminine impulse is just beginning to have a real influence on youth culture. The stunningly sexist attitudes in pop music, so prevalent in the simplistic days of the Sixties, that at first unwittingly exploited and then wittingly maintained the general misconception that libidinous expression is confined solely to the sex act, and then only amongst heterosexuals, are now mostly contained in a few areas of teeny bop and heavy metal music, where adolescents still seem to require romantic matters to be set out as simply as possible. Most adults know that sexuality is more complex. Now more than any other time, all areas of society need the balancing influence of the female understanding of life.

I thought about it some more. I've learnt so much from gay people. They have encouraged me not to be so restrictive in my thinking, helped me reassess my own sexuality and be able really to enjoy it – all of it, not just the bits you're supposed to.

Possibly one of the reasons I relate so readily to gay issues is that I sympathize strongly with their search for identity in a paranoid society which, in order to protect its own sense of self, prefers you to conform to its idea of normality rather than be a happy, fulfilled person in your own way.

When I finally returned Kris's call I had come to the realization that I was not singing in the third person. I was not imagining how someone else would feel. I was doing something far more revolutionary than that: I was drawing not only from my present life but from all my multifarious past lifetimes as a woman, man, cat, tree, speck of dust or spark of light in the universe. I was attracted to each song because it was resonant of an aspect of first-hand experience. So for the truly creative person, the more in touch they are with the eternity of their life and all its manifestations, the richer their work becomes. Inside our minds we have an endless source of material and inspiration.

I was really grateful for Kris Kirk's question. I have continued to support Gay Pride ever since. Now, with that performance over, I had completed the first leg of my 'second coming', and for a while it was back to the drawing board and family life for me!

PART TWO

Losing My Step

Barefoot Contessa

THE WORD SPREAD THAT I WAS SINGING. I was alive and kicking. Other colleges started queuing up for dates. I was happy to oblige. More and more dates were added until I had both an autumn and a Christmas tour scheduled. I took a short family holiday in Spain to recharge my batteries and to restock all the discarded shoes that had been pinched off the stage during my performances.

On my return I discovered that Polydor had decided to release 'Frederick' from the Westside Studio session as a second single. This did not make me too happy as they had booked no television promotion to go with it and I felt that without this exposure the record would sink without trace. I was right. I raced up and down the country trying to save it with a regional radio tour, but, although it was great fun to find out more about the latest surge of new radio stations, it was not the answer. 'Frederick' was stillborn.

An A and R (artist and repertoire) meeting was arranged at Polydor with Carol Wilson, the head of that department. Carol had not been there when I originally negotiated contractual terms with the company. Her arrival had happened in a some-what curious manner . . .

After working with the Smiths on the independent label, Rough Trade Records, in 1984, I decided that as soon as my son, Jack, was a year old I would have a go at recording again. I fancied joining a bigger international company that could afford to invest some real money into my planned album and would have the worldwide facilities to promote and distribute it. Polydor seemed to fit the bill.

My chart success with the Smiths on the single 'Hand In

Glove' in 1984 had been considered unusual, to say the least. I was aware that the record company fraternity were intrigued as to where I would go next. To stimulate their imagination I put together a tape of the songs I intended to record. Instead of following the obvious option of returning to the middle-of-the-road formula material so enamoured of second-time-around pop stars doomed to 'act their age', whatever that might mean, or emulating those encouraged to pretend they are nineteen again and re-release a golden oldie, I chose songs from new writers whose work I thought merited a wider exposure, like Lloyd Cole, Matt Johnson, the Waterboys and more from the Smiths. Charles and I took this tape to the head of A and R at Polydor at the time, Malcolm Dunbar. He liked it! Contracts were drawn up.

Then, overnight, there was a change in management. Maurice Oberstein, who had successfully run the UK operation of CBS records since the days of the dinosaurs, was brought in to take over the running of Polydor. This was a pleasant shock. Maurice Oberstein is a colourful New York anglophile and former chairman of the British Phonographic Society. I had known him for many years as Obie. If it were not for Obie I would not be a Buddhist today.

We had met in 1977 through Mike Mansfield, the television director and producer. Mike had been a trusted friend since he first directed me in 1965 in the TV series 'Ladybirds', and nicknamed me Sandwich, after a tea break.

At the time I met Obie I was at my lowest ebb ever. I had been trying desperately not to drown in a sea of deepest depression ever since the bankruptcy of Jeff's International Clothing Company a year or so before. The bills seemed never-ending as we tried to set up house again. The more money we earnt the more there was to pay. I bitterly resented the drain on my resources, particularly as I was on the threshold of a creative renaissance when it happened.

I had spent the previous few years setting up a musicians' workshop called Tatham Music, with writers, arrangers, musicians and a booking agency for recording sessions run by

Martyn Ford. We were based in one of Jeff's old showrooms in the rag trade area of the West End. The place was soon bulging at the seams, buzzing with musical activity.

Two people who became a welcome part of the furniture were Roger Cook and Herbie Flowers of the group Blue Mink. Over the lengthy period I had been writing and developing a musical with them, based on a story I had written called *The Alchemist*. Erte, the renowned Russian artist, had been commissioned to do the designs. I regularly visited his flat in the Bois de Boulogne in Paris and joined him on holiday in Majorca to discuss and oversee his work. He was a remarkable man; ideas tripped out of his head with breathtaking ease and fluidity, and he was always anxious to please. I have often noticed, with all the specially talented people I have had the good fortune to meet, that the greater the talent the more effort and application they put into their work. Genius is not a *fait accompli*; it requires constant attention and development. Even though Erte was in his seventies he took a daily run followed by a swim before we settled down to work.

The writer and stage director John McGrath had loved the idea. One of our music publishers was talking to an animation company in Los Angeles about it and was just about to jump on a plane to discuss it with the film director Fellini, when I called and stopped him.

Quite suddenly I had run out of optimism. I woke up one morning and all faith in myself had disappeared. I could not see the point. It would not happen. Nothing would. I was deeply embarrassed to think that I had ever imagined it could. I just felt an awful squirmy feeling in the pit of my stomach. Fear. Even Jeff's usually infectious enthusiasm was no longer catching.

I then spent a joyless year working in nightclubs to make money to pay debts. My sense of identity had become so inextricably merged with Jeff's that I carried his business failure around with me like a heavy load, as if it were my own. In one sense it was, as I had signed a personal guarantee for the company, although Jeff tried his best to shield me from the full impact of the repercussions. Eventually he was able to negotiate for him to take total responsibility for the debt. A few of the clubs who were also going through a hard time financially, which was common among many businesses in the Seventies recession, took advantage and did not pay my fee. They knew I did not have the money to sue and that I did not want to draw attention to my predicament.

I was not proud of the work I was doing. I functioned like a zombie, just going through the motions, until the pain began to seep back into my consciousness. Then, in a rush of manic energy, having realized that Jeff, my hero, was vincible, I began to fight back at his angry outbursts in a series of blazing, tortuous rows.

It was after a hellish New Year celebration in 1977, when the emotional strain of our disagreements proved too hard to bear any longer, that I lost our expected baby. I remember coming round after the operation and begging the doctor who, only a few years before, had delivered our wonderful daughter Grace into the most idyllic world full of sunshine and promise, to let me stay in hospital for ever. Anything was better than the reality I had to go home to. Incredulous people always ask, 'Why didn't you leave?'

Firstly, no one likes to admit to failure. Secondly, what would I do? I had never had to fend for myself before. I knew nothing of the small practicalities of daily living. Where would I start to find out? My past legal and financial advice had led me to my present mess. My few current connections were Jeff's, hardly likely to be sympathetic to me. Eve? She would really gloat – 'I told you so . . . All men are shits . . .' etc, her usual script, and try to entangle me again in her poisonous web. I did not agree with her and did not want to end up like her either. My parents? They are simple, honest folk, and were ill equipped to comprehend or deal with my kind of everyday megadramas.

And where would I go? The last of my savings were tied up in a trust fund that bought our house in Ireland. So with no means and no one to turn to for advice, I was helpless. People like me are not expected to turn up at the local Citizens Advice

Bureau. Then there was the overwhelming feeling that I did not want to betray Jeff. I could not leave him at such a time. It was him and me against the world, wasn't it? But more than anything else I was seized by such terror at the prospect of day-to-day life on my own that I was immobilized. I was beginning to feel that each day was booby-trapped with unpleasant surprises that I could no longer take in my stride.

I could have saved myself and everyone else so much pain if I had known then as much as I do now about the insidious workings of the selfish ego that lives inside us all, eating away at the energy that replenishes the spirit, the impetus to start afresh, robbing us of the confidence to take responsibility for our own happiness, feeding us with illusions that justify our blaming others for our problems and consequently blinding us to the power and beauty of our true nature and capabilities. If only I had known how to become master of my own mind. If only I had known how to become strong.

During the summer holidays when I was a little girl I used to stay with my Auntie Marje, my mum's best friend from the war, and Uncle Geoff on their free-range chicken farm in the Hampshire countryside. One day I went missing. Auntie Marje found me sitting in the middle of the road, blissfully unaware of the real danger I was in. I was so convinced by my fantasy that I had managed to persuade two local friends to join me. This inadvertent compulsion to self-destruct was so overwhelming that no amount of reasoning could make me budge. Eventually I had to be forcibly removed.

I was dangerously back on that road again. My operation had been serious. I had been close to death. I was bedridden for a month afterwards. At weekends Jeff borrowed a wheelchair from the London clinic to whisk me round the empty streets of the West End at breakneck speed to cheer me up. I desperately missed Grace, who stayed behind with Jeff's parents in Ireland, and begged Jeff to let her come to London to be with me. I was inconsolable until her grandmother brought her over.

I failed to give myself a chance to mourn my loss. The grief remained locked inside, unspoken, unexpressed. Like an impotent passenger I looked on in complete bewilderment at the rollercoaster of disasters that destiny was taking me on.

I disappeared deeper and deeper inside myself. In an effort to shake me out of my depression, to give me some sense of purpose, Jeff and Eve, not understanding the cause, conspired together to get me a recording contract. This would also ease our financial situation. My friend Mike Mansfield mentioned me to Obie and, without a clue about what I wanted to sing, I was signed to CBS records with a reasonable advance.

I made two tracks for CBS records. Barry Blue, the producer, did his best to mould me musically into a viable marketing formula. I went passively along with everyone's well-meaning suggestions, feeling exposed and vulnerable and unconfident. I remained uninspired. The recordings were mechanical and unsatisfying in every way.

In a final valiant effort to put some meaning into my work, I contacted Ann O'Dell. I have no idea why. It was an instinctive gesture. Annie is a musician and arranger who had done some brilliant work for Bryan Ferry which I much admired. She was also a member of Blue Mink and had been introduced to me a couple of times at Tatham Music by Roger and Herbie.

At my suggestion we tried composing with each other. The results of two headstrong women meeting head on were strange and awkward, but interesting none the less. We booked a small studio and demo'd some of the songs. Soon after, Annie came round to dinner with Jeff and me at our modest flat in Harley Street.

I will never forget the surreal quality of the evening. It was dark. It was always dark in that flat. There was no electric lighting. The smoked glass dinner table was lit by two large round candles cupped in transparent bowls. A lot of vodka was consumed. At one point in the boozy conversation Jeff fixed his eyes on one of the globe-shaped candles and wondered out loud why we were all on this great big ball of earth spinning around in space.

To our complete surprise Annie started burbling on about buddhas: Shakyamuni and Nichiren Daishonin; time periods:

shoho, zoho and *mappo*. She kept repeating a phrase, '*Nam-myoho-renge-kyo*'. She told Jeff that if he wanted to know why we were here, he should chant this phrase. Then she turned directly to me as she swayed in her chair and said, 'If you chant this you can have anything you want, anything, even if you don't yet know what it is.'

Jeff and I stared at each other. This was a sobering thought. So we all had another drink and ignored her strange outburst.

A few weeks later I rang Annie up and asked, 'Anything? Did you say I could have anything?'

'Yes,' she confirmed. 'Just chant "*Nam-myoho-renge-kyo*".'

'How long for?'

'Until you get what you want.'

'Is it like magic?'

'No. Chanting "*Nam-myoho-renge-kyo*" brings out your Buddha wisdom so that you know what action to take and gives you the courage and compassion to take it.'

Oh Christ! All that Buddha stuff again.

'Do you have to do anything weird like stand on your head or go on a diet?'

'No. Just be yourself.'

'Uh-huh. Mmmm, interesting. Do you close your eyes and think of worthy things like the sound of one hand clapping?'

'Sit upright, back straight, palms together, eyes open, and chant out loud, clearly and rhythmically, for what you want for your happiness. This desire will then naturally begin to harmonize with world peace. Focus on a plain wall, no distractions. Until of course you get a Gohonzon . . .'

'A *what*?'

'A special mandala to help you concentrate. Why? Thinking of doing it?'

'Oh no, no, of course not. I wouldn't dream of doing anything so crackpot. Just checking that I hadn't finally flipped and imagined what you said.'

'Oh.' Silence. 'Bye then.'

'Bye!'

I ran straight upstairs to the spare room, set up a candle on a large dinner plate, kicked my shoes off and knelt down to make my first fumbled attempt at chanting. It felt really good. I went out and bought some more candles, all different colours. I continued secretly for an hour a day, sometimes more, for a week, until all the candles had melted together into a mountainous multi-coloured wax sculpture. Life had never seemed as wonderful. I felt hopeful, confident even. There was only one problem. I knew what I wanted all right but what action to take? Twenty thousand pounds does not just fall out of the sky.

The following morning, with heart pounding, I rang the boss at CBS Records, Maurice Oberstein. I had never approached someone like that directly before, having always gone through a business manager or a lawyer. I didn't even know if he would take my call, especially as all I had given his company so far was two flop singles. His secretary picked up the phone. He was busy. My heart stopped pounding and sank . . . but was I free for lunch tomorrow, his secretary asked. My heart rose again . . . Why, yes, I was free.

'Call me Obie,' said Maurice Oberstein as he ushered me into the smart Italian restaurant.

Even in those days Obie was no spring chicken. Nevertheless, he sported a luminous baseball cap, which remained on his head throughout the meal. Obie was easy to talk to. He told me about his father and his childhood in the States, and about the punk bands he had recently signed whose music he did not like or understand, and I found myself telling him unselfconsciously that I had started chanting. What a coincidence . . . his upstairs neighbour, a ballet dancer, did the same, all hours of the day. 'What a racket! The chanting and her dancing!'

We came to the end of the meal. Obie asked for the bill and turned to me. 'Now, what exactly is it that you want?'

'I would like twenty thousand pounds to make an album.'

'OK. It's yours,' he laughed.

I was dumbfounded. 'But I'm only signed to make a couple of singles. I don't have a contract to make an album,' I reminded him.

'You do now!' he grinned.

His driver chauffeured me home. In the Seventies, twenty thousand pounds was a really decent budget to make an album. I flew up the stairs to my flat and immediately phoned Annie.

'It works! It works!' I screamed excitedly down the phone.

'What does?'

'The chanting. Obie just gave me twenty grand! What do I do next?'

Of course there was much more to it than that, but it was a beginning. I had been '*shaku buku'd*'! What a gloriously suggestive turn of phrase to describe being introduced to Buddhism. As I continued I realized I was not yet ready to make the kind of album I envisaged. I had some heavy changes to make in my private life first – and then I had to work on my mental and emotional stability.

A few months later, at another amicable meeting with Obie, I asked to be released from my obligations to CBS so that I could take time off to sort myself out. Obie wrote out my unconditional release on a table napkin. The legal department were a bit thrown by the unorthodoxy of it all, but eventually they honoured the napkin and returned all my old Sixties masters.

Now, here were Obie and I again in 1984, this time at Polydor together. The first thing he did was to implement the suggestion of Richard Ogden, head of marketing, to bring in Carol Wilson to run A and R. This made her responsible for all the signings and artistic development of the artists. Malcolm Dunbar promptly left and joined another company.

Working with Carol was another strange twist of fate. I knew her well, through Nik. She had successfully run Virgin Publishing, putting together and signing bands like the Police, and had then started a subsidiary record company with Virgin called Dindisc.

Shortly after Nik sold up his share of the Virgin group of companies in 1981, Carol also left, following a serious disagreement with Richard. She became a frequent visitor at our little seaside cottage.

Carol and Nik were great, longstanding friends. I don't know what she made of me. I seemed always to be heavily pregnant, breast-feeding, changing nappies or performing some domestic chore. She certainly couldn't have seen me as a glamorous international superstar; more as a harassed, homely supercook. I pottered around the garden tending the herbs, while Nik and Carol went off for hour after hour of therapeutic sailing. My mother was convinced it was a case of all hands on deck and that they were having an affair. I knew for a fact that this was impossible. Nik and I had already tried it. The cabin was far too cramped – unless she was double-jointed. The only thing that Carol ever dropped was the anchor.

Carol rang me herself to tell me the news of her appointment at Polydor. 'I consider you my own signing. Let's pick up where Malcolm Dunbar left off.' That was a relief; traditionally the new person dumps the old person's acts immediately and starts establishing their own style of operation.

'Let's go out for an extravagant lunch and drink buckets of champagne to celebrate the deal!' she suggested.

I picked Carol up at her new office. I had never seen her behind a desk before. My last memory of her a year before was of a shivering, sniffling heap huddled around the Calor gas fire in our cottage, socks hung over the back of the chair to dry, feet in a puddle of seawater, her oilskin dripping noisily on to the floor while I, heavily pregnant with Jack, made the tea.

I waded through a sea of deep pile carpet to greet her. Surprisingly, her hand was soft and manicured, not muddy and chapped as I remembered. She edged out from behind the desk and sashayed across the room to turn off the wall-to-wall stereo. 'My God, she's got legs!' I thought, as she exhibited her tailored, miniskirted, Katharine Hamnett suit. It clung efficiently to her hips.

'I can wear it with a casual polo neck during the day, and change it for a beaded top if I have a dinner appointment,' she explained, looking more like a *Cosmopolitan* fashion feature than a windblown yachtswoman. She teetered forward on her high heels and sailed past me to the door. I followed cautiously, buffeted by her wake.

In the Ladies she chose carefully from an assorted array of cosmetics that she had stashed away under the wall mirror. The Carol I used to know never wore make-up, and had a vengeful disdain for fashion; that lady had only the one pair of mudcaked jeans, wellies and a tube of lip salve. This one had grown and bleached her boyish crop into a blond bob that swung across her face like calico sails as she ducked into the taxi after our signing photo was taken in Obie's office. I felt quite frumpy in my oversized beatnik jumper and black ski pants.

We really pigged out at lunch. None of our past parsimony was evident on this occasion. I began to think how much had changed in my life over recent years, how wide my horizons had become. Now I was embarking on a renewed recording career. Little did I know that this was truly to be a voyage on uncharted waters . . .

I was ushered into the demo studio, a dark, silent, windowless room lit by a single spotlight that shone on the gleaming grand piano. I was sixteen. I had seen only upright pianos before, in Nan and Grandad Goodrich's front room, at school assembly and in our local working men's social club when I was a kid.

We had wonderful dances there. Auntie Jen, my godmother, taught me the Lambeth Walk, the Hokey Cokey, and the Gay Gordons. She also taught me numerous saucy songs. Later in life I was to teach her how to practise Buddhism.

When I was very small, Auntie Jen and Uncle Arthur would perch me on their arms as they partnered each other for the waltzes, foxtrots and quicksteps. They span me round the dance floor till their arms ached and still I pleaded with them not to put me down. I looked forward to this all night. I suppose this explains my bizarre addiction to 'Come Dancing' on the telly.

I can still remember the sound of the Irish showbands, with their jangly discordant pianos, off-key saxophones and out-of-time drums – wonderful. It was all accompanied by the smell of Guinness and hand-pulled beer on the men's breath, and the cackle of the women's laughter as they exchanged gossipy chit-chat. I can also recall the feel of the bubbles of lemonade on my face and up my nose as I sat on a bench with my packet of crisps watching the dancing while the other kids rolled about on the cloakroom floor among the hats and coats. I would be all dressed up in one of the frocks made by my Aunt Helen in the flat downstairs. My favourite dress was made of white silk rayon patterned with coloured umbrellas.

Three generations of my family went to the social: grand-parents, mums and dads, sisters, brothers, cousins, kids and in-laws. My family was huge, or so it seemed; everyone was either related through marriage or an 'auntie' or 'uncle' through friendship. We all loved to sing along to all the sloppy romantic tunes and have a good 'knees-up'.

My mum is a bright and vital personality; she's always full of lively gossip, always just like a little girl despite her years. If you put her on a crowded bus, within five minutes she is on first-name terms with everyone, discussing their personal problems. She was often the life and soul of the party, along with her two sisters, Jenny and Dolly. I loved the tone of her voice, especially when she sang only to me. It tickled parts of my life that nobody else could reach. She also played the accordion. It was a beautiful instrument, inlaid with mother-of-pearl and kept safe in a musty box in a secret place. She played it at parties. There was something so awesome and powerful about her when she played that it frightened me. Her fingers would fly, her shiny black curls bounced from side to side, her eyes twinkled, especially at the men, and her hips swayed. Maybe it was her sensuality that felt so alien to me. This was another person, not my mother. I cried so much that eventually she stopped playing altogether. I wonder if my young children feel the same when I sing? . . .

The carpet in that demo studio was green. I know this because at sixteen I was so shy that I could not bring myself to look up. Tony Hatch, the head producer at Pye Records in the early Sixties, responsible for many of Petula Clark's hits, sat at the piano waiting to audition me. He asked for my music. I had some song sheets that Eve Taylor had given me – Kathy Kirby's version of 'Secret Love', and 'Bobby's Girl' by Susan Maughan.

These twee little tunes were not to my taste. My preference was for songs full of strident teen drama like the Crystals' 'He's A Rebel' or the Shirelles' 'Will You Still Love Me Tomorrow?' These were the kinds of song I could relate to, the songs I had been singing with local guitar-based bands in dance halls. I loved all the American girl groups. Nothing could compete with those chunks of cool vinyl shaking around in our big gramophone player/cocktail cabinet. It fizzed and bubbled – 'Da Doo Ron Ron Ron Da Doo Ron Ron . . .'

It was intoxicating stuff.

'Doo Lang Doo Lang Doo Lang . . .' I yearned back at the pulsating discs, clutching a Beatles album sleeve to my chest. Theirs was the first album I ever bought. I played it so much that the grooves were almost worn out and my parents' patience also began to wear thin.

'You really got a ho-old on me . . .' moaned John deliciously. I sang along, copying every quiver, bend and tremble in his voice. I loved his nasal leer. I skipped the tracks sung by George, Paul and Ringo. John was hip – he still is to me and ever will be, song without end . . .

Now here I was having to sing these stuffy Tin Pan Alley songs for Tony Hatch to get a record deal. I did my best but my efforts were firmly turned down.

Undaunted, Adam Faith kept pushing Eve to persevere. The main problem was that she could not see anything in me. She liked showbizzy Fifties female artists in sparkly frocks like Connie Francis and Lena Horne. Adam could see something far more contemporary. In an enterprising leap of the imagination, Adam suggested that Eve finance the recordings herself and lease them to the record company to manufacture and distribute. This would enable us to make the kind of records he felt I was capable of. He also suggested that Eve team me up with the writer of his latest hits, Chris Andrews, who also happened to come from Dagenham.

To Eve's great credit, she responded with entrepreneurial enthusiasm to Adam's suggestions and put them straight into action. This was a unique situation, the record contract being one of the first agreements of its kind. Unfortunately, nobody realized that a time should be specified for the return of the tapes; Eve just assumed that, as she had paid for the records to be made, they were her property, and would therefore be returned when the contract ran out. Nor was there an advance on sales given, as is regular practice now that such lease tape deals are commonplace. Eve was very keen to be with Pye Records and take advantage of all their connections – ATV, a powerful television network; London Management, the biggest booking agency; and the London Palladium theatre, *the* prestigious venue of its time to play.

When they drew up the contract with Pye Records, nobody dreamed that I would ever sell one record in the UK, let alone millions all over the world, or that they would continue to sell for decade after decade to come. Of course, at the time I knew nothing about all this. I did not sign the contract. At sixteen I was a minor, and my parents had to sign on my behalf. Even if I had known about the contract, I would not have had the expertise to understand it. I did not have a lawyer to explain the implications of its clauses and terms to me and look after my interests. I was happy in my ignorance, overjoyed with the sudden change in my circumstances. My meagre royalties from Eve – one halfpenny per record sold – seemed like a fortune to a former Ford's office girl on seven pounds, fifteen shillings and eleven pence a week!

I was not the only one to be exploited. Great producers like George Martin were employed on a weekly wage by their record company and never received royalties for the hits they produced. George told me that his move to become independent after producing hit after hit for EMI Records was precipitated by the denial of a request by him and fellow producer John Burgess for a modest rise in salary to reflect their chart successes. This is the kind of everyday practice of yesteryear by which fortunes were amassed by some, and from which today's record business has grown. Can you imagine Madonna or Stock, Aitken, Waterman putting up with any of that!

On the other hand, who would have imagined that, instead

of the Sixties tradition of struggling new artists going on tour to earn a few quid and find a few more fans as part of an exciting package of up-and-coming acts, support bands nowadays actually have to pay the star act huge sums out of their recording budgets or publishing advances for the opportunity to perform on the same show and be exposed to a bigger audience? They end up grossly in debt to their record company, while the megastar adds to his or her millions.

My first singles probably cost a couple of hundred apiece. Nowadays, that piece of vinyl would cost a minimum of around £10,000, plus the inevitable video costing upwards of £30,000, plus a UK marketing budget of around £20,000 – and we are talking modest sums here. This, understandably, inhibits record company investment in new acts. Opportunities are open only to the very lucky few, and with a diminishing audience there is such competition for sales that the more successful those few are, the more expensive – but not necessarily better – the process becomes as they desperately try to hang on to their slice of the market.

With the massive outlay involved in launching a new artist, only those with immediately obvious global appeal are signed to sing songs with immediately obvious global appeal – like a golden oldie. The charts are full of them. It is vital for the healthy growth of the industry to maintain a creative undercurrent of artists and writers who have less immediate and less defined audience appeal, but who have the ability to invent, originate, initiate new styles and avenues of creative endeavour – we must be able to afford to experiment. Why are people today so concerned with the immediate and superficial? You cannot create a whole new culture like the Sixties overnight. Of course different things need different lengths of time and circumstances to grow. But the reality is that an alarming polarity is increasingly evident: the handful of workaholic megastars earning megabucks on the one hand, and the hordes of starving, out-of-work wannabees carving out a sordid existence from their left-overs on the other. The possibility of making music shrinks further and further away from the grasp of the people in the street yearning to communicate with each other. It stinks of stagnation. At some of the concerts I've been to lately, a team of zombies could have been performing to an audience of corpses and not one rock reviewer would notice. We are so used to and taken in by consumerism. I believe that popular music is dead – we have to reinvent it. How? We have to discover the joy of living in these exciting, explosive, exhilarating times and express it in our music. Nothing can hold back the enormity of that power. This is a very very special age in which to be alive . . .

I adored Chris Andrews from the first moment we met – which was at his parents' house, just round the corner in Dagenham. I loved his raucous piano style, quite unlike Tony Hatch's. We liked the same music. We were particularly influenced by West Indian ska, blue beat and black American artists, which seems to surprise everyone, considering the pure pop we produced. We stomped and screamed together for hours thinking we were the bee's knees. Chris came up with two songs I liked – one was called 'As Long As You're Happy Baby', the other 'Ya-ya-da-da'.

I borrowed money from my dad to come up to London for the recording session. I was accompanied by my mum's blonde bombshell friend, Jean. I didn't tell the girls at work where I was going – they had already taken the piss out of me when I told them I was going to be a star. Both Adam and Eve were in attendance.

I had to wear these huge earphones on my head that mucked up my hairdo. I felt really silly. When I looked up I could see them all upstairs in the control room through the glass panel discussing my performance. Eve did not look at all happy. Suddenly her face changed, became animated. She made a remark to everyone, pointing at me as she jumped up and down with excitement.

I heard them all laughing and squealing down the talk back, 'Your feet! Your feet!' I looked down at my oversized pair of plates.

'What's the matter with them?' I asked defensively.

'You've got no shoes on!'

I apologized and began hunting round the studio for my slingbacks.

'No, no. Keep them off. You may not look better, but you sing better that way!' laughed Eve.

'Suits me,' I said, and kicked them off again. Three takes and the song was in the can. From then on, whenever I sang I was barefoot. *Et voilà! La chanteuse aux pieds nus; la cantante scalza;* the barefoot contessa!

For hardcorn Sandie Shaw fanatics, here are the reasons why:

1. It is more comfortable – I could never find shoes to fit my size seven-and-a-halfs in Dagenham.
2. It is one less thing to think about when getting an outfit together.
3. I am extremely shortsighted and it helps me make my way around the stage without falling off the edge.
4. Its symbolic potency is immense.
5. It feels sexy.

The following weekend the *Dagenham Post* came round our house and photographed me in the back garden – barefoot. This was the first time, apart from school pictures and wedding groups, that I had been in front of the camera. I felt so daft, posing in the grass, flanked by my dad's London Pride and multi-coloured pansies. The neighbours peered out from behind the curtains, wondering what all the fuss with Sandra Goodrich was about – had she joined the Dagenham Girl Pipers?

My mum was horrified when she saw I had no shoes on. 'But your feet are so ugly, Sandra. You've got bunions and corns, and they're so *big*,' she fretted. Then she had a brainwave. She discovered a local chiropodist and engaged him to come round every month to do my feet. He handled them so lovingly and took such care that I began to think that they did not look so bad after all . . .

I studied the deep pile carpet around my feet in Polydor's offices as I waited for Carol Wilson to finish her calls and continue the

A and R meeting we had arranged. After the 'Are You Ready To Be Heartbroken?' and 'Frederick' singles, what Carol wanted me to make was another single. I wanted to continue making more tracks with Clive Langer at Westside and complete the album I had originally planned with Malcolm Dunbar, so as to be able to choose a single from a more substantial body of work. Creatively, with the tour going so well, I felt this was the right thing to do. The audiences wanted an album from me. Also, on a practical level, I knew my great strength was in the foreign markets and that the international companies do not bother with singles unless they are promotion for an album.

Carol and I continued to hold to our different opinions. She took another phone call – from Bucks Fizz. Carol then suggested that a suitable song for the single would be the old Beach Boys' number, 'Going Back'. Charles caught my eye. We both knew there was no going back for me. I decided then and there to leave.

I hauled up the anchor and set sail into dark and troubled seas to complete my tour alone with no record company as a life raft.

All About Eve

RESTARTING THE TOUR without a record company was depressing, to say the least. I did not know whether or not I should or would record again; whether this was hello or good-bye. It was hard to keep the triumphant torch of the first dates burning through the second leg. Sometimes the flame was barely a flicker and sometimes it threatened to go out altogether; then a particularly close communion with an audience or a series of backstage conversations with fans would rekindle a surge of new hope and belief in myself and set the internal fire roaring and crackling once more. The crowd were not inhibited by such concerns; they were just happy to see me, most of them for the first time.

I visited Manchester again, this time the University, and also Newcastle, this time the Polytechnic. The audiences continued to be amazingly enthusiastic and appreciative, but I was struggling inside. Going on stage I felt like I was throwing myself to the lions that prowled negatively around my mind; each performance was an effort to tame these beasts of self-doubt.

Of the band, the guitarist Mark E. Nevin proved to be the most supportive. He had the inner resilience to back me up, to look out for himself and not cruise on other people's efforts. I knew that he was quietly nurturing ideas about his own band, writing his own batch of songs, rehearsing with his own singer, Eddy Reader. But when he was with me he never failed to be there for me a hundred per cent, never held anything back, and was fiercely loyal too. People with the right attitude always accumulate good fortune; talent on its own is not enough. These qualities of Mark's probably contributed considerably to the success of the first venture with his own band, Fairground Attraction.

At a creatively vulnerable time such as this was proving to be, a sympathetic, encouraging but realistic business manager is essential. I was lucky to have Charles and Cathy Negus-Fancey to give me that support.

I was thinking this over while I prepared for the Newcastle date. I had my usual last-minute confrontation with the mirror before I went on stage. A final sweep of lipstick reminded me of Eve, who had a fascinating make-up ritual. There is no doubt in my mind that she had a profound influence on me in my early years, right up until her death, and even after. It's difficult now to imagine the emotional hold she had over me . . .

I met Eve when I was sixteen and she was in her mid-forties. She was married at the time to a man as Jewish as matzo balls, nick-named Moishe, who was also her business partner. He smoked big cigars and called ber Boobella. They lived in an expensive apartment by South Kensington tube with his son, Stephen, from a previous marriage and a Spanish maid called Lucy. Lucy was slavishly at the husband's and stepson's every beck and call, but she organized Eve and the flat to her own convenience. Eve always had to ask Lucy's permission before she did anything in the home in case Lucy threw a fit at having her domestic regime upset.

The first time I visited Eve's flat to sign our management and agency agreement, I could hear Eve screaming at the top of her voice in the kitchen and Lucy screaming back even louder in broken English. I had come with my parents and boyfriend (the one with the Ford Prefect from the Ilford Palais). We all huddled together in embarrassment in the lounge, waiting for the shouting to stop. As their voices rose we sank ever deeper into the feathered luxury of the silk sofas. Eventually Eve emerged, all smiles, victorious, followed by Lucy, who scowled at us sullenly behind Eve's back as she served us the tea that had been the cause of the argument.

The tea came in bone china cups as big as soup bowls. Our eyes were like saucers. The contract by comparison was much smaller, consisting of one page written in very small print. My parents, feeling awkward about their lack of sophistication in business matters, signed on my behalf without any contention. I have never seen the contract from that day since. Every attempt to acquire it from Eve's lawyer was deemed outright mutiny and therefore absolutely out of the question. I think my parents must have had a copy, but that got lost along the way.

Moishe sat in the background smoking a huge cigar and cracking corny jokes. He glanced casually through the contract.

'You'll have to change your name. Sandra Goodrich is a bit of a mouthful,' he said.

'Any ideas?' asked Evie.

'Well, my friends call me Sandie,' I ventured.

'Sandie . . . Sandie . . . Black, Sandie Maugn, Sandie More,' toyed Moishe. 'I know,' he joked. 'How about Sandy Shore? Especially with those bare feet!'

Eve, not recognizing his pun, clapped her hands together enthusiastically, 'Yes, that's it! Sandie Shaw!' and I was reborn and christened in her living-room. From that moment I became the daughter that Evie never had.

Although on matters of taste we fought a lot, I really loved Eve. I know all the worst about her and I still love her. If it were not for her bullying and pushiness I would never have achieved any of my early successes; they would have remained a Dagenham girl's teenage dream. When I was away working I would write her fond, appreciative postcards and always left little thank-you notes and drawings in her office.

She was ill a lot. Looking back I think she must have been on the change of life for as long as I knew her, which was around twenty years!

When I visited her fifth-floor Regent Street office I could hear her screaming down the phone as I came up in the lift. I would rush in with a cup of tea and her headache pills. Eve liked to have a boiled egg and toasted soldiers with me for lunch, which we ate at her desk while she continued to field heavy business calls from her many telephones. These often gave her heart palpitations and I would open the window for some fresh air and then stroke her hands until she felt better. Also there was Eve's back problem; she was always complaining about it. One day I decided to surprise her by having a splendid black leather relaxing chair delivered from Heal's.

Eve somehow managed to convince me that she was perpetually on the brink of death. I began to feel guilty if I gave her any problem or anxiety that would bring on one of her illnesses, in case I sent her over the edge. Her other way of keeping me in control was to tell me everybody hated me. If I met someone I liked and felt a rapport with, Eve would immediately inform me that they had told her something really awful about me and I should therefore not trust my own judgement. Then she would tell me a 'piece of dirt' about them so that in future I would trust only her. She was especially vehement about people she saw as business competitors.

Increasingly Eve took over my life and, as much as she could, my public identity. At one point she was doing my press interviews for me, and even did a series for a Sunday rag, with headlines like 'WHY SANDIE NEEDS MORE BOYFRIENDS', confiding, 'I'm the only person she can pour her heart out to,' and admitting, 'I nag her, but only for her own good.' She proudly showed off to the journalist her latest present from me, a diamond and platinum watch.

Eve's other artists were often jealous of the attention she gave me. One of them, knowing that I could not swim, once went so far as to push me in the deep end of Eve's swimming pool one dark Spanish night. I did not find it funny at the time, but on reflection these feelings were understandable.

As Eve grew more fond of me, her tyrannical efforts on my behalf became less of a business activity and more of a personal crusade, and any rejection she took as a mortal blow to her ego.

'He's a shit!' she would pronounce as she slammed the phone down on an unforthcoming agent. 'All men are shits!' She would cast a scathing look across the office at Moishe sitting at his twin desk, smiling, unperturbed.

Eve and Moishe had bought a holiday flat in Majorca. On

one occasion when I joined them, I saw Moishe from the balcony of Eve's bedroom bonking one of his young mistresses on the balcony of the flat below. The affair was the talk of the communal swimming pool. Shortly afterwards they divorced.

Eve's saucy red MG sports car went out the door with him. So did the South Kensington apartment. They were replaced by a silver Mercedes and a house in Knightsbridge. Eve kept the Spanish flat. Despite the change of car, Eve's driving did not improve. Passengers clung to the dashboard in terror as she drove erratically and chatted animatedly, flicking her cigarette ash out of the window and gesticulating at the same time, oblivious of the havoc she was causing to her fellow road-users. Eve had learnt to drive during the war and consequently had never had to pass a test. She took Hyde Park Corner like a blind tank driver taking Alamein.

After her divorce, Eve and I became even closer. As my personal insecurity and isolation grew apace with my increasing celebrity, her influence on the creative content of my work became stronger. I became frustrated and angry about this and we argued long and loud, but finally I felt powerless to change the situation – Eve held all the reins, financially, emotionally, and socially. I stayed overnight at her house, watching telly in the same bed. Lucy, the maid, continued to work for her for a while, serving us breakfast with the special contempt she particularly felt for other women. A white Scottie from Mike Mansfield took the stepson's place.

Sitting on her bed, the floor strewn with her old remembrances and keepsakes, Eve confided in me all the secret hurts of her life from when she was a little girl. I sat outside the bathroom on the stairs while Eve bathed, passing her soap, towels and tissues for her tears, and listened to her stories about her childhood, her mother, whom she adored, and her father, whom she despised.

Her father was a stage impresario of the Thirties and Forties. As a young girl, Eve went on tour with some of his shows playing a soubrette, the glamorous girly interest in the package. It was on these tours, Eve said, that she watched her father gambling away the family money and witnessed his continual infidelity to her mother.

Eve showed me all the wonderful publicity photos she had had taken. My favourite was of her wearing nothing but a giant pink powder puff. Eve was incredibly beautiful as a young woman. To help achieve this she had had a nose job. As we talked she was continually examining it in front of the mirror, moaning, 'It's dropped! It's dropped! Come here, Sandie, look at this old photo. Can't you see how it's dropped!' Then she would gather up the extra folds of flesh around her face and stretch them up and across her cheeks asking, 'Shall I get a face lift?' I was fascinated.

I loved watching Eve's elaborate make-up application in her dressing-room. She perched on a pink, frilly stool in front of pink-tinted mirrors, wearing a nylon negligee and fluffy high-heeled slippers. She started by smoothing moisturizer on her skin, followed by a dark-tan-coloured pancake powder, which she patted and wiped straight on top. Her eyelids were then smeared with sparkly ice-blue shadow, and her eyes outlined by thick black eyeliner stroked across the top of the lashes and turned up at the outside edges. With a dot of the brush she made a false beauty spot beneath her pencilled brow-line. Then . . . her lips. In order to make them appear thicker, Eve first brushed a line all around, just outside her natural line, with a big cupid's bow sweep at the top, and then filled it in with her favourite colour – bright Schiaparelli Pink. In wonder more than admiration, I sat at her satin-slippered feet observing the proceedings, just as I used to sit on the edge of the bath, watching my mum get ready to go out when I was small, making mental notes so I could dress up and do it for myself when she left the house. Eve never changed her make-up routine in the twenty years I knew her, all the while telling me her life-story.

In her stage-act, Eve began to do comedy routines and had one particular piece of business with two cymbals strapped to her thighs that is fondly remembered by the few old-timers who are still around in the business. She tap-danced with the Grade

Brothers when they were on the boards and did gags with Paul Raymond, before he went on to more titillating things.

Eve told me her first big romance was with one of her stage-door Johnnies; that he came from an aristocratic background and did nothing but drink. Her initial impressionable regard for his stately home and social standing gave way to disappointment when the effect of his drinking rendered him unable to fulfil his husbandly duties. The relationship went quickly down the hatch.

Evie was not too fussed about his problem, though. She confided in me that she always felt that sex was a waste of time and only useful as a means of holding power over men. 'Men are not interested in love and romance,' she informed me. Eve regarded my liking for things physical as an aberration that had something to do with class differences.

I was goggle-eyed at these sophisticated tales of emotional embitterment and sexual disillusionment. It was clear that Eve saw me as a second chance in life, that she was trying to relive her ambitions through me.

Mike Mansfield, who, because of our similar ages, I had naively thought was pursuing me, began to hang around a lot after Moishe's departure. The reality was that he was besotted with Eve. My initial shock and confusion at the unusual arrangement gave way to support as he patiently showered her with enough roses and romantic attention to make up for all her barren, loveless years. For a while she seemed quite happy, but neither she nor the times were yet ready for such variations from the norm in relationships, and although they remained close friends they did not marry. How sad.

One of the reasons marriage to Jeff was so attractive was that it gave me a chance to escape from Eve's increasingly strong clutches. I saw Jeff as the brave knight come to rescue me from the dragon. Then Eve met her next husband, Harold. I watched their exciting courtship quickly degenerate into a difficult marriage where she insulted the poor man mercilessly as dinner guests listened in sheer amazement to the depth of her calculated vitriol.

After the birth of Grace, I had a wonderful reason to give up any active interest in my career. Eve ceased to manage me, although we remained in touch. Unfortunately my emotional dependence on Jeff began to grow and fill the gap Eve left.

When I became a Buddhist I began to see the unhealthy side of my relationship with Eve. As my way of seeing things changed, Eve's grip on me started to diminish.

It was not until Nik's advent on the scene in 1981 that I realized how much I had changed. Nik was not taken in at all by Eve's histrionics, and coming from the 'new school' of Virgin Records was completely ignorant of and unimpressed by her old showbiz reputation. His immediate, honest response was, 'She's quite definitely crazy!' For the first time she appeared to be that way to me too. Eve had a lot of ideas about life and people that were completely twisted. Now, instead of being dragged into her paranoia, I would stand on the outside feeling confident of my own truth, maintaining my point of view however much she disliked and disagreed with me. This was probably one of the hardest things I ever managed to do – to trust that, just because the emotions she engendered in me were so strong, it did not necessarily mean that they were well founded or valuable; there was a deeper reality in my life. Consequently Eve no longer held any sway over me.

When Nik and I married, Eve was among the limited number, through lack of space, of close friends who were invited to witness the Buddhist ceremony. To our amazement she turned up with her grown-up stepson, now an accountant. His father, Moishe, had died and Stephen had only recently re-entered Eve's life. Eve insisted with her usual forcefulness that we squeeze him into the ceremony. Nik and I reluctantly obliged.

We had spent the previous week clearing out the kitchen and getting rid of our cooker to make way for a new super-dooper model that Eve insisted on giving us as a wedding gift. I was not supposed to know; it was to be delivered the day after as a surprise. I had been wary of Eve's generous gestures ever since she obtained a stereo unit on discount for Jeff and me one

Christmas. A week later she sent us the bill. 'The discount was the present!' explained Eve.

I had another unrehearsed shock at the wedding party – a singing telegram. In front of hundreds of bemused family and friends this poor girl had to sing a message from Eve made up of Eve's rewritten lyrics of my old Sixties songs. It was well meant, but was painfully out of touch with the passage of time. Eve had really built her 'part' up; her new words pointedly enhanced the importance of her influence in my life. Most of our guests were unaware of this piece of my past and the atmosphere was decidedly uncomfortable.

As the telegram girl finished off, Eve approached me from across the dance floor, arms open, Schiaparelli Pink lips puckered ready to kiss. Out of the corner of her eye she espied Harold, her long-suffering ex-husband, who was also a guest, standing in the ring of onlookers. She stopped, transfixed. Then the puckered lips turned into a scream as she shouted at me, 'How could you do this to me? How could you spoil my special day!' and stormed out, her stepson in tow.

Eve never spoke to me again. The cooker never arrived, and the empty space in the kitchen glared accusingly at me the next morning.

I applied the lipstick slowly and deliberately, smiled back at my born-again reflection and went on stage to greet the Newcastle crowd.

In the late Sixties I had a wonderful friend, an ageing Viennese psychoanalyst called Walter Schindler, whose desperate desire to get his hands on my psyche went unrequited. Every time he saw me he chuckled, 'How are you? Have you killed Eve yet?' I know he meant it symbolically, but I have never wanted to eradicate Eve from my life. She was a remarkable, courageous woman. A woman full of love with nowhere for it to go.

Not long after the wedding, Eve died suddenly and unnecessarily. Feeling unwell, she had called her doctor, but as her flat was so thoroughly burglar proof he was unable to gain access until it was too late. At the close of her life she had almost entirely run out of friends. The few that remained found her paranoid ramblings very difficult to handle. She had become impossible to relate to sensibly and managed to make life unpleasant for everyone. She had started seeing her stepson again – he was the closest thing she had to family. As far as I know he was the major beneficiary in her will. He did not inform me of her death or her funeral.

Eve Taylor lies in an uncelebrated plot in a Jewish cemetery in North London. To this day no stone has been placed on her grave.

This is not exactly *all* about Eve . . . but it is more than enough for now.

Beyond the Fringe

MY SECOND APPEARANCE IN SCOTLAND was at the Queen Margaret's Union in Glasgow. My hair, which had grown half-way down my back during the tour, was becoming a problem. The heat of the shows necessitated washing it daily. I discovered that, for some odd reason, a large percentage of my fans were hairdressers when Cathy pointed out to me that I had a lot of letters from young men expressing their desire to 'do my hair'. This was far more useful than some of the strange requests concerning my feet!

So wherever I travelled Cathy made sure that a local fan who was a hairdresser could come up and see me some time before the show and blow-dry my hair. I thought, why have your hair done by a total stranger when you can have it done by someone who really cares? Yes, I know this seems a bizarre way to 'meet your public', but it's far more fun than sending an impersonal autograph through the post. It proved a really popular move; and I was able to include them and their ideas in my work. As my hair-style was really simple and just required drying, there was not much risk of things going wrong. Occasionally the more impressionable ones had to be fortified with a stiff drink beforehand to stop their crimping fingers from trembling too much, but I came out of it all relatively unscathed.

I tried it first in Glasgow. I had been receiving letters, phone calls, flowers and presents from John for more years than I could remember. He was overjoyed when I started recording again; his enthusiasm stretched the goodwill of his clients to the limit. He played my latest releases continuously in his Dundee hairdressing salon, while boogee-ing around the backwash and singing along, accompanied by the hum of the hairdriers.

I have always had a thing about my hair. I just do not feel right unless my hair is clean and shiny. A person's hair-style tells you a lot about them. My mum, Rosie, always had lovely thick dark hair that hung in sensuous curls around her face. I used to watch her elaborate getting-ready-to-go-out ritual, the laborious unwinding of her old-fashioned metal clips and pipe cleaners and the pinning of the curls into little sausage-like bangs round the edges. Later she had it cut in an 'Italian Boy' and started using plastic curlers held in place by balls on elastic. She dressed in high-heeled pointy-toe shoes, pencil-slim skirt, skin-tight, hand-knitted sweaters, black, lacy, well-filled bra barely visible underneath. All this was topped by upturned, Vernon's Girl specs and a halo of hairspray. She was a real head-turner.

Rosie would never be seen dead in her curlers and would have thrown a fit if she had seen me doing TV dress rehearsals with my hair in those huge jumbo rollers that we all had in the Sixties to straighten our hair. Evie used to try and shoo away the photographers on set who were trying to get a scoop, but I did not care, as long as it looked good for the transmission.

When I was a five-year-old just starting school, I had two long pigtails down to my bottom. As my parents both worked I stayed after school at 'Aunt' Daph's over the road, with her two daughters, Linda and Maureen, who also had waist-length pigtails. All three of us dreaded the evenings when 'Aunt' Daph lined us up to brush out and re-plait our tangled tresses. We protested loudly, screaming like a chorus of howling banshees as she bravely tugged and pulled.

To my deep distress, the desperate kind that only newly self-conscious little girls experience, these pigtails stayed right up until junior school. I pleaded endlessly with my mum to let me have a ponytail like some of the other girls, to no avail.

One day, while flirting in the playground with a red-haired, freckle-faced boyfriend called Ronny, an argument developed over who should have the last pip in the pomegranate. I won. It was an unpopular victory. Ronny ran into the classroom, returned with a set of scissors and swiftly cut off one of my plaits. He ran around the playground, whooping and swinging it about in the air like a Red Indian brandishing a scalp. Furious, I grabbed the scissors back and started hacking away at his thick mane of red hair, only stopping when we were interrupted by the school bell.

Ronny hid his ravaged carrot top under his cap and I tucked the stub of cut pigtail under the other one and then forgot all about it. It was not until Ronny stood on our doorstep cowering alongside his outraged mother that Rosie discovered I was minus one plait. My mum let out a cry of heart-chilling agony. Then an almighty row broke out as each proud mother bemoaned the loss of her child's crowning glory. I was glad to see the last of it, and more than happy when the other pigtail had to be cut off to match.

At senior school my best friend Kathy took charge of my hair, cutting, colouring, curling and straightening it to go along with and often to start off the current craze. It was not until the age of sixteen when I walked into Vidal Sassoon's ultra trendy salon and, whilst seated nervously among a row of sophisticated models, had it all chopped off into that famous shoulder-length bob of mine, that I found a style that was really 'me'. 'For heaven's sake cut that awful fringe,' Eve constantly moaned. 'I can't see your eyes.'

To this day there are still a few forty-year-old Sandie Shaw clones around, but mostly the plagiarists are young girls eager to adopt the 'look' of the Sixties. I am alternately flattered and pissed off when some up-and-coming pop star copies me. On the one hand it is nice to be admired; on the other it smacks of a lack of originality. They don't seem to understand that it is a whole culture they are trying to emulate, but that was the Eighties, wasn't it? All style and no substance. I cannot remember ever wanting to copy anyone; my generation had a pronounced aversion to anything of the past, we wanted to do our own thing. A lot of young people now lack that essential thrust, that inner confidence to try something new, to challenge their limitations, to change their circumstances, make their reality different. Theirs is a generation obsessed with its own impotence. I suppose that is what draws me to them. I want to remind them of their power. The human race continually needs that surge of rejuvenation, that persistent drive of questioning and reassessment that should be intrinsic in the young. I get so frightened for the future at the way they so easily accept their lot when they could change the world if they wanted . . . but then I speak as a Buddhist. On my twenty-first birthday I was not, and I certainly did not feel like mistress of my own destiny.

Eve wanted to get the maximum amount of press coverage for my coming of age. Jeff, who always likes to do things big, helped to plan it. Our relationship at that time, although ascloseasthis, was not yet public knowledge, and we went to great lengths to keep it secret. Emotionally, creatively and business-wise, Jeff already wielded a great influence over me. He answered my doubts and insecurity about my looks by introducing me to a make-up artist and a wig maker. In retrospect I wonder why I felt so insecure, so inadequate; judging from the photos and the TV film footage of the time, I looked stunning. It was probably the subtle insinuations projected by the images and values of the fashion world that intimidated me. In fact, true confidence can never be based on having fame, beauty, success, money or a skinny body.

Eve, along with Jeff, who had previously stage-managed the launching of the Sandie Shaw dress label and shoe range, decided to have the party at Madame Tussauds. I was happy to go along with all their plans. I just loved being directed; I did not want the responsibility of coming up with ideas and having them go wrong. I was more at home making decisions in the studio than thinking up extravaganzas for the press. Eve had it stuck in her mind that I would arrive in a horse-drawn carriage – just like some fairy-tale princess or Cinderella . . . I dunno, whatever her fantasy was. Jeff was also embarrassed by her showbizzy taste. To counteract it he designed and had made for me the most beautiful dress and jacket. It was so-o-o sophisticated that it immediately brought out my sense of inadequacy. Cue the make-up artist and wig . . .

Hundreds of guests had been invited to the party, none of

them close friends. I didn't have any. I prepared at Eve's new house in Mayfair. I was not sure about the heavy make-up that Gordon applied. It made me look so much more grown-up, almost a different person. When he plonked on the curly wig and combed it out the transformation was complete. Why on earth I should want to make myself look like somebody else to celebrate twenty-one years of my existence on this planet could only have been a reflection of my excessively unconfident and malleable frame of mind. Ironically, one of the following day's newspapers featured a picture of Eve and me seated in the Chamber of Horrors, captioned 'Sandie and her mother'. My mum, understandably, was really upset.

Jeff and I had piles of wigs in hatboxes in our flat in Blackheath: the leftovers from the Sandie Shaw Shoes launch. The one I had worn on that occasion was white. There were also green ones, orange ones, purple and pink, curly and straight, long and short.

One of my long-lasting memories of Jeff will be his impression of 'King Charles And His Trusty Spaniel', which he executed in the bedroom, scantily clad in tight black briefs. He entered carrying under his arm the bassett hound on whose head he had placed a long curly green wig to complement the pink one he was wearing. Jeff's sense of humour always had me in stitches. How many other husbands keep their wife waiting to go out while they finish sewing her into her frock?

Some other occasions when I have worn a wig and acted out of character are for meeting the Queen, singing on a Royal Command performance and at my first wedding. In fact it would seem that on every important date I had an identity crisis that sent me reaching for the hairdresser. My present managers, Cathy and Charles, always know I am feeling insecure when I begin proposing drastic changes of hair-style. Whenever I fancy a radical reappraisal of my life I make an appointment to have all my hair cut off and dyed. So far I have always cancelled at the eleventh hour. One day I will go through with it and let the crop-haired blonde in me come out!

Luckily for John from Dundee and the audience, I wanted to stay myself for the Glasgow show. But nobody knew how long

I would keep my hair on; I felt like tearing it out in frustration for most of this part of the tour. The ardent longing of the fans for an album coupled with my lack of a record company was not only depressing but really gave my self-confidence a blasting. Why was this happening to me? I began to wonder again who I really was, whether I had anything of any contemporary worth to offer, whether there was any purpose in singing any more . . . you know, the usual hair-raising rubbish.

Between the Pope and
Archbishop Tutu

GEOFF TRAVIS, FROM ROUGH TRADE RECORDS, came to
the next show at the Royal Holloway College in Egham. He
had been waiting in the wings throughout the tour, offering
support and encouragement and, recently, a cassette for me
from the Jesus and Mary Chain. This contained a demo of a
new song they had written, and unlike their usual performances
which were drenched in torrents of feedback, this was played
only on acoustic guitar. The song was called 'Cool About You'.
It was wonderful.

I worked out an arrangement with the band and began to
include 'Cool About You' in the act to devastating effect. At
Holloway, Geoff heard me sing it for the first time and was
bowled over. When I came off stage he was all starry eyed.
I was impressed with Geoff's initiative. He knew exactly
what I was looking for, was a teetotaller, and also sported a
very nifty black caped coat that swept portentously around
his ankles. This made a pleasant change from the usual record
company uniform of jeans, checked shirt and beery breath.

I signed my autographs, chatted to fans about music, the
media, Thatcher, sexual politics, nuclear disarmament, ecology,
metaphysics, love, the universe, the past, the present, the future,
our role in it – all the normal backstage banter – and then
changed out of my stage clothes in a campus bedroom, returned
the bra I had borrowed from the student, and was driven off
into the night.

The following day we played at Bradford University. Once
again I was driven, as I had never learnt to drive myself. In
spite of this Jeff and I used to have two cars. A burgundy,

smoked-glass Bentley and a matching Mini. Jeff drove the Mini in his manic hell-raising way. I always trusted his driving, so much so that I often fell asleep alongside him as he raced home up the A2 in the small hours, clipping lights and hurtling round corners. On one such journey he nudged me awake and suggested I step carefully out. Still half asleep, I threw open the door to discover we were suspended on top of two traffic islands.

Jeff acquired a chauffeur for the Bentley, complete with colour-coordinated uniform. Unknown to me, Terry was new to the job; they both omitted to tell me that he had a slightly iffy past, and that Jeff wanted to give him a break.

On our first drive, Terry insisted that I sit in the back with the BBC executive to whom I had offered a lift. Terry ostentatiously held open the door for us with an exaggerated tip of the hat. I was lost for words. As we drove along, he turned round and with a staggering impersonation of Parker talking to Lady Penelope, asked, 'Is everything all right, madam?'

'Is this for real?' I thought. As he took his eyes off the road he rammed straight into the car in front. We pulled up with a jolt that sent me and the BBC executive rolling around on the floor on top of each other. Terry then slammed out of the Bentley, pulled the other driver from his car and threw him on to the well-polished bonnet where he slithered as Terry punched him on the nose. The two men laid into each other, filling the air pungently with rich and imaginative expletives. The exec and I crawled out of the back of the car while Terry was still preoccupied with his boxing bout, and hailed a taxi to our appointments.

The next morning Jeff tried to fire Terry, but was convinced by him that he could change his ways. He ended up saying Terry could have a second chance, provided he could convince me too.

Terry stood on the doorstep fumbling with his chauffeur's cap, mumbling apologies for his behaviour and especially for his ripe language. He chose his words very carefully. The effort got him all flustered and tongue-twisted. Finally, in frustration, he threw his cap at the wall and exclaimed, 'Oh fuck it madam! I'm so bloody sorry!'

From then on Terry called me Sandie, we ditched the poncey uniform and I sat in the front with him. He even secretly started to teach me to drive. We bought an old banger and decided to give Jeff a surprise.

I pulled up outside Jeff's offices and offered him a lift home. He presumed I had a taxi waiting. When he saw my old banger he thought it was Terry's and amiably jumped in. I don't know how long it took for it to sink in that I was in the driving seat, but as we stopped at the traffic lights at the end of Wells Street he jumped out and ran down Oxford Street screaming, 'Help! Murder! My wife's trying to kill me!' This did wonders for my confidence.

So I found a qualified driving instructor who had previously taught Prince Charles and would not be daunted by the prospect of teaching me. As we risked life and limb negotiating Hyde Park Corner (*before* those traffic lights were put in) he chewed on indigestion tablets. I don't know whether I was a good driver and he was highly strung, or a terrible driver and he had nerves of iron. I suspect the latter to be true. When my test date was confirmed his face dropped. I think he thought never was too soon, but I decided to go through with it.

On the morning of the test I was booked to go on the Pete Murray radio programme. Stupidly, not realizing that millions of people were listening in, I explained my nervousness by telling Pete about my driving exam later that morning. 'Oh really? Where?' he asked. Even more foolishly I told him.

We pulled up at the test centre. The streets were lined with hundreds of curious wellwishers who actually expected me to take my test in front of them. They cheered as I parked outside . . . they cheered again as I pulled away with the examiner. That was enough. I was out of the car and on my way home in shock, leaving the poor examiner alone in the passenger seat. Shortly after that my driving instructor retired. I don't know if it had anything to do with me. I did not attempt to take the wheel again.

One day during the tour we passed my old house in Blackheath. The drive looked sad and empty without the two matching cars. A bus stop and lamppost stood in what used to be our front garden. When the council had started to widen the road into a motorway I had been furious. Every time they tried to relocate the lamppost Terry and I tied a rope around it, attached it to the Bentley's bumper, and drove off, rooting it out again.

We stopped so I could take a closer look. A road had been built alongside the house and our wonderful garden was now a housing estate. They had even pulled down my beautiful gazebo where I had hidden with the dogs in the summer and painted in water colours in the winter.

I sat on the steps and tried to picture the garden – the trees, the pond, the long grass in the orchard, the mountains of apple blossom, the butterflies, the ladybirds, the pair of robbins in the holly bush outside my bedroom window, and my dogs: Olly the St Bernard, Porky the bassett hound, Peggy and Blue the Great Danes, and Cassidy the Pyrenean mountain dog, all huddled together in the gazebo.

In 1970, when I was pregnant with Grace, I used to sit and dream in the garden in my sunhat, excruciatingly happy. Joni Mitchell's bright intelligent songs had come to my attention. I loved them, but I felt that I could never do anything as exciting as all these new emancipated American lady songwriters were doing. I really did not want to sing any more. I just wanted to stay in my safe little world among the chestnut trees.

Unfortunately I was due to appear in Italy at the San Remo Song Festival. In Rome, the record company kept changing their minds about the lyrics of my original Italian song. I told Eve time and time again that this made me nervous and I did not want to go, but she kept talking me back into it. The day before I left, yet another new version was sent for me to learn overnight.

> Dimmi, dimmi se domani,
> Io dovrò restare sola.

Dimmi, dimmi non ho paura
Di guardare la vita in faccia . . .

But I could not face it any more. I had had enough of the
travelling, the hanging about, the dramas, being dressed up and
brought down, forever worrying about hit records, forever
trying to be what Eve or Jeff or the public wanted me to be . . .
I just wanted to stay at home in my cosy little cocoon and have
my baby. It's amazing what a few hormones can do to your
outlook.

The night before the flight to Italy, I lay in bed pretending to
be asleep. At midnight I crept quietly out into the garden and
hid under the hay in the gazebo with the dogs. In the early hours
I heard the car pull up in the drive to take me to the airport,
followed by voices calling for me. Somebody was walking in
the grass. They stopped outside the gazebo. I snuggled even
closer under Olly's lovely fur coat, and hoped and wished with
all my heart that they would not find me.

'She's not in the garden,' shouted Jenny, my roadie, who was
living at the top of the house. 'Don't worry, Jeff, you go off to
work. I know where to find her.' When they called off the
search I breathed a sigh of relief. I stayed put until I was sure I
had missed the plane.

Jenny's silhouette stood in the gazebo doorway. 'It's all right,
you can come out now. I knew you were there all along.'

'Did Eve do her nut?' I asked worriedly.

'Yes. It was so funny! I think I've got the sack.' She pulled
me up on my feet. 'Come on in, have a cup of tea and listen to
some Leonard Cohen. That should cheer you up! Don't fret,'
she comforted. 'Fame and fortune aren't everything. Let's look
after the baby.' I followed her hippy footsteps back into the
house, and, at that moment, as far as I was concerned I had
officially retired from singing.

By the time we hit London and played at the Mean Fiddler and
finally at the University of London Union, I was feeling much
stronger as an artist, much more committed. I had experienced

such an open and honest rapport with the audiences that a very definite on-stage persona was coming into being – pure essence of the real me! I had really benefited from all that battling with myself.

A pleasant surprise was added to the end of the 'Freshers' leg of the tour – a date in Portugal, singing to backing track for TV, a real doddle. So I invited Cathy, Charles and Nik to come along too for a weekend break.

Just before we left I heard about the United Nations' efforts to create an event called 'A Million Minutes of Peace'. They had a great idea – instead of asking people to give money they were asking them to donate three minutes of their time on a specified day to thinking about peace.

Inspired, I went straight along to Doreen Davies, who had been head of programming at Radio One for many years, with two Buddhist friends, Mark Parker who was then a plugger for Arista Records, and Connie Fillipello, George Michael's PR. We asked for three minutes' air time to be donated in the weekday lunch programme so that millions of listeners could join in during their break. To our surprise she agreed immediately.

In order to bring attention to this international peace initiative, the UK branch of the United Nations wanted to join the press and TV link-up in which all the other countries were taking part. Each country was launching hot-air balloons at dawn with celebrity passengers on board, like Billy Connolly in Sydney and Jack Lemmon in New York.

Although there was an amazing response from the rest of the world – some governments were even stopping in mid-session for three minutes of thoughts on peace – in Britain the media and celebrities who had been approached were not the least bit enthusiastic. Concerned, the UK office of the UN rang me on the night before the flight to ask if I knew anyone who would accompany me in a balloon. I thought somebody from a different walk of life who adored publicity would be best. Nik's ex-partner, Richard Branson, sprang to mind.

The following morning, at the crack of dawn when I got up

and dressed for the flight, it was dark and freezing cold. At times like this you begin seriously to question your own sanity. I left a note at home on the fridge door – 'Nik, just popping up in a balloon with Richard – back for breakfast!'

It was damp and miserable in Hyde Park. Luckily Jeff had given me a fashionable warm flying jacket to wear. Richard pulled up in his car, all jolly hockey sticks, and noted first me, the only celebrity, and then the feeble press turn-out.

'I thought there would be more of us,' he drizzled. 'I don't want to be the centre of attention.'

'Strange!' I thought.

After much huffing and puffing the balloon was ready to go. Richard clambered expertly into the basket, then pulled me in head first, so that I landed upside down with my legs in the air. We must have looked like Andy Pandy and Looby Loo. The aviator prepared to take off. He turned to Richard.

'I don't suppose you've been up in one of these before,' he said proudly.

'Oh yes I have!' crowed Richard. 'I've got my own one – I'm learning to fly!'

The atmosphere deflated. At this point the meagre press crew sidled into position and aimed their cameras and questions our way. I then witnessed the most extraordinary performance from Richard. He painstakingly turned his back on each camera directed at him and ignored all the questions, pretending to be engrossed in conversation. As the photographers shifted around the balloon trying to get a better angle, he avoided them by shuffling around the tiny basket with me, squashing the aviator like an overripe gooseberry. It was all getting very silly. He must have been as disappointed as I was at the poor response for such a great cause after all his early morning efforts.

Richard suddenly announced, 'I'm frightfully sorry, but I have to rush off to a big press conference – about my own balloon enterprise.' This transpired to be his fateful transatlantic effort.

Richard baled out and left me to finish the photocall alone. I realized that he had intended to use this as a little supplementary publicity for his own stunt. When the plan had failed to get off the ground, the ever-buoyant Richard had decided to save himself for his next press call. I suppose it's one way of getting your projects up and away.

The Radio One piece went out at lunchtime and it was brilliant. The thought of sunny Portugal cheered me up even more. The contract came over to be signed. Charles gave it the once over. He rang me.

'Guess what? This is a bit more like it . . . It's a massive peace concert for the United Nations organized by the Portuguese Government, part of the "Million Minutes" project,' he told me excitedly. Then he laughed. 'You're going on between the Pope and Archbishop Tutu!'

A Sight for Sore Eyes

ON THE WAY TO THE AIRPORT, bound for Lisbon with
Cathy, Charles, Nik and the band, my contact lenses became
uncomfortable and my eyes itchy. Unfortunately I had packed
my lens case in my suitcase. Nik went to the rescue, scouring
the airport terminal for a chemist. He returned with a case and
a bottle of liquid to store them in.

The plane was about to leave. I rushed into the loo and
whipped out my lenses. Having no glasses to wear I could not
read the instructions on the bottle so I popped the lenses into
the liquid and hoped for the best. I was looking forward to
seeing Lisbon. I had been once before in 1968 to do some
concerts. The trip had been total madness . . .

As the plane landed and the doors opened on that first visit,
I was greeted by a deafening roar from thousands of Portuguese
fans, all squashed together like sardines in the tiny airport.
Tentatively I descended from the steps of the plane on to the
tarmac. A surge of bodies engulfed me. The police formed a
tight circle around me, but the crowd just pushed harder and
sandwiched us all together. I could not move.

'They all want to touch you,' chuckled a police officer.

'Oh no,' I thought. 'There's not enough of me to go round.'

You must appreciate that there were none of the sophisticated
security and crowd control systems that we have developed
today. The frenzy of the Sixties took everyone by surprise.
Happenings like this were unprecedented. In Europe I was the
first real live British pop star they could get their hands on and
each person was determined to do just that.

The police were as hysterical as the crowd. In the mêlée I
was separated from Eve and my entourage and surrounded by

impassioned admirers screaming at me in Portuguese. We were all welded together by their intensity and body heat.

Gasping for breath, I seriously thought I was about to die. Then, miraculously, I was lifted into the air and laid out across the upheld hands of the policemen. Around the airport I went, passed gently from person to person across a vast sea of arms, through immigration, customs and luggage arrival. Thousands of people touched me in this bizarre laying-on of hands.

Outside I was lowered into an open-top car. I was accompanied to the hotel by the whining sirens of a motorcycle escort, press and TV cameras and carloads of fans with their radio stations blaring my records out into the night. I had certainly arrived in Lisbon.

Another notable arrival around that time was in Berlin. I travelled very early in the morning with my father, sitting at the back of the plane hoping to remain unnoticed. I had not had time to bother with make-up so I flew 'incognito' in huge dark glasses and a floppy hat. As the plane descended we noticed this massive welcoming committee gathered on the runway – photographers, camera crews, and a fifty-piece brass band.

'Oh no!' I cried, and dived under the seat for my eyeliner. The other passengers filed out of the plane while I put the finishing touches to my face. As the queues of businessmen disembarked a trigger-happy band leader noticed the only other female traveller standing at the top of the plane steps.

To her complete shock the band struck up a rousing medley of all my hits, marching up and down alongside her on the tarmac as she was showered with roses and blasted with popping flashlights. When they realized their mistake, the red-faced band-leader had to start all over again for me. The welcome somehow lost its sparkle the second time around.

My departures have also been noteworthy. Like the time I appeared at a festival in Edam, Holland. The townsfolk were anxious that I should be aware of their famous cheese and presented me on stage with two large red balls of it. Unfortunately the show was running late and I was about to miss my plane home. Deciding to make a dash for it, I zoomed off stage in my bright, sparkly minifrock, into a waiting car, a big, red cheese ball tucked under each arm. We sped to the airport.

The sight of me racing desperately through the departure lounge in full stage-gear, dropped cheeses rolling alongside and knocking down fellow travellers like ten-pin bowls, must have been too much for the airport staff. My plane stopped in mid-take-off and returned to pick me up.

Ground staff, quite rightly, were not always so accommodating. After finishing a TV show in Paris while still in the early lovesick stage of romance with Jeff, I tried everything to talk them into letting me on to the last plane home to see him – but to no avail. I had worked my way past check-in, passports, departures and through the boarding gate. There, nose pressed against the plate glass windows in dejected 'I Who Have Nothing' stance, I watched the plane's passenger bus unload on to the tarmac, the boarding steps being pulled away from the doors and the engines rev up ready for take off.

In a final rash bid, I dashed on to the runway and stood in front of the cockpit, hair flying in the wind of the propellers, waving up at the pilot. I mimed out my plight to the captain and crew. Suddenly someone flung open the plane door and threw down a ladder for me to climb up.

'C'est Sandie!' announced the stewards to the other passengers.

The captain turned and smiled at me as I clambered on board. 'O, l'amour, l'amour,' he sympathized over the intercom. I slid down in my seat to a round of applause.

My arrival in Lisbon this time, at two in the morning, was a lot less feverish. I had an early wake-up call a few hours later. I got up and crept quietly into the bathroom to get ready, and closed the door so as not to disturb Nik. My eyes stung as I put my lenses in. This was not too unusual, as I had had little sleep. The bathroom was very steamy so I fumbled about, dressing and making-up from memory.

It was dark in the hotel lift and I could not see the button panel. I felt around the walls until I found it. Downstairs the lobby looked misty, as if touched with an impressionist's brush.

As I was still only half awake I had not yet registered that I could not see. Unconsciously I must have slipped back into my childhood, when I always wandered about in a myopic haze.

How I ever managed to get around before my short-sightedness was discovered at the age of six is a mystery to me. I went for a school eye test and was found to be as blind as a bat (hooray for State schools and the National Health Service!). The way I had 'seen' things up till then was the way I believed life to be.

It was a profound shock to me when I first donned specs and went outdoors. The wonder of discovering that the grass was made up of tiny individual blades of green, or that the rusty hue of the houses on the council estate was made up of uniform little red bricks in intricate patterns. I could see people's laughs and frowns – the way the world actually reacted to me instead of the way I imagined it. I could wave to a friend across the playground. I could see words on the blackboard. I could distinguish the harsh way things ended and began. Everything had dark lines around it, separating one object, one shape, from another. Previously my subjective world had all washed together, around me and in me, mingling textures and colours.

I could not make up my mind which world I preferred. I still can't. The experience on stage, blinded by spotlights so that I can't see where I begin or end, everything seeming to be part of me, is exactly the same.

By the time I arrived at rehearsals on the Lisbon harbour I knew something was seriously wrong. My eyes were weeping and hurting badly. I took my lenses out and put them back in the liquid Nik had bought me.

Cathy examined the bottle. She read the instructions. 'It says here – "WARNING – do not soak or leave lenses in this solution"!'

Mine had been soaking in it all night. By now my eyes felt as if they were embedded with crushed glass.

Paolo, the Portuguese student assigned by the organizers to look after me, said not to worry. 'I'll get you to a hospital.'

'Let's keep this quiet until we know the damage,' advised Charles, 'or else the promoters will panic.'

Cathy and I sped off in the car with Paolo while Charles and Nik nonchalantly lunched at a harbourside restaurant trying to pretend that nothing was wrong.

It was Sunday. The main streets were full of people making their way to the concert. The backstreets were dark and deserted. We drove across town, past silent whitewashed walls screaming with red political graffiti, to the dusty outskirts of Lisbon.

When we arrived at the crumbling hospital I was on the verge of hysteria. Panic can play terrible tricks on the imagination.

Our entrance was barred by a mustachioed official seated behind a tiny window in the wall. He leisurely swatted flies as he interrogated us. In his nervousness, Paolo's grasp of English worsened. I hung on to him fiercely for comfort.

We were allowed in and then separated. I was deposited in a blurry queue of women patients who shuffled compliantly forwards, taking me with them. Suddenly I was seated at a desk and asked various questions in Portuguese. I was really frightened but I managed to tell the woman that I had hurt my eyes and could not see properly. I was then led back to Cathy and Paolo who were given directions as to where to take me.

We walked through miles of corridors until we arrived in a cool room. Someone sat me down and began to attend to my eyes. Having your eyelids pinned back is not the most pleasant sensation in the world. By now sightless, I clung to each sound: the cold clatter of medical instruments, the trickle of water, the soft whirr of the fan, all singing in hellish harmony. When the doctor had finished, both my eyes were thickly bandaged.

'Is there any permanent damage? Will I be able to see properly again?' I asked anxiously.

Paolo translated, 'Tonight, just for the show, you can take the bandages off. After, you must put them straight back on again. It will be painful but you will be able to see again in a week or so.'

When we were outside I could feel the sun on my face. Back at the hotel I stepped cautiously into the lobby, Cathy and Paolo on either arm to guide me.

'Don't worry. There's no one here to see you,' Cathy lied,

and helped me stumble up to my room. Later I learnt that the whole band had been standing in reception. The sight of me returning like a wounded soldier from the Crimean War had stunned them into silence. I wish I could have seen their faces!

It is very important to be able to see people's faces. I learnt this while acting in my first two stage plays. I had spent the first ten years of my singing career fumbling around the stage gazing myopically (some say sexily) into cameras, bumping into mike stands and tripping over leads, all the while managing to make it look entertaining. Then, at my first rehearsal to play Ophelia in *Hamlet*, it became clear that I needed a pair of contact lenses.

I met the bard through Roy Hodges and his then wife, Glenda Jackson. They were our neighbours in Blackheath. We shared the same glazier and between us kept him in business replacing the broken windows and doors caused by our families' penchants for smashing things during angry exchanges and dramatic exits.

Jeff had known Roy ever since Glenda was a struggling actress and Roy had started visiting Jeff's boutique, Clobber, to borrow outfits for her auditions. I had met them socially a few times and apparently I was often the subject of their bedtime discussions – they thought I should be acting.

Roy came round with a copy of the inevitable *Pygmalion* tucked under his arm. Too clichéd, I thought. Then came Blanche Dubois in *Streetcar*, followed by Bette Davis's *Little Foxes* – both far too American. How about something English?

'Then it *must* be Shakespeare!' Roy proclaimed.

'Oh no! Not that boring rubbish!' moaned the ex-Ford's worker from Dagenham. Roy, highly amused at my ignorance, then felt duty-bound to convert me into a thespian.

A dog-eared copy of *Hamlet* arrived on my doorstep. I flicked through it. I did not understand a word, though when read out loud the text really 'sang'. I agreed to play Ophelia and then, petrified at the prospect, attended my first rehearsal. I managed to talk through my part with all these incredibly wonderful and experienced Shakespearean actors without making an absolute fool of myself. In fact they took me to their hearts and really looked after me. I especially enjoyed the bits when we discussed the meaning of the text. To my surprise I found it unashamedly sensual, subversive and scathingly perceptive. Suddenly those dreary meaningless words remembered from the English Literature classes at Robert Clack Technical College sprang to life and leapt off the pages at me with the ferocity of a mean and funky bass riff.

My performance of Ophelia was most certainly different from the self-conscious efforts at Portia that Miss Parrot of the pleated crimplene frocks with twin icy mountain peaks, padded and precisely pointed, coaxed out of me in class.

When she was sane, I played Ophelia with the quiet passion of a committed folk singer like Joan Baez, and when she lost her marbles I played her like a tragic Janis Joplin figure. At one point, to illustrate Ophelia's insanity, I carried on walking in mid-air as if there were still ground under my feet. I did this from a rampart fifteen feet up, falling into the arms of the 'astonished' players below. My short-sightedness meant that I could not see further than my nose, so falling was an act of faith on my part as I could not guarantee that the actors would be in place to catch me. During rehearsals Roy worried himself into a tizzy about it, and the suspense eventually became too much; so off I went to the optician for my first pair of soft contact lenses.

What joy! With the lenses, not only could I see ahead of me but I could see to the side as well, which you cannot do with glasses. I could get close to people's faces without poking them in the eye with my frames. Better, I could avoid that awful clack of two sets of plastic as heads collide in a kiss. Even better still, I could run and jump around like a real soldier without fear of my bins falling off, when I subsequently played Bernard Shaw's Saint Joan.

St Joan came about because Roy got fed up with my complaining about the smallness of Ophelia's part. I stood in the wings mouthing all Hamlet's lines with him. Jeanne d'Arc was certainly a *tour de force*. My first sight of the length and wordiness of my part really shut me up.

This all happened around the time of Jeff's business crash

when we had gone to live in Ireland. It felt right to be in Bernard Shaw's birthplace to learn my part. With nobody around for miles, I rehearsed out in the fields in wellies, delivering my lines at the top of my voice. I stood in the hollow of the lightning tree for the scenes in the dock, my inquisitors the cows who gathered around curiously. Shaw's eloquent text was punctuated by their insistent mooing and chewing of cud. My audience were the rooks who nestled in the tall trees shouting 'Cor!'

In my irreverent hands Joan became a twentieth-century guerrilla freedom fighter, complete with army camouflage gear and Sten gun. Before the play opened I was invited on to the 'Six O'clock News' on TV to act an excerpt from the trial scene. I must be the only actor who has given such a public sneak preview of a play.

Unfortunately the precarious state of our finances meant that I could not afford to pursue my new-found career on the meagre wages from repertory theatre. In retrospect this was a short-sighted move, but at the time I felt that I had to go out and sing – this was the only way I knew of amassing a large sum of money quickly without hurting anyone in the process; but I did it grudgingly. I would have preferred to be elsewhere – maybe Elsinore . . .

Cathy found a huge pair of sunglasses to go over my bandages so that I would not frighten anyone backstage. The atmosphere that night was magical. We were performing in the old harbour overlooking the giant mastheads of ancient ships. Although I could not see anything, I could feel the warm sea breeze in my hair and taste it on my tongue. The hypnotic clanking of the sheets against the masts and the soft Portuguese accents drifted sensuously on the night air.

Pepsi, from Wham!, a fellow Buddhist, visited my trailer to give me encouragement and offered to chant with me. I had already done my evening practice of *gongyo*. Luckily I could recite the two chapters of the *Lotus Sutra* off by heart. I was not frightened; if I could remember my way through *gongyo* then

I could find my way through anything. I had no idea how much or how little sight I would have when the bandages came off.

We broke the news of my accident to the TV director and discovered that he had been my director on that first frantic visit to Portugal all those years ago. He was sympathetic and agreed not to do any close-ups.

Charles paced out the stage for me, to check how many steps I would be from the edge. He briefed the band to surround me like a protective cloak and discreetly prevent me from bumping into things, or worse, falling off the stage.

At last the dreaded moment came to take off the bandages. AAAArgh . . . the white hot pain. Huge tears plopped uncontrollably down my cheeks. I could not focus. I could only make out blurred, dark, hovering shapes. The medication I had been given stopped my pupils from dilating so as to inhibit eye movement and enable them to heal quicker. The prospect of performing like this in front of millions of people was daunting. If it had been anything other than a peace concert, I would never have attempted it.

The crowd roared as I was led on stage. I was left standing in a pool of bright light. I could feel the excitement run through me. Their peace candles appeared to me to be a galaxy of sparkling stars in the blackness. As Ophelia, triumphantly trusting in her own reality, I had stepped out into the unknown, believing that someone would be there to catch me. Now I felt like an astronaut walking in timeless space, absolutely free. It was exquisite.

When I landed back on earth in my trailer, a large circus of photographers, press and fans paraded outside asking excitedly for a 'picture', 'quote', 'autograph'.

'I'm afraid we can't help you,' explained Charles. 'She's had an accident . . . she can't see.'

'But she sang!' piped up an incredulous reporter.

'Yes, she did, didn't she?' said Charles, with a smile in his voice.

Benefits

I FINISHED THE TOUR with three Christmas shows, one in London at the Imperial College, and then at Sheffield and Keele Universities. By this time the CND motif had taken over my stage outfits. An art student friend called Jeannie took all my clothes and painted them with random 'Ban the Bomb' symbols. I was determined to use every opportunity to put across the things I believed in. At each concert, filled with aspiring young lives, I added more kindred souls to my collection of humane revolutionaries.

On New Year's Day, through a hazy hangover of tour memories – struggles and discoveries, disappointments and triumphs, and, more than anything, the glimpse of expectancy on so many fresh faces – one sobering thought kept nagging at me: 'What Happens Now? I might think I have something valid to say, all those fans might think I have something valid to say – but I don't know how to say it.' End of the rainbow.

I plunged into an abyss of excruciating self-doubt. Only consistent Buddhist practice enabled me to keep my head just poking out at the top, while my legs continued day after day to wade through fathoms of deep hellish mire. My normal inclination during these times is to curl up into a tight foetal ball of self-loathing and withdraw from the world. This time I did the opposite. I fought every day to open up my life, not to close up to the pain. If I felt I had no direction, I would find a new one, but not by trying to use my past experiences to rationalize my next move. I decided to go for complete creativity, true originality, to trust myself and say 'yes' to the very next thing that presented itself to me – regardless.

Lo and behold, the next day, Morrissey, conspicuously absent throughout my tour, appeared on my doorstep just like the first time – with doleful look on face and cassette in hand. Would I come and sing on a Smiths track they were recording just down the road? Well, it was not exactly what I had in mind, but he left the tape with me and asked me to think about it. I listened to the song. It was not one of their better tunes; in fact I sensed there was something seriously wrong. However, I said 'Yes.'

On a freezing winter's evening I stepped eagerly into the warmth of Solid State, the studio owned by Paul Weller. I was taken aback by the dull throb of inactivity. The recording equipment hummed vacantly like the constant bleep of a life-support machine for a comatose patient. People sat around silent and inert as if waiting for a charming prince to cast off the wicked fairy's spell and kiss life back into the session.

John Porter, the producer, waved 'hello' from behind the mixing desk where he was reading the music press. Andy Rourke and Mike Joyce bounced in, grinning awkwardly, leaving it to Johnny Marr to explain Morrissey's absence. I caught sight of Johnny's boyish figure for the first time since our trip to Germany to plug 'Hand In Glove'. He now wore the haggard look of a man tired of making excuses for his ill-mannered playfriend, tired of trying to salvage some sanity from manic situations. Was this what they had dreamed of on those dark Mancunian nights, plotting and thrashing out their path to fame and fortune?

Morrissey had become renowned for his 'no show' antics. Of course there was always a good reason. He was ill. I had recommended almost every specialist in Harley Street since stardom had wrapped itself around his frail shoulders.

Finally Johnny located Morrissey on the phone, and yes, he was desperately unwell, and could I suggest any treatment. 'A long spell of anonymity,' I thought, but kept it to myself. We arranged all to meet up again when Prince Charming was feeling better.

At last, a few weeks later, I rejoined them at Matrix studios wondering what on earth I was going to do on the song. Morrissey had written the melody of 'Sheila Take A Bow' around the fifth harmony of Johnny's tune, and because of the key and my range all I could sing was the third below. This put Morrissey and me in a two-part harmony reminiscent of the Sinatras' duet, 'Something Stupid'. It was squirmy. Shortly afterwards, John Porter was replaced by Stephen Street who, I was relieved to hear, wiped my efforts and started again.

Meanwhile I was asked to join the Red Wedge women's tour at the Shaw Theatre. Although not fully supporting their party politics (I'm a Green by nature, if you're interested), I still supported their optimistic feminism, so again I said 'Yes.' I sang, in total freedom and complete empathy, with a house-full of women. It was a wonderful feeling; I would love to do it again.

Soon after this I was asked to take part in the first major charity concert to raise funds for people living with AIDS. It was to be held at Wembley and called 'The Party'. At a press reception to launch the idea, I met, or rather collided with, Richard Coles, one half of the Communards, in the unseemly rush by our fellow hopeful participants for the press cameras.

Richard picked me up and took me off to a more sedate corner of Groucho's for a cup of coffee, leaving the other over-anxious lads at the photocall to make their grab for fame. The Communards were an openly gay and politically active band. Richard straightaway began to hone my sensibilities to sexual politics. Within seconds he had me falling about with laughter, his sense of humour as incisive as his profile. We decided to work together for my spot in the show – Richard would accompany me on the grand piano as I sang my Heaven 17 version of 'Anyone Who Had A Heart'. This was the start of one of those beautiful friendships . . .

I needed some singers to cover my multi-track parts from my recording of the song. I wondered who to use. A few weeks previously my friend Beryl Marsden had asked me to join her in a duet of 'Stand By Me' at the Liverpool Empire for the Liver Aid Concert, to help the famine victims in Africa, to which I had also said 'Yes.' I had never worked with Beryl professionally before, even though I had known her for almost ten years.

I first met Beryl, the scouse scalliwag, on the Northern

line – I was being followed. On leaving Ann O'Dell's house in Hampstead I walked anonymously to the Underground. I had just attended my first Buddhist discussion meeting there. That annoying, chirpy, Liverpudlian woman who had been sitting opposite me in the circle of people gathered around Annie's Buddhist shrine was still insisting on getting my attention. I pulled my scarf lower over my face, wrapped my raincoat tighter, head down to avoid any eye contact, and hurried quickly down the platform.

Click, click, those spiky heels of hers pestered me along the side of the train and into the compartment. She sat down beside me. I concentrated on staring out of the window, trying to ignore her presence.

'Hi! I'm Beryl Marsden. I just saw you at that meeting didn't I? Are you a Buddhist then?' she intruded cheerily.

I wriggled in discomfort. I had never been on the tube before, let alone had a conversation with a fellow passenger, a total stranger. I did not want anyone to recognize me in the state I was in. I did not want to be confronted with the reality of my life on the bloody Northern line.

I froze in panic.

'Well?' she persisted, extending her offer of friendship further.

'Yes, I am,' I volunteered grudgingly.

We travelled in icy silence. Sensing my extreme discomfort, Beryl must have been relieved when we arrived at her stop.

'Stuck up cow!' she thought, as she told me later when we had become best friends. 'You looked more like a frumpy school ma'am than a pop star!'

After my initial success at chanting for my twenty grand, Annie had encouraged me to go to some Buddhist study and discussion meetings. Here, for the first time, I heard people reciting *gongyo*. I was stunned. I had heard nothing like it and yet it touched me in the most familiar places. The power was incredible. I felt this intense yearning. A kind of home-sickness. For what? I couldn't say. All I knew was that I wanted to learn to do *gongyo* so that I could join in this wonderful sound.

Annie gave me a *gongyo* book crammed with squiggly Chinese

characters and explained how to pronounce the phonetics printed underneath. It looked really hard but I was determined to get my tongue around it so that I would not have to sit around like a wally at the next meeting.

I practised in America, whilst accompanying Jeff on a business trip to New York and Los Angeles. Day in and day out I wandered off with my little red *gongyo* book mumbling to myself. I was resolved to be word perfect by the time I returned. On Thanksgiving Day 1977, while staying with some Jewish friends at their beach-house in Connecticut, I finally cracked it. I was so happy, I recited *gongyo* all day between delicious mouthfuls of pecan pie.

Our friends must have thought I'd flipped. Jeff was used to my unusual behaviour by now, and anyway he was too preoccupied with his mountainous business problems to take much notice. Both he and my parents regarded it as a temporary aberration, a new fad to take my mind off things. They did not realize that as far as I was concerned I had stumbled on the secret of life's infinite mysteries.

When I returned to England and did *gongyo* for the first time with a group of people, I was astonished to find I was sitting alongside the guitarist Hughie Burns, who had simultaneously been learning *gongyo* in America. I had not seen Hughie since he had played guitar on my last lot of unreleased tracks for Obie at CBS.

To everybody's great surprise I continued to practise, developing a deeper faith. The following year, with Jeff, who had by then begun to practise too, I received a Gohonzon, just like the one Annie had enshrined in her front room. A Gohonzon is a copy, made by the High Priest of the Nichiren Shoshu sect of Buddhists, of a mandala inscribed by the original Buddha, Nichiren Daishonin, in 1279. It depicts Nichiren Daishonin's own enlightened life in all its multiple aspects, both negative and positive, but centred on the life condition of Buddhahood. Anyone who chants '*Nam-myoho-renge-kyo*' to this Gohonzon as Nichiren Daishonin taught is able to observe their mind clearly, like a mirror enables you to see your face. This process brings out their own state of Buddhahood, inherent but untapped in everyone's lives.

There are no commandments and you don't have to be a special kind of person to be a Buddhist. Just three things – the regular morning and evening practice of *gongyo* and chanting, supported by the study of Nichiren Daishonin's writings in order to understand how to change those attitudes which cause us and other people to suffer, and teaching other people to the best of our ability – ensure enlightenment in *this* lifetime, not next lifetime, not when you are dead, but *now*. Not in some expensive holy retreat, but *here*, in this street, on this planet. Not as some holy person wearing foreign clothes but as you are, be it secretary, nurse, lorry driver, business tycoon or even pop star.

In everyday terms, 'enlightenment' means that you are able to perceive the truth of any situation and take wise and compassionate action on all your daily problems and dealings, based on the absolute freedom of being completely true to your higher self, and not bound by the limitations of your ego. There is no obstacle that cannot be overcome with this practice (it's very practical!) and challenging obstacles leads to an even deeper understanding of life. In short, it is the means of becoming absolutely happy and fulfilled, and simultaneously creating a great world for everyone else to live in. Sounded good to me!

When Jeff and I agreed to separate, he stayed in Annie's district, Hampstead, and I joined another district of Buddhists in West Hampstead, called Fortune. The district was looked after by a lady called Dawn, and Hilton Valentine from the Sixties rock group the Animals! I was quick to notice that at that time there were no Buddhist groups practising in central London where I lived, and I immediately determined to change that.

Meanwhile, up and down the Jubilee line to West Hampstead I went, attending discussion and study meetings and bringing along my friends. Beryl had since moved into the flat with Grace and me. Together we went on special courses in Maristowe and to Trets, the European Buddhist centre in the South of

France. For the time being I put thoughts of my career aside and concentrated on learning about myself, developing my life, and taking care of Grace, who was then eight years old.

It was not easy, but right from the start I had a lot of help from some truly great people. At the beginning a huge giant of a Buddhist called Alfy, a chef, introduced me to Kazuo Fujii. Although Kazuo had the lofty title of Vice-General Director of Nichiren Shoshu of the United Kingdom (NSUK), the organization was pretty small-time. Our centre was in a tiny flat in Swiss Cottage and Kazuo was not employed as a leader; like everyone else he did it voluntarily.

In those early years Kazuo worked at Burberrys in Piccadilly. At least once a week Alfy and I would go and pick him up from behind a rail of macs for a chat, and listen to his pearls of wisdom over a cup of tea in a Soho café. We made a bizarre trio trailing past the theatres and sex shops of the area, the diminutive Japanese sales assistant, the gigantic Bohemian chef, and the faded heavenly body.

Kazuo was extremely unusual in that he was the first completely scrutable Japanese I had met; he had a peculiarly endearing combination of profound sagacity and wide-eyed innocence. He had, and still has to this day, the most disastrous English accent. Alfy and I puzzled for weeks over a strange principle he introduced when advising how to chant. He called it the 'Law of the Ryan'. We looked it up unsuccessfully in all the text books. Some time later we discovered that he meant the 'roar of the lion'.

Although I did not always grasp the complex theories he expounded straightaway, I quickly recognized his earnest desire to help people enable themselves to become happy, to change society, to create world peace. Trusting this, I gradually put the theories into practice, and chanting twice daily with the 'Law of the Ryan', I began to make sense of the shambles I had made of my many existences.

Then there was Roberta. Multi-marriages and a desire to experience everything the Sixties had to offer had given this Buddhist housewife from Ealing a rich past with which she

*I was just sixteen. I had recently been to
Vidal Sassoon to have my hair bobbed.*
(MICHAEL WILLIAMS)

*The reality was that I was an older woman
in a business overrun by deliciously
pubescent bimbos . . . At 39. Time Out*
mistakenly printed this as a Sixties shot.
(JILL FURMANOVSKY)

If you put my mum on a crowded bus, with[?]
minutes she is on first-name terms with eve[?]
. . . My nan was a woman of great spiritua[?]
stamina, and a fantastic cuddler.

'It's dropped! It's dropped! Come here,
Sandie, look at this old photo. Can't you see
how it's dropped!' Evie's nose.

'But your feet are so ugly, Sandra,' said Mum.
(MICHAEL WILLIAMS)

I felt like a giant switchboard, completely plugged in to the individual lives of the audience, that we were fused together in a mesh of cosmic energy. The last leg of the tour, 1986. (HERMAN NIJHOF)

There were no wrinkles around my eyes, but the world-weary sadness of them belied my youthful looks. As Ophelia during my 'Dark Ages'.

Jenny seeped into and freed my soul like pure fresh spring water. My best roadie.

INSET: *They had even pulled down my beautiful gazebo where I had hidden with the dogs in the summer and painted in the winter.* Blackheath. (GORDON MOORE)

'Stuck up cow!' she thought, as she told me later when we had become best friends. Backstage at the Liverpool Empire with Beryl Marsden. (LIVERPOOL DAILY POST & ECHO)

I'm fussy about who I wait on. At Rosc
(EXPRESS NEWSPAPERS)

He has the knack of bringing opposing elements together into original alliances. Nik with partner Steve Woolley.

On our first date he was so shy he kept slipp his chair and under the table. Nik with Ale: Pigg and Margi Clarke from *Letter to Bre*

'e must have looked a formidable pair. Eve picking my first backing group. (REX FEATURES)

. like a cuckoo's egg in a sparrow's nest. Mum, Dad and me. (REX FEATURES)

'Sandie, you can no longer be pretty . . .' My heart sank. *'But you can be beautiful by having confidence in yourself and your purpose in life.'* Hello Angel. (PETER ASHWORTH)

could relate to all manner of problems suffered by those of notorious disposition. Luckily, nothing could shock Roberta. I felt free to unravel any carnal episode of my life without fear of judgement or ridicule.

Karen Laurenti, with her pure faith and devoted support of all the women practising in Hampstead Chapter, encouraged the more sensitive, spiritual side of my nature to come out. I'll never forget those early women's meetings at her flat off West End Lane. I was agog with all their courageous struggles and experiences. We also fell about laughing a lot. These Buddhist principles had never before been applied to the British way of life and it was so exciting to be part of this ground-breaking energy.

I was inspired by the outright feminism, without a hint of aggression, of Nichiren Daishonin's teachings. It is the only religion I know that treats women not only as absolute equals in every way – they are not excluded from anything – but also with such deep and special respect. Apart from Jenny, I had never had any close women friends before because I had chosen a professional life where I was always surrounded by men. When I overcame my initial dismissive attitude and disrespect towards the female sex, I made huge leaps and bounds in my understanding of things and I began to really admire the incredible qualities of other women. The hidden bonus was that I started to like and respect myself.

A chapter consisted of about three districts of about forty people each, which in turn were made up of three to four groups. My enthusiasm did not go unnoticed and it was not long before both Beryl and I were asked to become group leaders.

I held my first group meeting on the second day of February, 1979. I spent all week preparing and getting keyed up. On the night, Beryl went discreetly up to her room and left me to it. I sat and waited nervously for the meeting to start at 7.30. By 8 nobody had turned up, so I called up to Beryl to come down and join me for *gongyo*. I carried on as if the room was full, reading out the guidance, passing on the study notes and information and discussing the evening's subject with Beryl as my only guest. Beryl's first meeting went along the same lines, with me reciprocating the favour as her only guest.

Not to be beaten, I got the list of addresses of the group members. If they would not come to me, I would go to them. I arranged to visit them one by one at home so that I could get to know them. There were several faces stunned to find Sandie Shaw standing on their doorstep clutching her prayer beads and *gongyo* book.

Visiting a different person each night, travelling by bus or tube, and more often walking because money was tight, I managed to meet everyone within a month. This way we all began to become friends, and I became aware of their individual struggles and was then able to encourage them in their practice. I spent hours copying out guidance, sending information or supportive postcards, taking calls and learning how to listen to their problems. It was exhausting, but it was also one of the happiest times of my life.

So, although the beginning was a bit rough, the group eventually taught me how to become a good friend. As my earlier years were not exactly riddled with chances to form close friendships, you can understand how grateful I was for the opportunity to overcome all the painful isolation experienced in my youth . . .

At my first school, my vivid, only-child's imagination did not endear me to my more prosaic classmates, who shared my confusion as to where my fantasy ended and reality began. The difference was that I actually enjoyed the confusion. I was always being reported to teachers for things I had not actually done, just fantasized out loud that I had.

My teacher disliked this fertile imagination of mine so much that he made my life a misery. My impersonations of him became more and more merciless. Although I always had good marks, usually in the top three in the class, he never singled me out for praise or gave me any encouragement. So here too I had problems wondering whether in reality I had any ability or if it was another private fantasy. I felt sure my work was good, but his complete and determined lack of response made me doubt myself. He must be right, mustn't he? He's the teacher. I tried harder and harder. Still he ignored me. He told my parents that as far as he was concerned, I was not eleven-plus material and that was that. I came home in tears almost every night. Fortunately for me, in Rosie I had a gutsy mother who stuck up for me and boosted my confidence.

It's funny that these incidents happened so many years ago and yet the pain is so real to me to this day. Whenever I find myself in a position that depends on outside assessment, particularly from a male figure of authority who seems to have the power to inhibit or discourage my personal growth, my self-confidence drops to zero, and I find myself in a mindless, inexpressible rage. It's only when I remind myself that I am no longer that little girl, I am a person with my own inner authority, able to give myself permission to do or be whatever I want, that the anger subsides. It's a great pity I did not learn this sooner.

Just three people out of the entire year passed the eleven-plus exam, and I was one of them. I'll never forget the look on the teacher's face when he heard the result.

Senior school was just as difficult. I had no idea how to deal with my rebelliousness and anger; it was most unfashionable then for girls to have ideas of their own. I remember when I discovered the fine art of swearing. I curled my tongue round the power-packed words with wanton relish – for me it was just play-acting. This was not appreciated by the prissy members of the class and I was sent to Coventry for weeks. In order to be liked, accepted, I tried to make my life smaller and repressed my fantasies so that nobody could hurt me with their thoughtless ridicule. My innermost dramas developed into mythological proportions in a land which I had invented, inhabited with characters I dreamed up, and which only I was allowed to visit. I was able to cut myself off completely . . . mmmm . . . Heaven . . . especially during the maths lesson.

In order to feel loved, to be accepted, we tend to twist and contort ourselves into all manner of odd shapes to try to fit in. This only serves to alienate us further. Nobody feels comfortable with a contortionist! However, introversion and shyness are not character traits that we are saddled with for ever. They are learnt habits and can be changed. Kazuo once said to me that whenever he walks into a room of people he feels that everyone likes him, not because he thinks he is so fantastic, but because he is so open to liking everyone else.

The members of my Buddhist group came from all over London and from all backgrounds. There was a young guy who worked in Junior Man at Harrods, another who was a roadie for a heavy-metal band, a Dutch lady married to a film producer and her two daughters, a 'difficult' woman living in a tower block, a carpenter from Dagenham, three girls from a music publisher's office, a Knightsbridge fashion shop manageress, an Italian recovering from heroin addiction in a hostel – talk about seeing life.

Today most of them are senior leaders in NSUK and have changed their circumstances almost beyond recognition. Our organization has grown steadily and Kazuo, along with other administrative staff, is now employed full time. From his office window at our new centre, Taplow Court in Maidenhead, Kazuo can gaze out over acres of beautiful grounds that roll majestically down to the Thames.

From those small beginnings my Buddhist group grew and grew until, joining with a co-leader called John Wadsworth, who lived close by and ran the café at the Pineapple Dance Studio, it became Harley District. This also grew and grew and became Westminster Chapter. We seemed to have a natural affinity with creative people – artists, writers, dancers, musicians. These people grew and grew in number until most of them went on to form an Arts Division. All this did not happen magically; it took great effort – introducing new people, teaching and encouraging them, training new leaders, and two hours' chanting every day. John and I worked hard. We had meetings almost every night of the week. My flat in Harley Street was always bulging with enthusiastic new Buddhists and their guests. It was so exciting. To me, building a foundation of Buddhism in society was and is much more enjoyable, and infinitely more lasting, than building business empires. It was an opportunity to use my entrepreneurial, visionary spirit to its best value, and employ positively the energy of my passionate rebelliousness. I wanted it to happen so badly that, over the years, particularly during my last two pregnancies, I covered the whole of Westminster borough on foot, pacing every street, learning the road names, imagining who lived there, what kind of work they did, what kind of lives they led. I knew enough to qualify as a London cabby! At every street corner I chanted 'Nam-myoho-renge-kyo' three times – no one could hear above the noise of the traffic. I drew up a list of all the areas where I would like a Gohonzon to be established. Over the course of time all this has been achieved, and more; and I have gained deep self-confidence from learning how to turn my innermost dreams into reality. Nowadays my particular responsibility in our organization of NSUK is to the Arts Division.

Having Beryl as my best mate through all this made it great fun. We are an unlikely pair. I am tall, she is petite. I have long straight hair, hers is short and curly. I am shy and reserved, Beryl is warm and bubbly. I am a bookworm, she loves to chat. I like to sit and gaze at the horizon, absorbing the poetry of the sun melting into the ocean. Beryl can't sit still for a minute; she likes poetry in motion. Our differences make us a great team.

Beryl took a while to get used to. It drove me mad when she borrowed my earrings without asking, only to reveal later that her sister was wearing them. On the other hand, the way I often cut myself off from people really upset her.

Beryl would get up and sing at the drop of a hat without any inhibition; I would shrivel in the corner, petrified that I would be asked. I was not used to singing without all the paraphernalia of a pop performer. When we went on Buddhist courses together, Beryl kept coaxing me out of my shell until eventually I was able to get up spontaneously and sing unrehearsed for the other members in any situation, to the makeshift accompaniment of whatever was to hand, from a badly tuned guitar to a set of kitchen pots. To be able to perform without being hampered by the limitations of the ego was such freedom.

In fact I know of nothing that compares with the sheer creativity and joy of the impromptu entertainments at the end of a Buddhist course. I played characters as varied as a lovable tart to Old Mother Hubbard. I did backing vocals, rehearsed groups, wrote mini-plays and songs, and learnt to present, organize and produce the shows. We all took turns at supporting each others' efforts. It was here, in Trets, in the unlikely setting of the canteen beneath the *butsuma*, the hall where the European Gohonzon is enshrined, that I learnt to communicate directly from heart to heart, from life to life.

Some people use their special talent for self-aggrandizement, to further isolate themselves, set themselves apart from the rest of humanity. I discovered we can also use it to bridge the gap between people, to bring them together in the awareness of their shared humanity. There is nothing quite so exhilarating as singing in this way.

I see society's present trend towards schism reflected in its so-called 'live' popular music – that lone revered spot far away at the other end of the stadium where the current embodiment of our dreams struts around in disassociated animation to the programmed memories of their Synclaviers, accompanied by top musicians whose skills, being replaced by these computers, are reduced to the indignity of miming to their own recorded performance. It all seems so much more real on the video screen! All art should be a life-enhancing, life-affirming experience, otherwise it is not art but a lucrative commercial transaction. So let's not kid ourselves, eh? Our spirits need to be uplifted and inspired by the skilful, creative insights of humane, compassionate artists.

Beryl came up with three other girl singers to do backing vocals for me at the Wembley AIDS benefit, all of whom happened to be Buddhists. The concert promoters asked me if I could do some extra time in the acoustic slot to enable them to shift instruments behind the stage curtain. I had the idea of augmenting the team of female backing singers with some male vocalists to make an a cappella sound, thus forming the first all-Buddhist vocal group. It was called the Human Revolution. I talked the organizers of the event into putting them on after my song with Richard Coles.

On the day of the concert, Wembley was buzzing with the sound of chanting. The other artists, like George Michael, Boy George, and Holly Johnson, were all closely associated with practising Buddhists. Boy George wandered in and out to chant with us. He is often quoted in the press as being a Buddhist, but although he practised wholeheartedly while he was coming off drugs he has only ever toyed with the practice. None the less, George was a welcome visitor. It takes all sorts.

I watched the show from the side with two members of George Michael's band, Pepsi and Hughie Burns, and his PR, Connie Fillipello, dreaming about putting on our first Buddhist pop concert in the future. I felt so good I jived around with my 'stable-mate' Deon Estus like a teenager.

Richard Coles, the singers and myself all tumbled on to the Wembley stage like a football team. Richard's piano was not plugged in. He stared at me helplessly across the lid. While the electricians fumbled about trying to get it to work, I chatted to the crowd until it was fixed. More and more, instead of experiencing that awful heart-chilling, stomach-churning dread that many other performers know so well – the fear that something will go terribly wrong – I know that it doesn't really matter if it does; you can use everything that happens creatively. Since the beginning of that first University Tour I had felt like a giant switchboard, completely plugged in to the individual lives of the audience, that we were fused together in a mesh of cosmic energy. Whenever I sensed things weren't quite right, I felt more able to centre myself, and then I would somehow know what to do or what not to do. The important thing for me is to appreciate that everything that happens is for the explicit purpose of bringing my life closer to the lives of others.

A few days later I did another, longer AIDS benefit performance at the Brixton Academy, joined by Mark E. Nevin and again by Richard. While standing in the wings with one of the organizers from the Terence Higgins Trust, he told me tearfully that he had just received a positive result to an AIDS test that morning. Before I could respond, my name was announced to the audience. His words rang in my ears throughout the performance. They were words that were to become all too common.

I wore a 'Safer Sex' tee-shirt and reminded everybody to wear the free rubber johnnies given out during the show! I sang barefoot just for the hell of it. It was filmed by Mike Mansfield's production company – somehow he managed to pull off the ultimate miracle in lighting and shoot me to look about eighteen again, just like when we first met . . . or maybe the way I felt had something to do with it.

I watched the rest of the show in the artists' area out front. While the old Bronski Beat, rejoined for the evening by Jimmy Somerville, were playing, a member of one of the support bands crept up behind me. He must have been upset by his group's relegation to the lower end of the bill by the producer, for without any warning he spat such venomous remarks in my ear that I shivered in the icy blast. Although I could not see his face, I recognized his voice. When I turned he had slithered away. After the initial shock I just felt sad that someone could be eaten up by so much jealousy at such an event, and also grateful that I hadn't popped him one. I had not considered my influence powerful enough to bring out such a strong reaction; but these benefits are highly emotionally charged and can bring out the worst as well as the best in us. People project both their positive and negative emotions and ideas of themselves on to public figures. As if you were a cloakroom attendant, they heap their 'hats' and 'coats' on to you. I spend a great deal of my life returning people's 'clothing' saying, 'Yours, I think!' Fortunately they mostly give me their happy coats and not just their cast-offs.

After the concert, we all partied round the corner at my friend Lynne Franks' house. I had made friends with Lynne some years previously when Jeff had suggested that, as she was such a Sixties fanatic, she might be interested in doing my press for the 'Anyone Who Had A Heart' release. With her husband, Paul

Howie, she has represented the interests of people as diverse as top fashion gurus Katharine Hamnett and Jasper Conran, and the Labour Party. I visited her office in trepidation. Lynne sat surrounded by vases full of white lilies and the buzz of frantic activity. She launched into one of her endless streams of conversation, ending abruptly with 'You *are* a Buddhist, aren't you?'

'Yes,' I managed to squeeze in.

'In that case I'll do your publicity for nothing if you tell me everything you know,' announced the typically generous Lynne.

I took her to her first Buddhist meeting the following week, and we had a deal. It felt a bit like being a Freemason.

Sleeping With the Producer

IN 1987 MY OLD RECORD COMPANY, which had altered its
name from Pye to PRT, suddenly changed hands. It was bought
by a millionaire, who had made his fortune in disposable cups
after the war, as a present for his daughter, Kim Richards. By
chance, my manager, Charles, was a friend of the family, and
he arranged a meeting for me with the daughter.

Kim was a girl of roughly Grace's age. To be absolutely
honest, I felt initially a great deal of resentment that her parents'
wealth enabled her to own what I considered to be mine, both
spiritually and morally. But she was friendly and co-operative,
so at last, although not in legal control of my early recordings,
I was at least able to liaise with her over releases and put an end
to the tacky cheapo presentation of them. This was a step in the
right direction.

That summer of '87 I broke off a family holiday in Cornwall
with the kids and my parents to return to London to film an
advert. The product was a soft drink called Britvic 55. They
had a retro plot for the ad, and had hired a lot of Sixties 'golden
oldies' to give it an association with those 'fab', 'fun' times.

I don't know about the others taking part, but I did it for the
money – lots of it, for my one second on camera. I'm not sure
whether they negotiated decent fees or whether they were
satisfied with getting their faces on the screen again. Unfortunately, most Sixties people are infinitely exploitable. Current
business methods are so much more sophisticated – you have
to be really clued up – and most of those bygone artists are
poignantly out of touch with today's world. Sadly, some of
them don't seem to value their talent, so why should anyone
else? For the most part they have already signed their commercial

lives away decades ago for ludicrously unfair contracts that would give a modern-age megastar a seizure.

Around the time that I was recording with the Smiths, Dave Clark of the Dave Clark Five sold his copies of 'Ready Steady Go' to Picture Music for video release without informing the artists performing on the tapes. No one questioned whether or not he owned the video rights or attempted to negotiate permission and royalties with the artists. This is not unusual. One of the contributory reasons that Sixties music is so much in vogue is that it is generally assumed that these artists have no rights, because of those painfully short but all-encompassing Sixties management and recording contracts. The material costs next to nothing to acquire and sell to an already primed market. Most Sixties icons have no artistic or financial control over their early masterpieces.

I discovered their plans to release a video by accident when someone from Nik's video distribution company, whilst in the packaging factory, spotted the proposed box cover, which to his amusement included one of my appearances.

On enquiry to the perpetrators, one person had the nerve to suggest that the exposure would be doing us a favour. I suppose they presumed that we artists would feel so honoured by their attention that no one would have the nous to kick up a fuss. Or maybe they just thought of us as cheap programming – getting something for nothing. Well I felt differently.

Dave Clark certainly did not own the right to reproduce my performances, nor did he own any video rights. A fair deal for everyone was finally struck with Picture Music.

I get sick to the stomach of the way music business people think that recording artists from the Sixties are easy targets. Their original meagre royalties, the paltry amounts they earnt compared with contemporary performers makes it doubly sickening for them to continue to be ripped off so callously.

Luckily, by this time my fortune had changed. I knew what was going on now, and my involvement with current music practices made it easier for me to stick up for my rights. Most other artists do not have the money or clout any more, but they

should still be respected for being part of the incredible surge
of energy and talent of that time. These musicians laid the
foundations of the music business of today. If people can't
respect and appreciate that, then they can't feel good about the
business they are in or their part in it. Is the money really
enough? Is it truly fulfilling to make a pile at someone else's
expense? Is that all it is about, at the end of the day? I think not.

I did my first advert at the end of the 'Ready Steady Go' era
in 1966. It was for Lux soap and it was directed by Karel Reisz.
This was a major treat as he had directed one of my favourite
films, *Saturday Night and Sunday Morning*. I was completely
overawed by him as he sat in my dressing-room, waiting
patiently for me to utter the scripted dialogue for him. I was
never much good at rehearsing.

The finished result is the cutest thing, a real period piece. I've
seen it again recently and it is still wonderfully fresh.

Evie was so impressed with it that she immediately started
planning a movie career for me. She introduced me to a lovely
man called Cy Enfield. Cy had just finished directing *Zulu* with
Michael Caine. Unfortunately our intended movie was shelved
when I informed everyone that it was a definite impossibility
for me to simulate love scenes with the co-star. The chemistry
Cy had hoped for between myself and George Lazenby, an
ex-James Bond actor and chocolate-bar model, was explosive
in all the wrong ways.

More scripts piled in. For some reason everyone wanted
to see me in scenes with my clothes half, almost, or completely
off – maybe they wanted to save on wardrobe expenses. As I
knew they would be less than impressed with my credentials, I
proved an extremely reluctant movie queen.

A trip to Finland for a UNICEF concert provided an opportunity for Evie to introduce my 'acting potential' to Marlon
Brando, who was hosting the show. He sat alone in the stalls,
watching my rehearsal, apparently mesmerized.

Eve's hyperactive ambition projected technicolour visions of
all my great future screen roles and sideboards crammed with
Oscars. She seized the moment and slipped into the seat next to

him. As he gazed intently at me she leant over his shoulder and proudly ventured, 'What do you think of my Sandie, Marlon?'

Evie's world stood still as one of Marlon's famous pregnant pauses filled the space while he searched for the right words. Finally he drawled sexily (he was still slim then), 'She's got a great ass!'

This was not the response Evie had anticipated. For once she was dumbstruck. He followed this up with lots of suggestive notes pushed under my hotel door which I never dared to show Eve as it would have added to her disenchantment . . .

On the set for the Britvic 55 advert I recognized most of the crew. I had seen them recently on the sets of Palace films like *Company of Wolves*, *Mona Lisa* and *Absolute Beginners*. In fact *Absolute Beginners* had proved after all this time to be my first, unheralded, venture on to the cinema screen.

One night, while discussing the day's rushes, Steve Woolley, Nik's partner at Palace, and the director, Julian Temple, were bemoaning the fact that they had not found someone suitable to play the character of Baby Boom's mum in the opening scene. The problem was that because of an unexpected change in scheduling they had to film it at five the following morning. While this was going on, Nik rang home and tried to have a phone conversation with me as our four-month-old son, Jack, screamed for his dinner in the background. The two things came together in Nik's mind. Impetuously he suggested me as Baby Boom's mum.

'. . . *and* Sandie's got an Equity card!' he trumped. Everyone thought it was a great idea – except me; I was still breast-feeding Jack. But I wanted very much to be part of Nik's first big production. So at the crack of dawn, leaving Nik snoring, I hauled myself and Jack out of bed and into the studio car along with our two-year-old daughter Amie and the new nanny. The boot was crammed with nappies, baby food, toys and a pushchair.

I went straight to wardrobe where I was kitted out and dressed by Dorothea. I was given a frumpy frock, corset, stockings, hat and handbag suitable for a Fifties housewife. Then I went to the hairdresser and had a wig fitting. After this came the make-up: powder, rouge and red lipstick. By the time they had all finished with me I was unrecognizable as myself, and the spitting image of my own mother, Rosie. Somehow I had managed to fit all this in between Jack's feeds.

I was given my lines and then placed on set amidst a crowd of extras queuing around a Soho street corner. No one had the remotest idea who I was. As the camera technicians rehearsed for the complicated shot again and again, my fellow Equity card holders chatted amongst themselves about their hopes and aspirations and shared the wild elation they had felt on finding out that they had landed a part in the film. I listened with great interest as they discussed my friends in casting and production.

When it was my turn, one of the actors eyed me up and down, taking in my dowdy outfit and over made-up face, and asked inquisitively, 'And how did *you* get a part then?'

'I slept with the producer,' I replied.

At which point the nanny arrived on the set and presented me with the baby, ready for his feed.

Palace Pictures had begun to take shape three years earlier in 1982, coinciding with our daughter Amie's conception in Paris. Nik and I went there to see *Diva*, Jean-Jacques Beineix's first film, which Palace had just bought for distribution. Nik and Steve had just returned from Los Angeles with a film called *The Evil Dead*. The director of this infamous horror saga, Sam Raimi, a precocious nineteen-year-old with choirboy looks and a diabolical imagination, had bowled over Steve (who was himself a mere twenty-six at the time) by respectfully calling him 'Sir' throughout negotiations. Little did they know where such dewy-eyed innocence was to lead them all.

That spring we all attended the Cannes Film Festival for the first time. Nik and Steve were looking for films to distribute. A greener bunch of wannabees would have been difficult to find. I was really looking forward to all that Provençale food, but I spent most of the time in bed overcome by nausea. Half-way through a movie I had to leave and throw up. My

Buddhist friend Dini Glynwood was also there with her long-time movie mogul husband Terry, who was putting together the finances for a mysterious project for the producer Jeremy Thomas. I suggested that Dini and I visit the European Buddhist centre in Trets together since we were in the South of France and our partners were busy wheeler-dealering.

It was during the car journey there that Dini suggested that my nausea might be morning sickness. This was as much a shock to me as the suggestion had been some twelve years before that I might be pregnant with Grace. The cleaner, Mrs Gooden, had offered that possibility to me while I lay on the floor as she helped to zip me into a pair of trousers that had suddenly become too tight. I had spent the past month on my knees retching down the toilet bowl every morning thinking I had a stomach upset. Life is so full of surprises! Fortunately, by the time my third child, Jack, was conceived I knew all the tell-tale signs!

By the following year's Cannes Film Festival, Palace had bought the distribution rights to Terry's mysterious project with Jeremy – *Merry Christmas, Mr Lawrence*. Also Nik and I had married and Amie had arrived. She came with us and stayed in our little *pension* just off the Croisette, along with the Palace outfit. All the big-time movie people were staying in the luxury of the Majestic or the Carlton hotels on the front, but Palace were still very new and counting the francs.

Since selling his forty per cent in Virgin, Nik had invested the money in Palace and we had struggled happily along with our lack of private funds. His departure had been precipitated by a disagreement with his partner shortly after we became an 'item'. Nik had been supported by the rest of the board over the issue of his colleague's disastrous desire to spend huge sums of money starting up a magazine called *Event* in opposition to *Time Out*. It was not so much the amounts involved or the idea that Nik objected to as the timing. He thought it was asking for trouble to take advantage of the crippling difficulties *Time Out* was then experiencing as a result of its highly profiled industrial disputes. Shortly after that meeting, his partner, being the major shareholder, overturned the board's decision and went ahead with his plans regardless.

Everyone knew that although Nik had been fiercely loyal since childhood and was happy clearing up after him and getting him out of scrapes, he was not cut out to be somebody's yes-man, especially at the expense of the company's wellbeing. Nik had no doubts – he wanted to leave. This could not have been an easy decision. Nik was devoted to his partner. They had grown up together, shared their first business venture when they were still kids, started Virgin together in their teens and built it in their own individual, idiosyncratic ways during their twenties, and even married two sisters. Nik was also devoted to the company and the people who worked within it. He did not want his departure to put it under any financial strain.

'Will you leave me now?' Nik asked me.

How could I? Why should I? He was the same person with or without Virgin.

Nik was paid for his share of Virgin – the company he had co-founded and built – the modest amount of £1,000,000, plus the Scala Cinema and the video editing suites. These were the bare bones he needed for his vision of creating a film and video production and distribution business.

It seemed to me to be an unrealistically small settlement for forty per cent of such a vast, thriving company, but Nik, who considered Virgin to be his 'baby', was highly emotionally charged about leaving it, and was not capable of making rational decisions.

On reflection, Nik, who had begun chanting regularly by then, made the right decision for more right reasons than he imagined at the time. His incredible skills as a financial and entrepreneurial operator meant not only that Palace never suffered from its initial lack of huge capital, but that, paradoxically, it flourished, since he could now exercise these skills fully on his own ideas. Suddenly he was able to develop a different kind of confidence in himself. Plus, starting from scratch made me feel I had contributed to his success by supporting and encouraging him. It made me a real part of his future.

After Nik's departure his existence and role within Virgin was systematically written out of its history. The impression given, if any, was that Nik had been some kind of managerial employee. But the people that I continue to meet who have had personal involvement with him during his Virgin years hold him in such great esteem. You can feel the warmth of affection and the depth of respect from those he enlisted and trained and who have since taken their own place within the entertainment industry.

A year or so later, Virgin was valued for its City flotation at £217,000,000. While Nik never received the financial return for the immense efforts he put into building Virgin, through leaving and starting Palace he was able to realize great qualities in himself – the kind that no amount of money can buy. It also gave me the opportunity to see the man and not the tycoon and start to love him. No, Nik is certainly not a yes-man.

When the film *Merry Christmas, Mr Lawrence* was shown at Cannes, the Japanese director, Oshima, was praised and fêted like a medieval shogun. The Palace contingent wore exclusive 'Oshima's Gang' boiler suits and tops. On the seafront, punters were offering fortunes to buy them off our backs, enough to get a decent room in the Majestic! But no one succumbed; these were real collectors' items.

The European press clamoured hysterically for interviews with Oshima and David Bowie, one of the film's stars. In the furore of the press conference, they were falling over and tripping each other up for a word, a quote, a photo of the maestro and his protégé. Oshima was so s-u-r-r-e-a-l. David was so c-o-o-l.

Everyone dressed up to go to the Gala screening. In the brand new Festival de Palais the pictures flickered and the reels of film turned, underscored by the strains of Ryuichi Sakamoto's magical soundtrack. I shivered with excitement. The end titles rolled, the emotion welled up in my throat and tears stung in my eyes. I still feel the same thrill every time I hear the music played. It was my first inside experience of the glamour of the film industry.

Afterwards I picked Amie up from the *pension* owner and his wife who were babysitting. The next morning, feeling like a movie queen, I swept through the hordes of busy film-makers doing their deals on La Croisette, pushing Amie along in her Mothercare fold-up pushchair with nappies and babyfood in a bag swinging from the handles. Amie and I accompanied Nik to all his lunch appointments and negotiations. It never occurred to him that this was somewhat unusual behaviour for a business-man.

Nik's eccentricities have grown over the years. At first it was odd little things like forgetting who he was calling by the time they answered the phone, his mind, not wanting to waste any time, being already on to the next item on the agenda. Nik's associates, when picking up the phone only to hear a self-absorbed 'ummm . . .' on the end of the line, always answer, 'Hi Nik.'

Then he gave up smoking cigarettes for health reasons and contrarily began lighting up huge Havanas over dinner. To keep fit he runs five miles to work every morning in his shorts, with his pinstriped suit for appointments in the City in a backpack. In the summer he takes a change of shorts for his meetings. Recently at Cannes, Lenny Henry kept staring at his legs and asking him, 'What are those two pieces of string hanging from your trousers?'

What really unnerves people is his habit of using public transport to get to business meetings. While his counterparts mooch around in their BMWs and vintage Bentleys on their fancy expense accounts, Nik often turns up on the bus to discuss million-dollar deals. Sometimes he saves time by negotiating on the bus on the way. He often takes calls on his mobile phone from Los Angeles or New York on the number 88. Oblivious of the effect he is making, he throws the kinds of figures around that his curious fellow passengers only ever see in a telephone directory. I'm too embarrassed to sit with him. His latest thing is jogging to the shops and calling for a car at the check-out point to pick up the weekly shopping while he runs round the park.

They banned his mobile at The Groucho Club. He has to surrender it to the receptionist on arrival as it upsets the members who come to relax and forget about such mundane matters. Nik, on the other hand, is never coy about discussing or asking for money, in any situation. It's his favourite pastime. To him it is just a means to an end, the end usually being a movie. (I wish it were a new kitchen!)

On the rare occasion we take a taxi home from a function, he always infuriates me by asking the driver to stop at the end of the road, never outside the house. He says it's to make it easier for them. I know it's because he's trying to save 5p on the meter (forever the cost-cutting producer). Nowadays it is only because of the risk of my temper that he lets them drop us at the door, and even then it's a toss-up who wins.

When I made the track with Heaven 17 for their album *Music Of Quality And Distinction*, and Nik was still at Virgin, I was asked to go to Birmingham to promote it on telly. Trisha Whitehead, who was then head of promotions there, sent me a rail ticket. It turned out to be second class. Surprised, I pointed this out.

'No one at Virgin travels first class – not even Boy George!' she explained awkwardly.

'Well they had better start now or I'm not going,' I informed her. 'They can't honestly expect artists to perform at their best after signing autographs and having tea spilt over them for two hours.'

Ten minutes later Trisha was back on the phone offering a first-class ticket and roaring with laughter. Apparently the artist and staff travel directive had been issued by Nik in an economy drive. He was puzzled at my request but knew me well enough to believe I meant it. Trisha was wriggling with amusement at the irony that it was me who had given her the opportunity to force a policy change.

I have learnt a lot from observing Nik's business behaviour. In all situations his mode is conciliatory, while mine tends to be confrontational. It is very unusual for a successful businessman in the entertainment industry not to be motivated by ego. Nik seems always to identify so totally with the task in hand that emotion or arrogance never get in the way of accomplishing the project. He has the knack of bringing opposing elements together into original alliances. He is also very brave at being able to look an unpleasant truth in the face and take the responsibility of doing something about it. He has two major attributes which turn me on. The first is his mind: his mental stamina and ingenuity continually fascinate me. The second is his hair. It is black – not dark brown, but black, like a raven's. One day it will be grey like his father's, but hopefully never bald. I would find it very difficult to love a bald man.

Without a business deal to focus his attention on, Nik is an intensely shy and modest man. Which is why he surprised us all at a recent birthday party during a Palace company weekend in the country. I sat and watched him breakdancing on top of the banquet table, Chianti bottles and brandy glasses flying everywhere. Waitresses stopped serving and bemused kitchen staff ran out to see what was going on. When he simultaneously tried to dance and balance his birthday cake, which was alight with sparklers, the hotel manager lost his nerve and ran alongside the table trying to grab the cake from him before it turned into an incendiary device.

The girls from accounts egged him on mercilessly. When he stripped off to put on his birthday present of a luminous tracksuit and jumped off the table, they followed him out of the private room and on to the disco floor next door, causing such a rumpus that the other diners refused to pay their bills.

Certain faces turned apprehensively in my direction during this free-spending frolic. I refused to interfere . . . it's up to him how he enjoys himself on his birthday with his own company. I don't mind what he does, it's just so good to see him coming out of himself. On our first date he was so shy he kept slipping down his chair and under the table.

After that second Cannes Film Festival, Palace applied for and received an '18' classification and a theatrical certificate for Sam

Raimi's horror movie *The Evil Dead*. As video was a brand new industry and had no classification regulations, everyone presumed, reasonably, that theatrical certification covered video too. So the film was released simultaneously in the cinema and on video. Then all hell broke loose.

Nasty ghouls appeared horrifically and unexpectedly out of the woodwork. The media, in their frenzy to amass their lucrative pounds of fleshy readership, seized their gory moment. 'VIDEO NASTIES!' their headlines screamed. 'CHILDREN UNDER THREAT!' the copy splattered. The pages oozed with stomach-churning images. In their hysterical ignorance they lumped *The Evil Dead*, a film straight out of the classical horror movie genre, with uncertified hardcore exploitation rubbish.

The Director of Public Prosecutions, without any further investigation as to the appropriateness of *The Evil Dead*'s inclusion with these other types of video, took all the titles straight from the newsprint and put them on a hit list. Nik, believing in the validity of his movie, refused to withdraw it from sale. Instead, he supplied all the video outlets that bought the movie with a legal defence pack and a promise to stand the court costs if they were prosecuted. The DPP, with its bottomless pocket of taxpayers' money, then started a series of local prosecutions of dealers stocking *The Evil Dead*. Up and down the country legal cases were going on, funded by Palace. Sinking even deeper in to the manure for his point of principle, Nik still refused to withdraw his film from sale.

Finally they raided Palace's distribution company, and with their haul of copies of *The Evil Dead* personally prosecuted Nik as chairman of the company for contravening the Obscene Publications Act. This could not be taken lightly; it is an imprisonable offence.

On the day his case came up, I stood on the doorstep and waved goodbye with Amie at my side and Jack in my arms. I can't deny I was frightened. I wondered whether they sent you straight down or let you come home first for a change of clothes and a toothbrush. At lunchtime Nik rang to say that he had been blessed with an extremely well-informed judge and the case had been thrown out. The DPP's office had been ordered to pay Nik's costs and told off for wasting public money.

A few weeks later, at a charity screening, Palace premiered *Absolute Beginners* with Princess Anne as their guest. Nik's task was to be host, look after her, and present all the stars and film-makers in the line-up after the screening. As he has a terrible memory for names, I stood behind him ready to prompt him in case he was tempted to do his usual and call everyone 'darling'.

The same year Palace released *Kiss of the Spiderwoman, Nightmare on Elm Street*, and co-produced *Letter to Brezhnev*. The year before they had put out *Paris Texas* and *Nine and a Half Weeks*, and had produced Neil Jordan's follow-up to *Company of Wolves, Mona Lisa*, featuring Bob Hoskins' Oscar-nominated performance. Almost every month there was a film to premiere and masses of interesting people in town to entertain.

By this time Palace had become the hottest film producer and distributor in the UK and headed the new wave of 'young guns' in the industry. At Cannes they were now chased around by directors, writers and foreign distributors who wanted to work with them, and instead of a *pension*, Palace stayed in a huge apartment on La Croisette, overlooking the Festival de Palais.

I would sit on the terrace in the evenings, watching the sun go down over the Mediterranean and the flashlights pop as the glamorous audiences tripped along the red carpet to the various premieres, picking through invitations and choosing which party to attend.

The premieres are all a bit posh and dickie-bow. Nik and Steve are always having to blag the doormen to let in their unsuitably dressed film stars and directors. The same old dress suit or pair of evening shoes goes round and round the Palais, in and out of the Gents and through the front entrance again on different people. Steve spent the whole of one screening barefoot . . . we were grateful he did not lend his trousers.

My favourite part of the day was always the early hours rendezvous at Le Petit Carlton where the less salubrious end of the industry, particularly the English, gathered and crowded out into the street for a spot of low-life fun. Along with everyone else I let my hair down. I have been known to sing arias from the upstairs balcony with the barman down below. The Palace contingent takes it in turns to be carried back to bed. One morning I got up to go to the loo and tripped over Neil Jordan snoring happily on the floor along with various other film notables. Another pile of people, having been unable to fit their key in the keyhole, lay asleep outside the front door.

At home, our bedroom has been taken over by scripts. I have to negotiate vast stacks of them in order to get to bed. I put my favourites on the top. One evening, over a drink, the director Peter Richardson, for whom I had just played a brief cameo part in *Eat the Rich*, asked me how he could ensure that Nik read his script of *The Pope Must Die*. I suggested that I could put it at the top of the pile if he wrote in a scene requiring a handbuilt eco-friendly kitchen, which I would promptly grab after the shoot.

'But the film's set in the Vatican!' he remonstrated. 'And anyway the Pope can't cook!'

It took two years to prepare *Scandal*. A lot of the old Establishment people did not want the film made and did their best to stop it. Nik and Steve realized that the event was an important precursor to the 'Swinging Sixties'. It signalled the fall of the Establishment and set the scene for the explosion of creative talent from the young working masses, a radical social and economic change. Regardless of the sometimes devious and often blatant pressures put on them to stop, Nik and Steve pursued the project with relish. It was meant to be a TV production, but as each successive door mysteriously but firmly closed on them, it was decided that the subject was hot enough to make into a film. They had ample encouragement from me, Christine Keeler being one of my adolescent fascinations.

While Nik was setting up *Scandal* a persistent stream of late-night production phone calls from LA, which started as soon as my head hit the pillow, began a Freudian association for me between the name of Profumo and bedtime. Coincidentally, one of his relatives was living in the same street. One morning she accidentally rammed the backside of her jeep into my car whilst parking. In all innocence she immediately gave me a cheque to cover the damages. Nik, his imagination fired by other more serious efforts to stop the film, refused to cash it, pinning it on his office wall as a memento.

All in all, you don't get much sleep sleeping with the producer.

Wheel of Fortune

AT THE BEGINNING OF 1987 I had taken the brave step of starting driving lessons again. Of course everybody laughed, thinking that because I was so scatty it would take me years. But I was determined. The secret of learning anything is to find a teacher you can trust completely, then let them do their job. Nothing is more inhibiting than criticism, either for a teacher or for a pupil. I found an instructor who was a real nutter, but he was committed, and was not offended by my loose tongue in times of crisis, which usually started as soon as I sat at the wheel. This was a major plus.

We drove around Regent's Park and Westbourne Grove while he calmly recited his poetry to me and expounded on his philosophy of life. He had great insight into people's characters and how they expressed it in their driving. When I told him I was worried about my inconsistency, he said I was consistent in that I could be relied upon to be completely inconsistent! When I had trouble getting the feel of the clutch he suggested that I took my shoes off – this worked wonderfully, so I continued to drive barefoot. After thirty-eight lessons (one for every year) I took my driving test.

This time I was not hampered by an audience – or shoes. Just before we entered the test centre I witnessed a car crash. With this in mind, I drove as slowly as the Park Lane traffic flow. I was on continuous alert, so keen to anticipate any sign of danger that I could almost sense people coming out of their front doors. My heart was thudding so loudly I could hardly hear the instructions. When he said turn left I pulled into a pub driveway by mistake and he fell about laughing. To everyone's surprise

207

(except my instructor's) I passed first time. I rushed straight out to buy a car.

I drove over to Morrissey's Knightsbridge flat. He looked dishevelled and worry-laden, his familiar high stiff quiff flopping at half-mast. Although it was almost summer, a fire blazed in the hearth and 'Top of the Pops' blinked silently at us from the TV screen. The Smiths had managed to complete *Strangeways*, their last album for Rough Trade Records, amidst much personal discord, before swapping from this Indie label to the comparative luxury of EMI. The move brought the disagreements between Johnny and Morrissey to a head. The magnificence of their inspired musical collaboration was now reduced to painful disharmony, accompanied by the wretched orchestration of legal wrangles.

I felt sick. I had watched them grow from young, green hopefuls to full-blown pop heroes, and now to see them withering towards disbandment was truly depressing. I am fascinated not only by what factors contribute to the creation of a great phenomenon – how it emerges and develops – but also by how long it lasts and what eventually destroys it. There are so many lessons to be learnt. Everything goes through the cycle of birth, maturity, decline and death. Whether it leaves behind it something of value depends on what it was based on, just like a person's life. The Smiths was no ordinary group; they had had something original, something special – they really touched people's lives. I could not believe it was happening. Nor could Morrissey. I'm sure he thought that things would just blow over and Johnny would come round like he had always done before. I tried to cheer him up by playing him some of the material I wanted to record. I left him the tape and promised to bring round some new tunes by Chris Andrews, of whom he was a great fan.

This was a time when Morrissey really needed a close friend. Johnny is fairly easy to get along with, but Morrissey can be exasperating. He seemed never to have learnt the art of friendship, and I felt desperately sad for him, imprisoned in his self-imposed solitude. Of his acquaintances I had met, surprisingly none was his intellectual equal or shared his emotional depth, and certainly none had the experience to relate to his current predicament. So he was stuck with paid professionals who were not attuned to his wavelength and cared little anyway. This all struck many familiar notes in my own tone scale.

I was careful not to take sides as I did not want to alienate Johnny. Nor did I offer any business advice as I felt my best qualification was as an unbiased friend offering support. Having vowed not to interfere, I groaned each time a new 'expert' came on the scene, further complicating matters. From where I was standing, all Morrissey's problems started with himself – his insecurities and the way they made him behave. It was during this dark period for both him and me that we shared some of our closest exchanges. There is such a warm heart beating under the stylishly affected exterior with which he protects himself from the world – honestly!

That summer of '87 I performed again at the Gay Pride Festival, with Richard Coles, Mark E. Nevin and the lovely Tom Robinson. Tom's famous anthem, 'Glad To Be Gay', which he updated and sang along with the crowd every year, had taken on a new slant since he had recently begun his first strong relationship with a woman. He was quaking with fear in anticipation of the audience's reaction. Of course they adored him, they do every year, and every time he still gets frightened that they won't. We had rehearsed Lou Reed's song called 'Perfect Day' in Tom's studio the week before, but he was unprepared for me to start singing it all wrong in front of an audience. It was just such a lovely atmosphere, with the warmth of the sunshine and the people, that I forgot myself and started daydreaming. I looked round at him and stopped the musicians. I thought Tom was going to explode with sheer terror. 'No worries,' I told the crowd. 'If it's worth doing we can always start again and do it properly.' Mistakes don't bother me too much. Everyone makes them. I knew everybody loved me anyway. We then performed a heartfelt version. The sun shone. It was such a perfect day . . .

I followed this by an appearance at the Women In Music concert at the Hackney Empire with artists like Girlschool and

Shelley Anne Orphan. On the way home I heard announced on the car radio Dusty Springfield's intention to sing on a Pet Shop Boys single. This seemed like a rerun of my partnership with the Smiths on 'Hand In Glove'. People started nagging me again about working with Johnny or Morrissey. I did not consider this an option. If I was to record, I had to go forward and establish my own style first. There was no point, no personal satisfaction, in going over old ground.

Cilla Black continued her mega-blast Eighties comeback, assaulting our living-rooms with her family TV shows 'Blind Date' and 'Surprise Surprise'. I was not tempted by offers in that area; I did not feel ready yet to become a celebrity presenting things. It would mean the kiss of death to my budding singing career.

All through the tour I had been plagued with requests by well-meaning but misunderstanding friends to release old material. The hit Lulu had with her uninspired revamp of 'Shout' that same year, and then Pet Clark's pedestrian 'house' version of 'Downtown' added fuel to the argument. I did not want my past turned into a seven-inch cliché. Moreover I was trying to launch a new career that had contemporary relevance, and in the long-run this short cut to record sales would prove counter-productive; it would just re-establish what I *used* to be in people's minds, and make it even more difficult to present something fresh. I wanted to go forwards not backwards.

It seemed no accident that Dusty, Cilla and Lulu had all surfaced again at the same time. We always did things together in the Sixties, we were always vying for the number one hit. I had the most – three (oops! ancient competitiveness popping out!) – but we all had different audiences. I wonder if anyone could have imagined then how we have turned out today.

Dusty used to frighten me. I never knew what to say to her. She seemed so much older and more sophisticated than me. When she sang she waved her arms around and posed as if directing traffic. She had old-fashioned make-up, high spiky heels, a bouffant hair-do that went out of style a decade before, and loved wearing those sparkly frocks that made me feel so uncomfortable. She was a real one-off. Her voice was wonderful and her songs were great. She spent much more time and money on her productions in the studio than I could afford, and had a reputation for being a highly strung perfectionist. In a man this would have been described as 'a professional attitude', but women were not supposed to care so much about their work then, and she pissed a lot of people off. However, her deep respect for her work means that we now have some wonderful recordings to remember her by.

Cilla was a bit of a frump when she first came down to London from Liverpool. A Raphael and Leonard haircut and John Bates clothes gave her a miraculous transformation. She did long stints at the London Palladium. I have this image of her there on stage, lit by a solitary pin-spot, belting out heavy-duty ballads, her pale skinny arms stretching up and out from her sleeveless long frocks like branches from a tree. During the years of pantos and summer seasons this impassioned *chanteuse* gradually turned into the chummy comedienne we are more familiar with today. To envisage that change would have taken a huge leap of the imagination.

Lulu was always a cheeky bum-wiggler. A lot of come-on with no pay-off. Her miniskirt and flick-ups shook in suggestive unison, but the songs were innocent enough. I never understood why she did not make a bid for international stardom when she had the American hit 'To Sir With Love'. Maybe her appeal was peculiarly British. Although her hips swayed, she never thrust her tits. She was the acceptable face of Sixties naughtiness, a 'nice girl'. As she matured, any hint of sexiness was quickly diluted by her BBC TV series so as not to offend the family. Lulu, more than any of us, has proved consistent over the years, always working, no tantrums or nervous breakdowns, a Mary Whitehouse supporter and a great all-round entertainer.

Dusty, Lulu and Cilla all emerged from the madness of the times relatively unscathed, in one piece. My heart really goes out to those others who were unable to survive intact, the ones who did not have luck on their side. There are plenty of them. One such performer was Kathy Kirby.

Kathy was out of step with the era's mania for contemporary teenage images. Hers was decidedly more mature. Although she was very young, she went around all tarted up like a thirty-year-old and was most famous for her red glossy lips which practically stuck to the screen as she oozed out of the television set. With her Marilyn Monroe curls and dresses that were unfashionably tight, inside which her figure curved round alluringly, Kathy Kirby was more of a turn-on for our dads. However, she managed to make a few hit records, mostly out of up-dated old tunes like Doris Day's 'Secret Love', and for a while was very successful.

Our paths did not often cross professionally. What we did have in common, though, was managers who had a penchant for gambling. Hers was an ageing band leader called Bert Ambrose. As we were both under age, Kathy and I would often find ourselves sitting side by side outside Crockford's waiting for our elderly mentors to finish on the roulette table.

Evie loved to book me to sing at casinos. These were the only times she would accompany me to work. Of all the glamorous gambling places in Europe at which I played, her favourite was Cannes . . .

As I went on, the sky was still alight with a gigantic celebratory firework display. The casino hall glittered with all the trappings of uninhibited luxury. The men wore tuxedos and the women wore sparkling indications of the size of their husbands'/ lovers' bank balances around their ears and throats. Each laced and ruched table was piled high with red roses and liberally dotted with brandy glasses. I wore a turquoise miniskirt, with a top cut off at the midriff and beaded with crystals that twinkled under the spotlight.

My entrance was greeted with absolute silence. It was more like walking into a morgue than a party. Luckily I could not see the fashionably disdainful looks on their faces as I went through the motions of my first song. The song was accorded no response whatsoever. For a moment I thought they had gone home, but there was no mistaking the glitter of all those diamonds. It occurred to me that when someone pays a lot of money for something, they feel they can treat it how they like. Before I had time to dwell on this, the resident band launched, somewhat too readily I thought, into my second number. This was also received in silence. Two can play at this game, I thought. I'll continue to sing, that way they are obliged to pay me. But that's *all* they've bought; I'll be damned if they can have my attention. So I broke the unbreakable rule of performance and deliberately turned my back on them, ignoring them entirely for the next song.

To my surprise I was greeted by cheers. When I turned they were all standing and applauding, throwing the roses from their tables. One man crawled on to the stage and threw himself *à mes pieds nus*. '*Now* we know where we all stand, we can enjoy ourselves,' I announced, and as a special concession finished my act in French.

When I came off, the casino manager was beside himself with joy. Apparently the previous acts had been a major American star who only managed to get through one song before leaving the stage, followed by an even bigger American star who had walked straight on and straight off in disgust. So this whole fiasco had less to do with Talent and more to do with Attitude. As usual I left by the back door, as I was too young to walk through the casino. I went to bed while Evie enjoyed the rest of the night at the roulette tables gambling away her commission.

One of the high points in Evie's life was when John Aspinall asked me to sing at his birthday party at Clermont's, his gaming club. As membership of this club was extremely exclusive and geared toward the more aristocratic gambler, Evie had so far been unable to gain admittance.

I shared the stage with some of John's famous lions. Whether they were drugged or extremely tame I don't know, but they were very well behaved, and just prowled majestically around like kings of the jungle do. I met and befriended many admirers there, most of whom chased me all over Europe, which was rather flattering. One in particular made a bit of nuisance of himself while I was in Vienna for the Euroyawn, following me around in his flashy sportscar. With the eyes and the ears of the world on me it proved extremely difficult to keep him away from the notice of the press. Somehow I have never found a weak chin attractive, which fortunately saved me from the fate of doing guided tours around my stately home instead of my rock tour around the universities.

Evie, on the other hand, had her eye on Bernie Van Cutsem, who in turn had his eye on me, because I made him laugh. I thought he was a really sweet man, but Eve, being a racing fan, was very impressed when she found out he trained horses for the Royal Family. When Bernie asked me to Ascot, Eve jumped at the invitation, dragging me unwillingly round the royal enclosure.

I was bored to tears, but Evie was a bookie's dream. Nothing, not even the British weather, could dampen her enthusiasm for gambling. For a while I presented endless cups and rosettes. She even had me giving away prizes to greyhounds.

Around the end of the Seventies I read that Kathy Kirby, whom I had not seen since our lonely vigils outside Crockford's, had had some kind of breakdown and had been admitted to a psychiatric hospital for treatment. Feeling extremely fortunate that I had not ended up there myself, I contacted Kathy through her new manager, a well-meaning man who found himself out of his depth when confronted with Kathy's 'theatrical' outbursts. I wrote and then arranged to visit her.

I went by tube and bus up to the hospital in North London. I was let in through a high security door, and asked by the matron to wait in a side room while she was giving out medication. During this time I was kept entertained by various patients who came in to get a look at me. One in particular, 'Gary', arrived in his pyjamas. Wanting to impress me, he went to get his best clothes and then proceeded to take all his things off and change into his suit in front of me. I was not sure how to behave so I tried to carry on as if I was backstage in the band's dressing-room instead of a medical establishment.

'Gary' was extremely interesting. His disjointed communications made a lot of sense to me. His random statements were beautiful and had a poetic infrastructure all their own. I was really enjoying our conversation when a nurse came in and disturbed us. 'Gary' was so angry at having lost my attention that he began tearing the leaves off all the houseplants to get it back. The nurse explained that he should not have been with me. I was told off and taken to another section which was also locked, and then on to Kathy's room.

The nurse left the door open behind me while I was there and I turned to take a look at Kathy. She was lying on top of her bed in a pink nylon negligee, looking the spitting image of Evie. I thought my eyes were playing tricks. Then she smiled and looked every bit as pretty as she ever had.

Kathy was desperate to talk. The words came tumbling out and the tears came tumbling down. Her story, which shall remain her own to tell, was enough to drive any sensitive soul round the bend. I truly sympathized with her experience. It is hard to keep a grip on reality when everything happening to you just does not make sense.

In the middle of all this a woman came charging into the room, tipped Kathy out of bed and started rummaging under the mattress for a musical score that she accused Kathy of stealing. Kathy calmly turned to her as if being thrown out of bed were an everyday happening and insisted that she had never seen her silly score and to please go away, she was entertaining guests. The fellow patient backed out of the door, still grumbling.

Kathy put the bed back in order and threw herself on to the mattress dramatically. 'That's "Edna". She's always doing that. She can't even write music.' I could not stop laughing.

'You get used to all that stuff in here,' she said matter-of-factly.

I went quite a few times to see Kathy. I told her how to chant, but she was so heavily sedated I'm not sure how much sank in. After a while the staff began to trust me and gave me permission to take Kathy out for a walk.

Kathy wriggled with pleasure when I told her the news and slung on her mink coat over her pink negligee. As soon as we were outside she grabbed my arm and asked me to take her to the nearest pub. It did not seem like a very sensible idea, but Kathy talked me into it with her girlish enthusiasm. After just one drink combined with her medication she was extremely tiddly. Frightened of attracting too much attention I tried to keep her quiet. I could just imagine what the papers would say in the morning. I got her out of the pub but she ran for a passing bus. I grabbed her by her mink coat and pulled her off the platform. We giggled all the way back to the hospital like any two girls on a silly night out. As I delivered Kathy safely to the nurse, the key turned in the lock behind her like the turn of a knife in flesh.

Shortly after that, Kathy suddenly checked out, and I have not seen her since . . .

There was something not quite right about the material writers were submitting to me for my planned album. I could not put my finger on it. I knew deep down that I had something original to offer. The trouble was that I did not know quite how to express it. I was not sure that these songs were 'it'.

A postcard arrived from Morrissey that started, 'Hello angel, Do you think I care too much? . . .' and then went on to express his doubts about these same songs. The message hit home. But instead of feeling depressed, I was inspired. I had a cassette of a tune Chris Andrews had written for Morrissey to add lyrics to – I played it. Out popped a melody and words from my head. Suddenly I had a song called 'Hello Angel'. Maybe this was what I had to do. Maybe I should try writing more myself?

I had nothing to lose.

Hello Angel, Do you think I care too much?
Hello Angel, Here's a vicious touch
Go on and be a devil, blaze a trail up in the sky
Like an avenging Gabriel, spread your wings and fly
But oh you seem to lack that essential thrust
You seem to lack that essential drive
And I want you to surge on upward
Purge the heavens and survive
Why do I want you to be so brave?
Why do I want you to lead the way?
You should know better kid –
Because you always did
Hello Angel, Do you think I love too hard?
Hello Angel, Here's a vicious barb
Go on and be a devil, blaze a trail up in the sky
Like an avenging Gabriel, spread your wings and fly
But oh you seem to lack that essential gnash
You seem to lack that essential bite
If you want I'll be your conscience
I'll push you upwards into flight
Charming all the birds out of the trees
Bring the doubters down to their knees
You should know better kid –
Because you always did –
Oh Gabriel spread your wings and fly away
High up in the sky away . . .

PART THREE

Spreading My Wings

Bath Nights

By September 1987, the Smiths had left Rough Trade Records, signed to EMI and split up with much acrimony. Morrissey was left on his own with the new record contract, while Johnny went off to play on Bryan Ferry's album and Mike and Andy started work with Sinead O'Connor.

Around the same time, I went to see Mark E. Nevin's brand new band, Fairground Attraction, play in the acoustic room at the Mean Fiddler. It was wall to wall with tartan-shirted, lager drinking A and R men, all pretending to be uninterested. I stayed for two numbers, and marvelled at how, considering Mark had not only conceived and formed the band but also written all the material, the singer Eddy could treat him on stage like an inconsequential background noise. It didn't seem to bother him. I wondered how long this could last. None the less, they signed a record contract for a tidy sum with RCA soon afterwards, and all in their garden seemed lovely.

In October, Morrissey rang to ask me to join him and Stephen Street in the Wool Hall Studio just outside Bath. Stephen was producing and co-writing Morrissey's first solo effort. I could take him a cassette of recent Chris Andrews tunes to hear. I packed a toothbrush and a biography of Virginia Woolf and drove westward in my brand new Mitsubishi, feeling wonderfully independent behind the wheel.

At the Wool Hall, a farmhouse idyll with recording studio *en suite* nestling cosily beside the towering remains of an old castle, I was greeted by Morrissey offering hot flapjacks and cups of tea. He fussed around the old pine kitchen like a broody hen. An EMI recording budget provided a working environment that was a far cry from the stark basics of Matrix, the last studio

221

in which we had worked together on the song 'Sheila Take A Bow', from what turned out to be the final batch of Smiths' recordings. The cook arrived and asked me to check the evening's menu and to choose my room. 'They've been so excited about your visit they've driven us all to a frenzy,' she confided.

Morrissey showed me around the place, mentioning past visitors, pointing out who had slept in which room. Peter Gabriel there, Joni Mitchell here . . . he stood in the doorway, eyeing the room fondly. I could almost see her fronds of golden hair curling over the bed's fat pillows. 'OK, I'll take this one,' I said, wanting to please him.

Dinner was an intimate vegetarian affair. Morrissey, Stephen and I sat around a large pine table supping burgundy. They had my stay all planned out. After the meal they would take me over to the studio and play me some tracks, then if I was into it we could drive into town and go to a disco. 'A disco!' I asked Morrissey, puzzled. 'That's hardly your style. I didn't know you could dance.'

'Neither did I,' he replied mysteriously.

'He's been out grooving almost every night,' Stephen informed me.

Morrissey continued to knock back the wine in uncharacteristically hedonistic fashion. He giggled and burped a lot. This was all going to be rather pleasant, I thought. Then to my amazement Morrissey leant forward and said, 'Tomorrow we can go for a work-out at the gym – did you bring your swimming cossie?'

'*You*! In the gym!' I was stunned. I gulped down another glass of wine.

'I've been teaching him how to train his body – it's good for his voice,' Stephen confided, adding, 'I'm a real believer in physical fitness.'

'Mmmm . . .' I thought. I shot a glance down his chair at his tight, neat little attributes and was very impressed. A nice taut bum is an asset to a producer as you spend a lot of time talking to it while he leans over the mixing desk. If he could do the same for Morrissey . . . the mind boggled.

We braved the cold night air to go to the studio across the courtyard. My chair was positioned with precision in front of the speakers, but I was too nervous to sit down. I prowled around trying not to be affected by the intense atmosphere, trying to make light of things. They played three tracks in quick succession.

Morrissey could not look at me; he could not look at anyone. He stood hunched self-consciously over the controls staring at the volume meters. During the last song, 'Maudlin Street', he turned and caught my eye with such a pained expression. His desire to be special, to be admired, to be brilliant, was so naked, so touching, so vulnerable. At that moment I dearly loved my delightful, delicate, delinquent friend. I cried, he cried. I sensed his fear and I felt so frightened for him.

I've never met a star who did not always know that one day they would shine for all to see. There is a kind of genius in certain people which at a certain time in their life, when all aspects fall into perfect alignment, creates an electrifying conjunction of quickening energy. They become a star. Gloriously they light up the midnight sky. We stand on the earth and admire their brilliance. Being unaware how to recharge this energy, their star all too quickly burns itself out and fades back into the darkness. Although they have always lived with the inevitability of this astral flight, because they don't know *how* it happened or what caused it to happen, only *when* it was happening, they just don't know how to recreate it. They spend the rest of their existence wondering how, trying unsuccessfully to make it happen again. Their star dissolves back into the universe in a desperate state of unfulfilled potential like a vast black hole. Heaven knows how many burnt-out supernovas are wandering around in the darkness looking for the 'light switch', the source of creative regeneration. Maybe Morrissey was scared that his star could also wane.

We were joined in the car by the engineer, nicknamed 'Psycho' for reasons best known to himself, who drove us to the club. Morrissey and I spent the night gossiping away in a dark corner. When he wanted a drink, Stephen, who looked after the cash, ordered him one, and when he wanted to go to the loo, Stephen, even though he didn't want to go himself, led him there and back like a doting father.

All I will say about the trip to the gym in the morning is that Morrissey has such good legs he should have been in Wham! . . .

During lunch Morrissey revealed the underlying purpose of my presence there.

'Would you sing some harmonies on a track called "Please Help The Cause Against Loneliness"?'

'Well, let's have a listen and I'll see.'

I drove around the Avon countryside learning the song from a cassette. Stephen took me into the studio, made sure I was comfortable, then went to the control room and left me alone, slamming shut the huge soundproof door and locking me in. I was a willing prisoner. Stephen turned down the lights and played the track to me. Sitting in the dark I felt like a baby in the womb, with the mike lead attaching me umbilically to the world outside. Instinctively I sang.

I listened to Stephen's disembodied voice float down the cans into my mind, coaxing, offering suggestions, encouraging this forty-year-old child like a paternal protector. A lot of young people (older people too, come to think of it) are too awestruck to direct me properly, but I felt comfortable and secure with Stephen. He told me that we had worked together before, although I had not noticed him, when he engineered my recording of 'Jeane' with Johnny Marr.

The mornings were spent taking leisurely breakfasts, talking artwork or admiring the first photos of Morrissey's budding partnership with Stephen Street. In the afternoons he and I browsed around the bookshelves of Bath, searching for inspiration, and singing Fifties pop duets in the car to take Morrissey's mind off my novice's driving skills. In the evenings, while they fiddled around in the studio, I sat in front of a crackling open fire and made notes for the first chapters of a book. Later, as a special treat, Morrissey, who understood and had great empathy for my competitive need to win, helped me cheat at Trivial

Pursuit. It was all so enjoyable that I was loathe to leave. I promised I would try to come back.

I flew home. I don't think my wheels ever touched the motorway, I was so inspired. My mind was all right, burning with ideas. As I drove past the Natural History Museum I realized I had forgotten to give Morrissey the Chris Andrews tunes. I put the tape on, and within two plays nearly had the lyric of a song. I drove round and round Hyde Park until I completed writing it. This made the collection of songs I wanted to record up to three – 'Cool About You', given to me by the Jesus and Mary Chain, and two of my own compositions, 'Hello Angel' plus this latest one, 'Nothing Less Than Brilliant'.

A few weeks later, on the spur of the moment, I decided to return to Bath. On arrival I asked about 'Please Help The Cause Against Loneliness'. Morrissey told me that they were not going to include it on the album as it did not fit the style of the other songs but . . . why didn't I record it myself? I liked it, and it suited my voice . . . 'Why not indeed?' I thought. Now I had four songs.

At the studio, along with Stephen who also played bass, were Andrew Paresi on drums and Vini Reilly on guitar. With those other musicians there, the chemistry was rather different.

'I can't tell you how much I love them all,' Morrissey gushed in an unaccustomed expression of deep affection. (He was later to have one of his radical changes of heart and blow them all out.) They all seemed deeply in love with him too. It was intriguing to observe each vying with the other for his attention, his laughter, his approval, or his admiration of their musical prowess. They tiptoed around in his presence as if on eggshells, not wanting to offend their maestro.

Andrew was the most profoundly affected, being an intensely emotional young man with enough unresolved hang-ups to fill a man-sized wardrobe – the stuff that Morrissey worshippers are made of. When this was channelled positively into his drumming, the result was a unique quirky style. When it was not, it was excruciating for him and everyone else.

That evening, when we had eventually decided we were all

going out clubbing, a socially unconfident, fashion-conscious Morrissey paraded around for me in his room trying on this outfit and that – What should he wear? How did he look? Did I like this jacket? It was an ironic reversal of the dressing-up he gave me for my first appearance with the Smiths in Hammersmith. He had long since lost his naivety and was now acutely aware of the impact of his formidable presence.

We assembled in the dark entrails of a slightly dated Bath nightclub, and huddled behind the warm familiarity of the throbbing speakers. One by one the musicians ventured on to the dance floor, peeling off the layers of self-consciousness with Wildean gestures. Stephen tangoed me expertly round the room with the practised precision expected of a physical training instructor.

Joined at last by their master, the acolytes encircled Morrissey in a tight protective mandala. Jokingly, the notorious celibate toyed with their flat male breasts in turn as onlooking eyes bulged with fascination. I stood aside, declining the public fondle. It was highly amusing to see him enjoying his charismatic effect on his audience.

The circle of nirvana was suddenly broken by a blonde who appeared from nowhere. We looked on, transfixed with undisguised jealousy as she brazenly ransacked our little clique, stealing Morrissey away for a quick shimmy, blasting him with cigarette smoke all the while. He returned sheepishly to his possessive flock, eyes glazed and reddened – probably from the nicotine.

To everyone's relief this episode was quickly superseded by a guest appearance by Morrissey and me on the dance floor. Everyone cleared a space as we jived to – of all records for the dee-jay to have picked – the Smiths' 'Sheila Take A Bow'.

Morrissey spent a lot of time locked away in his room, suffering the familiar last-minute torture of searching for exactly the right word to finish a lyric. I could almost feel the panic rising in his throat as each moment brought him closer to the end of his debut album, to the final word, the last say. Once I held him close for comfort, outside the studio, sinking into the softness of his red cashmere jumper. To my surprise he opened up and exuded back. Forgetting his usual jarring physical awkwardness, he allowed himself to melt into the oneness. Back and forth the sympathetic communion of spirit flowed. I knew he could not allow himself this luxury again. Although it was not quite goodbye, it certainly felt like adieu to the Morrissey I used to know.

I was beginning to feel restless at the Wool Hall. I found all the jostling for Morrissey's attention rather unbecoming. I thought I should be taking advantage of my resurgence of mental energy and getting my own album together. One morning I packed and left. When I got home another cassetteful of musical ideas from Chris Andrews awaited. I jumped into my car and played the tape at full volume. By the time I had driven up the Bayswater Road and back I had written my fifth song for the album, 'Take Him' – all about a curious incident in a disco . . .

Why Are We Waiting?

ON MY RETURN FROM BATH, on the basis of some excerpts from a couple of rough chapters I had written, I agreed a publishing deal for a book with Mike Fishwick from Collins, neither of us knowing quite how it would turn out. I was surprised how easy-peasy it all was compared with getting a record contract. A few discreet meetings with editors in darkened corners around Soho and Bloomsbury, offers proffered over the telephone and a quick drink at Groucho's, and it was all done. Nik bought me a word processor for Christmas and I started becoming computer literate. There's nothing quite like deleting a few thousand words by mistake to give one an incentive to learn.

In another burst of creative ignition I wrote a fourth song with Chris Andrews called 'I Will Remain'. Adding this title to my list of Things To Record, together with a re-mixing of 'Hand In Glove', and the incomplete track of 'A Girl Called Johnny', the Waterboys song, I now had a total of eight songs for the album. I put it on the back burner to simmer while I tapped out my meditations on Word Star.

In February, in response to a business visit I had made to Milan the previous year, the Italian impresario Claudio Trotta asked me to appear at the San Remo Song Festival for the first time in almost twenty years. My musicians had now disbanded, apart from Mark, with whom I had continued to make occasional appearances for various charitable or political causes connected with AIDS or Nuclear Disarmament. Mark had just finished his long-planned album with Fairground Attraction, so I was surprised when he jumped at the offer to come to San Remo. It was definitely for love, not money.

I didn't realize until I arrived how much I had missed Italy – the chaos, the melodrama, the food. In the Sixties I was in and out of Italy all the time. Pierro and Bruno from the record company always used to negotiate the restaurant and the lunch menu before money was ever mentioned. When they enquired about my work availability, Eve would say, 'She's been on a busy schedule. She's very tired. Tempt her with some pasta.' I have many sun-soaked memories of long languorous lunches seated under the shade of vines, peeling fresh figs and downing *espresso* after a scrumptious meal.

At work nobody thought you meant what you said unless you tore your hair out and screamed at ninety decibels. This suited me fine. Coming from the tight, prissy background of Britain, the Italian experience was a volcanic release of all those pent-up passions that had lain dormant in Dagenham. Italy was like an affirmation of life. I believe I became quite a different person when my feet were on Italian soil. The language made my singing looser, more fluid; I loved recording in Italian. Even in photos I looked different. Italians, along with most Europeans, have always made a big thing about their grand prima donna stars; in England, female artists were still thought of as bill supports and stocking fillers. My love affair with the countries of Eastern and Western Europe that evolved through my work pattern there, fuelled by my aptitude for languages and fascination with foreign culture, explains why the development of my particular style was so different from that of my Sixties contemporaries like Lulu and Cilla. It also saved me from the winter pantos and the summer seasons at the end of the pier, for which I am eternally grateful. The role of *La Grande Dame* has always suited me more than that of Aladdin tights. My friends take the mickey and call me Dame Sandra of Dagenham, and call Rosie the Dame Mother.

Twenty years later in San Remo not a lot had changed, except that the artists taking part in the song competition now sang to backing tracks. Along with the danger of things going wrong, some of the excitement and anticipation had disappeared. As a guest performing outside the competition, I was singing the way I preferred – live. This had its problems.

I rehearsed in the afternoon at the casino. A full orchestra of rhythm section, woodwind, brass and masses of strings was at my disposal. The sheets of music and genteel playing were a far cry from the hip-grinding sound of my band at the recent university gigs. I felt stuck in a time warp. By coincidence, the orchestra was led by the same conductor as on my first appearance on Italian TV in 'Studio Uno' when I was seventeen. This was cute but, although the parts still suited 'Girl Don't Come', a mammoth hit sung in Italian – '*E Ti Avrò*' – in the Sixties, they did not go with the stark Eighties realism of 'Jeane'. I managed to convince everyone, without hurting any feelings, that 'Jeane' should be accompanied only by Mark on the guitar.

That evening the audience, mostly toffs in tiaras, quickly recognized the first song and sang along as they do in Italian song festivals. Then, to my surprise, during 'Jeane' they began to pick out their own refrains and choruses, standing up and applauding wildly every few bars. 'I wish Morrissey could see this. It's outrageous!' grinned Mark in my ear while I tried to concentrate on keeping time over all the clapping. I doubt if anyone, least of all me, would have envisaged a Smiths song being received in such a way in such surroundings.

On the plane home, Mark had yet another drink and asked me how long it took before a pregnant woman 'showed' and if it were possible to sing when you were about to have a baby. So that was why he had been drinking so much – Eddy was pregnant, and before the band had their first record out. 'We daren't tell the record company, in case they drop us. Do you think they'll notice?' he fretted.

Fortunately for them they were signed to RCA, newly headed by Lisa Anderson who had broken all the rules and had two children and looked after four more while pursuing her career as a record mogul. While I was pregnant with Grace in 1970 I was made to sing sitting down on 'Top of the Pops' so that no one would notice my bulge, and maybe to prevent her slipping out unannounced while I was dancing around – I dunno. They had funny ideas in those days. When 'Perfect' was released it went zapping up to number one in the charts, and Eddy danced about wearing baggy clothes.

By comparison, my own recording situation was an uphill struggle. For some reason I was stuck half-way, immobilized by doubts. After all that hard work and preparation for the album, my self-confidence dissolved into thin air. I had a complete and utter block based on the usual questions – Is it all worth it? What have I got to offer nowadays anyway? Shouldn't I settle down and do something more 'becoming' for a forty-year-old going on forty-one? Was Japanese flower arrangement a more suitable pastime? I seemed to be waiting for something to happen – but what?

I went to talk things over with my friend Beryl at Manna restaurant where she was working. Traditionally, waitressing and singing seem to go hand in hand. Even I have done my stint of waiting at tables. Not when I was younger while building up a career, but much later when I was in my thirties and trying to feed and support myself and Grace, alone. It's not easy being a single parent, but to me, poverty was a reasonable price to pay for independence and the chance to restart my life before it was too late.

After Jeff left for a trial six months, which I must explain – in his favour – was of my choosing and not his, he looked after us well financially – although erratically, as was normal for him when it came to money – for a month or so. Then, following an argument concerning my wish to become an independent person and to retain privacy about my social life, even though I knew it might be at the cost of him withholding financial assistance, the payments suddenly ceased. So did communications. I did not think that this 'punishment' fitted the 'crime', but Jeff's way of dealing with disagreements and emotional pain was to stop talking to people, to cut them out of his life for hefty lengths of time, sometimes for ever. Gradually he started coming round to see Grace again, but the subject of money was now a no-go area. As he has never offered an explanation I can only guess at his reasons. Although he kept impressing upon me that he had little money, I came to my own conclusion – that when *I* began to value myself, he would come to value me too. I decided that, in the meantime, Grace and I would have to look after ourselves.

I had no savings as I had lost everything when his business went under. I kept telling myself that I had always had the ability in the past to make lots of money . . . but could I do it now? Alone? Without Jeff for emotional support? Or Evie to do the deals and push me forward? I felt such a wimp; such a novice; such an innocent in this world. I did not know the first thing about everyday dealings with money and the basic necessities of life, the kinds of things that most other people pick up in their teens. I had bypassed all these details as I was too busy being a star, cosseted from the small day-to-day realities. I did not know simple matters like how to open a bank account, how to get a loan, how to get a decent plumber or put curtains up, how to budget housekeeping (what *were* rates payments anyway?!), what an electricity meter looked like, what Calor gas was, where the buses stopped, where the tubes went, how to get a ticket, use a public telephone, buy my own drinks, find out about tenancy rights, legal rights, women's rights! I had a crash course in domestic ergonomics. I found energy where I had never looked before.

At first I was still finishing off some singing dates to help pay off bills, but without the business debts I had no incentive to continue. Being on show made me suffer acute discomfort at my marital and financial plight. Although nobody was actually aware of what I was going through, my performances could not lie. I could not bear people looking at me. I felt as if I was transparent; as if all my skin had been stripped off, that my insides were bare and exposed with no protection. I went through agonies under the glare of the spotlight.

Each morning I crept tentatively downstairs wondering if there would be any of those dreaded manila envelopes waiting on the doormat, whose imagined contents made my stomach lurch in fear. Was it another unknown debt presenting itself? A writ? A summons? For many years these were the reminders, the final demands, of my past with Jeff.

To make ends meet I started selling off our furniture, old clothes and jewellery. Not knowing how to go about it properly I did not get very good prices, so the money quickly ran out. In order to go on a religious pilgrimage to Japan, I sold the remainder of my art deco collection and art nouveau pieces, except for my set of miniature china nude ladies whom I could not bear to part with. Nowadays they display themselves seductively over the Adam mantelpiece with the knowing ease of women who've been there and back and survived to tell the tale.

With all my savings and possessions gone, the only option left was to get a job in order to feed, clothe and pay the rent for Grace and myself. I did not know where to start. I had never had a job before. Beryl was waitressing with a few friends in Roscoe's, a Soho restaurant where my old mate Alfy was the cook. On the spur of the moment I asked the manager for a job. He thought I was joking, so I pretended it was for research for a book.

On my first night I worked so hard that I ached all over. I put in a lot of effort and managed to get good tips. It was dark so nobody recognized me, and anyway customers never look directly at a waitress. I was so happy there and had such a laugh with all the other staff.

The restaurant was right opposite the *Evita* show, so a lot of theatre people came in. One night I served Andy Warhol a *crème de menthe frappée* when he sneaked out of the performance during the interval. The last time I had seen him was in New York where *he* had offered *me* a drink as a guest at his studio. He did not recognize me as a waitress. It was a strange experience to go from being a celebrity to a non-person. I loved the anonymity.

Su Pollard, who was then unknown but behaved as if everyone *should* know her, came in a lot. She kidded me that she was a great stage actress who was down on her luck and had been forced to work at the Co-op. She gave a wonderful performance –

tears, hanky-wringing and everything. Being naive enough to believe her, I offered to give her a meal; she had earned it. A few weeks later she was a TV star.

I used to finish work in the early hours of the morning. Strolling home through Soho past the empty fruit crates and the tarts and pimps in the doorways, with my treasured meagre wages in a money pouch slung round my hips, I felt as safe as houses. I felt like a princess. I felt like the world was my playground. I felt really in control of my life.

One day I took a chance and did the lunch shift in full daylight. Within minutes the place was full of tipped-off pressmen wanting to know what on earth I was doing there. It was really difficult. I could not leave my customers, and if they continued to hang around I was in danger of losing my job. I gave them the same story that I had given the restaurant manager, that I was researching a book, and they agreed to come back during my break. I collapsed in tears by the cake trolley in the kitchen with Alfy and Beryl passing me paper napkins to mop them up. There was no way I could tell the press the true situation. I did not want Grace's schoolfriends or my family to read about my predicament in the papers. My parents would be so upset with me and so angry at Jeff. They would not understand. I did not understand. I still don't understand – except that it was *my* problem so I had to deal with it.

Beryl rang Jeff to come and help. He rushed over straightaway and got rid of the press. He offered a shoulder to cry on and masses of sympathy but no financial assistance.

Once my cover had been broken I could no longer continue the job. People came in to buy coffees just to gawp at me. My heaven turned into hell. Eve, with whom I had kept in touch, not realizing that I was not well enough to perform any more, had tried to book me to sing in a flashy new nightclub. On reading the newspapers, the Greek owner rang to cancel the contract saying, 'Why should I want to pay all that money for her as a singer when I can get her cheap as a waitress?' I had news for him. I'm fussy about who I wait on.

I had overheard a couple of waitresses talking about social

security. I had no idea of its existence or what it was for. It's not the kind of information you pick up in Monte Carlo. I decided to find out more.

One morning I took Grace to school, then looked up the address of the local DHSS offices in the phone book. I joined a forlorn and desolate queue of humanity at Tavistock Place. I had never come across such misery all in one room. They sat vacantly, resigned to waiting all day to plead for assistance. The queue consisted of the mentally disturbed, the elderly, the sick and disabled, the jobless, homeless, hopeless, loveless, luckless, those unable to cope: society's take-away, throw-away, disposable population. I had to admit to the lady who finally interviewed me that I was one of them, if only temporarily. The next day Grace and I became a social security statistic, another 'burden on the State'. I was very grateful for the support. I needed a breather so I could get my house in order.

It would be reasonable to assume that I was very unhappy at this time, but, on the contrary, since becoming a Buddhist two years earlier, in spite of life being difficult I had never been happier. I had started on an incredible adventure of self-discovery, a re-sensitizing experience.

Up until this time, being unable to handle the problems that destiny was doling out, I had over the years of the Dark Ages systematically cut off all areas of my life that brought me pain. From the beginning of my Buddhist practice, bit by bit, at my own pace, I had worked up the courage to reassess, change and rebuild these areas.

At this point I was ready to deal with those parts that only deep self-challenge could reach. It was not easy. Some days I screamed, some days I raged, some days I spent locked up in my own private hell under the glass table unable to move or speak, immobilized by uncontrollable spiritual pain and fear. On the other hand, I often experienced such visions, such intense joy.

I know many Buddhists, more pragmatic by nature than myself, who have never had or desired to have a mystic experience, and yet still they have come to an understanding of the eternity of life in their own way. But for me, mystic experiences are essential. I could never have continued without them.

The process of purifying my senses had started quite naturally almost the first day I began chanting. I came to realize that I was a very delicate, ultra-sensitive, highly tuned being. While walking in a busy London street I would suddenly be captured by a traffic noise or a movement in the wind and be drawn into a whirlpool of universal ecstasy, sublimely orchestrated in never-ending loops of melodies and swirls of rhythms. I became aware of every sound – the breathing or sneezing of fellow pedestrians, the closing of windows, the hum of office machines, the nibbling of insects in the woodwork, the shouts of builders on scaffolding, the roar of buses; even the screech of arguing voices took on a divine dimension. I felt I could hear the noises from everywhere all over the world and the cosmos all blended in this outrageous harmony, this bizarre syncopation that set my heart and mind on fire; it was an exquisite feeling, far beyond my imagination. The simple act of breathing in and out was sheer delight. Sometimes it lasted for moments, sometimes hours.

It was the same with *déjà vu*. I've always had it, but as soon as I had become conscious of its happening, it stopped. Now it carried on for as long as I wanted. I stood outside and observed the wonderful symmetry of human beings interrelating, events unfolding.

I could play with my perceptions of this energy too. In my mind's eye I watched a screen of brilliant colours reforming and merging in shapes that I recognized as atomic patterns, though I'd never seen them before. I watched spellbound, never letting my own ideas interfere with the plot of this never-ending, self-perpetuating, quantum drama. I was drawn to the chemical constructions of objects like crystals, and geometric structures like pyramids. I noticed the same structures in the dynamics of people relating to each other, and saw that this beautiful synthesis of energy patterns was universal and repeated and communicated throughout all manifestations of life.

I saw colours and 'halos' around people, and found out they

were called auras. Simple objects like a chair or table glowed, each particle of life incandescent. I stopped in my tracks in wonder at the shape of a tree or a stone, or a tiny money spider, and marvelled at how perfectly their physical properties mirrored their spiritual characteristics, their oneness with the universe. It became glaringly apparent that matter and spirit are inseparable, pulsating with life. This is an important concept to understand if you are stony-broke! If I could develop and purify the spiritual aspect of my life, then the material aspect would follow suit!

I began to understand that everything was '*Myoho-renge-kyo*'. With my entire being I wanted to '*Nam*' to it – to devote myself to it, to harmonize with it, to be one with it, to be it.

I experienced spontaneous 're-birthing', during which I took form from latency, became a foetus, and went through the birth trauma again. I felt so clearly the cord tighten around my throat, and my resistance to joining this difficult planet; the fierce tug between my opposing desires for life and death. I questioned my mother on this and found her story of my birth corresponded exactly to mine. I usually had some kind of confirmation after these 'journeys' that I was on the right track from things like a passage in a book, a painting, a conversation, a news article, or an idea in a film, but not always immediately. It was wonderful to continue to have reassurances like these that I was not going bananas; or that if I was, then I was not alone. There were other people out there feeling the same. I reasoned with myself that even if there was an epidemic of insanity it felt so brilliant that I could not have cared less if I was completely off my trolley, and what's more I hoped it *was* catching.

On a more practical level, my increased sensitivity made me get tiddly a lot quicker and consequently I cut down my alcohol consumption drastically. Another unexpected 'perk' was that I always sensed where the bargains were in the shops, which not only saved money but helped me save precious time trudging round everywhere.

When I was little I always had to guess what my father was thinking or feeling as he was too shy to articulate it. My mum always used to say, 'You know how your dad feels.' Because of this I became sensitive to atmospheres and signs in an effort to understand the unspoken. Throughout my life I had had an ability to 'tune in' to my father's thoughts. I felt an uncomfortable feeling like an electric shock in my middle whenever I sensed something amiss, something that I could not identify but that none the less made me feel anxious. As I began to travel away from home to sing, this feeling transcended time and distance. I could be in another country, or on the other side of the world. I never understood what caused it or how to deal with it and never discussed it with anyone. It was part of my life, like a squint or a limp you don't notice any more. As I began practising Buddhism I noticed it was not exclusive to my father's thoughts. Suddenly, through no conscious effort of my own, I was able to do this with everybody. It was not very pleasant. My head was always full of random information, bits and pieces I 'picked up' from all over the place. I was a cosmic dustbin. This made me very confused. It gradually got worse and worse. Sometimes I felt as if I was plugged directly into an electric current. I would be debilitated by it and unable to concentrate on anything else. I had developed an unconscious habit of crossing my arms over my stomach to protect and comfort myself, or rubbing my hands together frantically to relieve the atmospherics.

One day I met an American Buddhist, an astrologer, in a friend's kitchen. She uncrossed my arms and told me I had nothing to be afraid of and that it was not her intention to hurt me. She pointed to my solar plexus and said, 'You feel it there, don't you?' She explained to me about things called *chakras*, openings in certain parts of the body that receive information that the five senses can't perceive. She told me not to fight it but to trust my intuition because, as a Buddhist in harmony with life, I would be protected by the universal forces and I would receive nothing that I was not able to deal with.

This was such an eye-opener. It was certainly not the type of information you'd pick up in a conversation on Dagenham Heathway or at the Wakefield Theatre Club. After all those years of confusion things suddenly began to make sense, to become clear. I realized I was not in the least bit odd after all. I was experiencing a common phenomenon, a lost form of communication, the awareness of which varied from person to person. Because it was such a part of my nature it was a problem peculiar to me that I had to overcome. Take heart – hardly anyone who becomes a Buddhist goes through all this stuff! On the other hand, there may be some sensitive soul out there waiting to hear this reassurance.

As I continued my Buddhist practice I learnt to distinguish between other people's thoughts and mine; to know my own mind. When anyone projected their thoughts or feelings on to me I was able to identify them and pass them back to their owner to deal with. I began to learn how to let people flow in and out of my life but not dump any of their rubbish there.

Gradually all these things balanced out and merged into everyday living and became just a normal aspect of life, no big deal. I was beginning to be more sensitive to other people's needs, not over-preoccupied with my own, which made me a more rounded, happy person. Becoming less self-absorbed and more self-aware, I started to become a more enlightened artist.

I still have difficulty coping with the pain of international tragedies and the 'buzz', the electrical charge, from the events of great import in our lives; and worse, the depression, the anticipation preceding some as yet unidentified occurrence. But now that I know what is happening to me, know that something is becoming, is about to materialize. I know what to do about it. I can, by chanting, relieve the pressure and fill the void with creative constructive energy.

There is a distinct danger that to the uninitiated all this mysticism might seem a bit like an acid trip. Let me be absolutely clear. IT IS NOT. Buddhism is better.

When I was staying with my student friend in Scotland, he discovered that I had a 'nose' for finding a certain kind of fungi – magic mushrooms. I had no idea what they were at the time and I helped by collecting them for him. He would dry them and package them and send them to his mates. Naively, I thought they were a special delicacy. And so they were . . .

I took my first nibble. Mmm, fun – but not for long. Soon my delicately tuned metabolism found it all too much. The tingling of all my senses in harmonious unison that my practice had helped me achieve quickly descended into a tacky cacophony as the mushrooms took hold. It was thoroughly unpleasant. I could not possibly imagine how anyone could want to be so brutal to the fragile make-up of a human being. You cannot open the doors of perception with a battering ram. Drugs achieve the absolute opposite effect of that intended – they *de*-sensitize. The continual bruising and abusing of the self creates spiritual scar tissue that builds thicker and thicker walls until all entry is prevented. Instead of purifying the senses, they pollute. The body has its own store of natural opiates and stimulants that it releases beneficially at the appropriate time. Over the last decade, medical research has identified at least fifty previously unknown hormones which affect our state of mind and body in different ways. We just need to get our minds and bodies working harmoniously. We don't need to clog up the system with artificial substances. Life is the ultimate drug.

I would also like to make it clear that while the content of my visions and revelations is the essential underpinning inspiration of my practice, the actuality of it is in how I struggle to apply my understanding to life's mundane problems. Because universal truths such as the eternity of life, the oneness of everything, and the Buddhahood in all phenomena are such an everyday reality to me, they give all my actions meaning and direction. In the final analysis, Buddhism is not religious mysticism. Buddhism is *action*.

My mundane problem was that I still had a creative block. I decided to take one step back before I pounced. I did not want to jump all over the place without direction. It was better to bide my time. Everything comes to she who waits . . .

Choose Life

I CANNOT IMAGINE NOW how Grace and I managed in those years without a washing machine. During that time I discovered the joys of the weekly visit to the Launderette. Every Thursday I plodded up Marylebone High Street tugging a shopping trolley piled high with dirty washing, pockets jingling with ten pence pieces. Sometimes Beryl came along with her infectious chatter to divert my attention from my latest 'heavy' book.

On one visit we sat next to what looked like a pile of washing someone had left behind. Suddenly Beryl started talking to it animatedly. She nudged me and said, 'You must meet my friend Phil Sawyer. I haven't seen him since we played together in *Shotgun Express*.' The pile of washing moved and a face appeared from under a woolly hat. 'Can you lend us ten pence for the drier?' he said. After that the three of us spent many a happy hour in the Launderette, talking about Buddhism and watching the washing go round. Phil, who lived locally, came home with us to take a look at our Gohonzons. Soon he was practising himself and received his own.

Phil said he was a guitarist and that he had played in the Spencer Davis Band during the Sixties. This was when he met his now ex-wife; after this his star-studded world had crumbled and disintegrated with alarming speed and efficiency. His musicianship was not that evident to me at first. His guitar, like his life, was in a sorry state.

We started chanting together for an hour and then writing songs for an hour. Added to some work I was doing with Don Gould, who had been my stage music director before, during and after Jeff's business problems, I had the makings of an album. I was still feeling too fragile, too raw, to go straight

241

back into the jungle of the recording industry, so I planned to raise the money and produce it myself.

I had kept in contact with some agents, through whom I began to book myself all over the country in small out-of-the-way venues that hopefully no press would hear about. I quickly learnt how to organize and cost out the shows in order to make a profit, which I put into the recording kitty.

To my relief I was able to come off social security and take responsibility for the family again. The first thing I bought was a new pair of shoes for Grace. In desperation she had placed them hole-side up on my desk. I started to treat myself to a visit to the local hairdresser before each performance. Chocolate digestive biscuits were on the shopping list again. We were back in business. Nothing fancy: we were still cutting corners and budgeting like crazy. Our regular shopping trips on the bread-line funds from the social security offices had turned Grace and me into pretty shrewd consumers, with a great appreciation of everything and anything we were able to buy. We get a great kick nowadays from zooming around the supermarket throwing whatever we fancy into the trolley, and reminding ourselves how we used to live 'When We Were Poor'.

Jeff also began to pay a small but regular sum towards Grace's keep. Although I welcomed his support I found it humiliating having to arrange the payments through some unknown person in the accounts department of his new company, Warehouse. In an effort to be practical, I struggled to overcome my pride.

That year I played mostly working men's clubs and gay bars up and down the country. For the live dates Phil came along as musical director with his battered guitar repaired and polished and sporting a borrowed dinner jacket. I sang through all the golden oldies and gritted my teeth at the end to do 'Puppet On A String' *and* a reprise. We used whatever house musicians were available – some who could read music and were familiar with my songs, and some who definitely could not and were not. A sense of humour was essential.

I sang in all kinds of odd places. Like the venue where the toilets were directly in front of the singing area so people had to walk across the stage to go to the loo. If it happened during a break in the music, everyone could hear them spending a penny.

I worked alongside all manner of weird and wonderful performers from apprentice comedians to drag acts. Often there were no dressing-rooms, so I usually arrived made-up and dressed. Before I went on I would sit in the manager's front room having a cup of tea and being shown through the family photo album, or else I would hang out in a communal backstage area with the other artists.

Once I waited patiently behind the stage curtains for the previous act, an exotic dancer, to finish. I was sitting on some old wicker baskets in the corner. To smatterings of raucous applause she came rushing offstage during her finale number, 'Gold Finger', played economically on a snare drum and an ancient trumpet. She was dressed minimally in a few chiffony bits and some oriental jewellery covering up her naughty areas. The triumphant smile abruptly disappeared from her face as she caught sight of me on the baskets.

'Freddy! Sheba!' she shouted as she lunged at me, pulling me off and extracting from the baskets two large, wriggling pythons. Lovingly she draped one around her bare shoulders and wrapped the other around her naked midriff. She flounced off, casting me a venomous look as she returned to the stage for her encore.

It certainly was not the Albert Hall, but it felt exactly right for me. The audiences were warm and honest, friendly and incredibly appreciative. They were ordinary, unpretentious people whom I felt at home with. I actually began to enjoy my performances. I did not always pull huge crowds, but those that came were ideal for reassessing one aspect or another of my relationship with an audience – like being equals, but at the same time retaining control as the performer they have entrusted with the task of uplifting their evening. I've seen so many artists give in to the tendency to try arrogantly to bully a crowd into submission or be dominated by an audience reaction. Everything depends on self-respect and mutual respect based on the dignity of life. I had a strong rapport with the audiences. Unbeknown to them, they were helping me to change my life.

The money was not brilliant, but it soon piled up. After a week's stint around the North, I finished with a large envelope bulging with cash payments. Feeling really pleased with myself, I took a taxi to the bank in Leeds to deposit it in my album recording account. When I arrived, I hoisted my bag on to the counter, but when I looked inside – the money had gone. I could not believe it. I looked again and again trying to convince myself that this was not really happening. It was like a recurring nightmare; maybe my luck had not changed after all. I was devastated.

I returned home empty-handed. The following week I was contacted by the Leeds police saying that a little boy had brought my money into the station. While he was playing in the street he had seen me drop a package in the road as I got into the taxi. Recognizing me, he had picked it up, and with his parents had gone to great lengths to return it. So there was an up-side to being famous after all.

With Beryl as my accomplice, I flew across the Iron Curtain once again to film performances of all my old songs to be distributed around the Eastern Bloc and shown on TV. We were accompanied everywhere by a State 'guide' employed to 'look after' foreign visitors. I pranced around every day in the snow for the cameras, and afterwards Beryl and I chatted in the bathroom with the shower turned full on to avoid being monitored. I bet they thought I was a nice clean act.

In a year I netted, after all expenses, twenty-five thousand pounds to pay for the album. I did deals on studio time, negotiated agreements with a producer, an engineer and musicians, and worked out publishing arrangements with my co-writers. Brian Johnson started to work for me, getting overseas record companies interested in leasing the tapes. I had come a long way from the clueless dolly bird of the Sixties.

Towards the end of the recording I met Nik. He introduced me to Carol Wilson, who was then running Dindisc for Virgin. She came down to the studio to listen and give an opinion.

She thought the tracks were 'fresh' and 'original'. She would certainly be interested in listening to the final mix with a view to signing it for her label. Phew!! Maybe I was ready to enter the commercial world again after all.

At the beginning of the following year, 1982, I finally finished the album. Brian Johnson took the tapes in to Carol's office. Oh yes, the tracks are still very 'fresh', very 'original', but there was 'no single' so she would have to 'pass'. I came down to earth with a thud.

We had various offers from foreign companies for the recording rights, but I had lost heart and could not raise the enthusiasm to traipse it around the UK A and R departments. By this time I was pregnant with Amie. Suitably diverted I put the album on the shelf alongside *The Alchemist* project to gather dust.

Just before Amie was born, NSUK, the Buddhist lay organization, decided that they would put on a world peace exposition the following spring. It was to be called 'Choose Life'. Its purpose was to incorporate all different art forms and means of creative expression from British Nichiren Shoshu Buddhists to illustrate the Buddhist view of life. This seemed like the perfect outlet for the album.

My friend Dick Causton, the chairman of the organization, suggested that I name the album after the exposition, *Choose Life*. Then Brian and I went about becoming record manufacturers. Jeff helped design the cover.

The world peace exposition was put on in Kensington, just after Amie's birth. It attracted some surprising attention. Katharine Hamnett used the *Choose Life* slogan in a tee-shirt range which Wham! teamed up with their little white shorts for their *Wake Me Up Before You Go-Go* video. Amie and I, as an inseparable couple, she being attached to the breast by her healthy appetite, helped with the public relations and were part of a team who showed visitors around. We did some low-key radio interviews together to promote the event and the album. Amie was happy to eat her dinner while I rabbited away to many a broadcaster's consternation or amusement, depending on their degree of social enlightenment. I also went on telly with Dick Causton for the first of his many broadcasts. These were the very beginnings of my re-emergence into public life after the 'Dark Ages'.

Phil had also begun to leave the Sixties behind. He had dumped the guitar and acquired two keyboards and a mixing desk. His tiny front room was choc-a-bloc with computers and leads. Soon he was writing and producing original scores and soundtracks.

Happily, Jeff's arrangement to contribute towards Grace's welfare lasted right up until the following year. Then, without explanation, a few months before his marriage to his present wife Sue, the payments ceased abruptly. I did not make a fuss. Jeff and Sue were expecting their first baby and I wanted to assist him in any way I could in establishing his new family. It was also vital to me that Grace and Jeff maintained a good father –daughter relationship. I would never do anything to jeopardize that; I was determined that relations between Jeff and me should not influence the way he felt about Grace. Eventually, in the summer of 1987, when Grace was sixteen, we worked out a proper financial arrangement for her.

Meanwhile, it's difficult to explain the enormity of joy, the exhilaration I experienced on receiving, at the end of 1984, the first big royalty cheque from my Smiths collaboration. It was a turning point. It meant freedom and financial independence again after almost ten years' struggle. I was able to afford a nanny, and to seriously, and hopefully more confidently, start rebuilding my career. I danced around the kitchen like the victorious Salome, carrying the cheque on a plate.

Life, Death and Everything

I HAD A PHONE CALL ASKING ME if I had some free time to visit a fellow Buddhist in hospital who was suffering from AIDS. I had plenty of time – thanks to my 'block' about singing. I took the Central line tube and got off at Whitechapel opposite the London Hospital. Outside the ward I was asked to leave all my bits and bobs, given a sterilized gown and asked to disinfect myself in the side room. The red disinfectant curdled menacingly round the sink as I scrubbed my hands.

My first glimpse of Martinus was a bit of a shock. He was having a blood transfusion. Later, as he lay in bed, I started to get to know him. He was Dutch, with eloquent, perfectly articulated English. He had started to practise Buddhism only recently to improve his energy as he was feeling so tired. He quickly discovered the cause of his fatigue – AIDS. He was aware that he did not have much longer to live. So, knowing time was so precious, I was as honest and open as I could possibly be, skipping all the frills and the dancing around of subjects that normally precede a friendship.

This is not as easy as it would seem with a total stranger, and for me particularly so, as I am very, very shy. It was an immense challenge, but the imminence of his death forced me to forget my silly hang-ups and concentrate on his needs. The only thing we had in common was that we were both Buddhists; he wanted to learn as much as possible as quickly as he could, and I was anxious to pass on everything I knew. I felt that my task was to help him to savour every moment of his life, to prepare for his death and to choose how he would like to live in his next lifetime. I had never spent time with a dying person before.

I was not aware of it when my grandfather on my father's

side died. I was told on the afternoon of his funeral, which had taken place while I sat my eleven-plus exam. To my surprise my Uncle John was waiting for me at the school gates. I was not deeply upset; I had never really had a strong relationship with my grandfather because he had always been so ill. I have some nice memories of playing dominoes with him, but mostly I remember him sick in bed. It frightened me when as a small child I was taken to visit him at his bedside. In the cold, damp, darkened room the only sounds were his agonized gasps as he lay on the pillow fighting for his breath. It chilled me to the core. I pulled away from his cheek when I was asked in hushed tones to kiss him. His pale, weary face was the colour of the chalk quarries where he had worked as a child.

My grandfather's mother had died when he was seven, and from then on he had accompanied his dad 'totting' for work on a horse and cart around Kent, while his sisters were put into service. At the chalk quarry in the mornings my grandfather, as a small boy, was placed into a bosun's chair and lowered down the quarry face where he chipped all day until they hauled him up at night. When the authorities discovered him at the age of twelve, his father was put into the workhouse because he had no fixed abode, and there he died. My grandfather was put on HMS *Warspite*, along with other young unfortunates and victims of circumstance, to be trained for the Royal Navy.

When he left the navy after the '14–'18 war, where he was in active combat in the Battle of Jutland and sailed in the trouble spots in Russia and Turkey, he was already suffering from weak health. To support his family he worked first on the barges on the Thames. Then, during the Thirties slump, he took any work he could get, and that was very little.

Eventually my grandfather found regular work as an electrician's mate, and took over his job when the electrician was called up to fight in the Second World War. To the family's dismay he had to give the job back after the war was over. From then on he did the firm's 'dirty' work, crushing stone into tarmacadum to make roads. At night his hair would be matted with the grey dust. His bronchial problems became chronic.

My dad's childhood memories are bleak and impoverished, both materially and emotionally. Nowadays, frilly aprons always make him laugh because when he was a kid the women wore Tate & Lyle sacks tied with rope around the middle for a pinny.

After a means test there was help of sorts for those short of money. My grandmother loathed and feared the assessors coming round to make sure they had nothing worth selling off. These men had the right of access to all your possessions. My grandparents had a second-hand, out-of-tune piano in the corner, which had been given as a present. Nobody could play it, it was just for ornament. It was worthless except as firewood, but the assessors always made a bee-line for it. My father remembers my grandmother worrying, 'That thing is more trouble than it's worth!'

My father was forever tearing his clothes while climbing. Out of necessity my nan was a very good darner and patcher and passed her expertise with the needle down to my dad, who passed it on to me.

When my father was around ten he had a nervous breakdown brought on by the strain of silently holding in the seething anger he felt at the poverty that singled him out from his schoolmates, the shame of forever queuing for handouts in patched clothes, and the frustration of being the eldest son helplessly watching his sick father crawl in to work in order to get the money to pay for his medication. He recalls going to the doctor to ask for some medicine that his father desperately needed, but being refused unless he could come back with a shilling.

My dad was taken to St George's Hospital for treatment for his illness. The best advice they could offer was for my nan to keep him in his bedroom for six months' rest. Bored, he climbed out of the window and hung on to the guttering, where he got stuck and had to be rescued by the fire brigade.

For me this is a horrific glimpse of what life would be like again without the National Health and social security services we have enjoyed since the end of the Second World War. My grandfather died at the age of sixty of chronic emphysema brought on by deprivation and the inhuman working conditions he endured during his childhood and youth, and the lack of medical and social care in his later years. He left my grandmother a widow for sixteen years. My dad now suffers from acute angina, exacerbated no doubt by his unvoiced childhood anguish and the sense of injustice which still haunts him to this day.

On the next few occasions when I visited Martinus in hospital, I chanted with him as he asked. He was finding it really difficult to concentrate on his own because of the drugs he was being given and the drowsiness that was a by-product of his illness. His over-riding concern was for the wellbeing of his boyfriend and another patient he had been teaching how to practise. While we chanted together, I tried to communicate to him as much as I knew, but most of all my strength of conviction – like a life-to-life transfusion. The nurses and doctors thought the effect on him was really valuable.

I was not there when my grandmother on my mother's side died. I was twenty-five. I called her 'Nan'. I adored her. I preferred her company to anyone else's when I was a child. She was a woman of great spiritual stamina, and a fantastic cuddler. I made her tickle me endlessly, 'round and round the garden like a teddy bear', up and down my arm until I exhausted her.

My nan had six children, one of whom died as a baby and one, my Uncle Ben, when he was thirty-two, of tuberculosis. Although I was only three months old when he died, I can remember him very clearly and feel a very strong connection with his life. I remember the sunshine, the curtains and the darkness of the room and I remember recognizing and feeling very close to him, although he never held me.

My mum explains that a few weeks after I was born she took me over to show to him while he was very ill in bed. However, he was so concerned that I should not come into contact with his illness that he made my mum stay outside and hold me up to his ground-floor bedroom window for him to see.

My mum says that Uncle Ben was so handsome that once,

when he took her on a trip to Petticoat Lane, an agent had spotted his thick black curly hair and pestered him with his card, offering him a modelling contract with Brylcream. When Uncle Ben smiled at the suggestion, the agent made another offer on his sparkly teeth. When he fell about laughing, he offered him another deal on his twinkly eyes, and when he walked off with my mum, the agent followed them to the station telling him his slim figure belonged on the catwalk. Uncle Ben shrugged him off saying it was a sissy thing for a man to do.

My Uncle Ben died before the National Health Service was established, in a hospital far away from home, where visits of an hour's duration were limited to twice a week. Nowadays nobody dies of tuberculosis. My mum remembers that despite their extreme pain and suffering, my Uncle Ben and my grandfather on my father's side had deeply desired to live.

My mum's grandmother, Nanny Buckfield, was by all accounts a tiny but exceptional woman. She lived in Stratford and gave birth to three girls and five boys, two of whom died in the '14–'18 war. She was widowed early and struggled to bring her family up alone. To do this she washed all the working overalls of the men in the fibre factory and also had a job at Tate & Lyle's.

My great-grandmother enjoyed a pint of stout on a Friday night, which she had brought to her from the local pub. She would send someone over with the jug from her washstand to fill up and then she would sit on the windowsill and drink whilst chatting with the other neighbours who were doing the same.

She delivered all the local babies just like my nan did after her. My nan brought all her grandchildren into the world except me. She left that to my Aunt Doll because she said my mum kicked up such a fuss about nothing that she preferred them to get on with it alone while she looked after my two young cousins. I took my time and did not join them for nearly twenty-four hours.

My nan and grandad were one of the first families to move out from Stratford in the 1920s to the burgeoning new housing estate of Dagenham. It must have been a joy to my nan not to have to share her house with another family; her own seven-piece brood had been crammed into two rooms and an attic. An inside toilet must have been sheer luxury. They were given priority housing because my grandfather was the foreman on all the electric cabling underground. When they first arrived, the milk was still being delivered in a churn over the field. Soon afterwards, my grandfather had to stop work because of an arthritic hip. I never saw him walking without the aid of a stick. His disablement was a financial blow to the family, but nothing they could not overcome by all pulling together. When he was getting on he often used his bad leg as an excuse to get out of doing things. Over the years my nan always had a sneaky suspicion that he was faking, but could never catch him out. He just sat there tapping his stick. They often stayed at my parents' dog boarding kennels in the country. The nearest neighbour was the pub over the next-door field. One Christmas, while everyone was busy preparing, he took his stick and hobbled over for a drink and, having had one too many, hobbled back. He was found sleeping in an armchair. The pub rang and told my mum that he had left his stick behind.

My mother's stories of her childhood are bursting with life and fun. Most of the activities centred around their house in Barmead Gardens where all the kids played safely in the street, which was shaped like a banjo. They played games like 'Hi Jimmy Nacker' which required them to pile on top of each other's backs until they all fell down, showing off their baggy knickers. Then there was hopscotch and throwing 'gobs', or making grottoes from stones and old shoe boxes. They got their toffee apples and coconut ice from the lady opposite who made them.

They were poor – like everyone else. I remember watching my nan doing the washing in a huge copper pot which bubbled on the stove. Then she wrung it through the mangle in the garden. There were no fridges, so a shady corner of the garden was also the coolest place to keep perishables, on a grid topped by wire meshing called a food safe. On Saturdays we ate toasted crumpets while my nan betted on the dog racing with my Uncle Arthur. Her son, my Uncle John, managed the local betting shop. On Sundays we had winkles and cockles and home-made cake for tea. All the front doors in the 'banjo' were left open and people popped in and out. My mum's family lived in a tightknit community of friends and offspring and my nan was at the heart of it.

My nan and grandad were overjoyed at my success in my teens. It gave them a new lease on life in their last years. They followed my career avidly, keeping up to date with all the current music, helping to run my fan club with my mum. I exchanged regular letters with my grandfather when I travelled abroad. In 1972 my nan died happily of old age, and was followed a few weeks later by my grandad, who could not live without her.

Martinus was feeling a lot better. At the doctor's suggestion he was allowed home so that he could spend his time in a more comfortable atmosphere. He surprised me with a telephone call from a new housing project for terminal AIDS sufferers in East London. He was trying the place out overnight to see if it suited him. But what really excited him was the news that they were making a wheelchair available to him so that he could come to a Buddhist peace exhibition the following week. This meant that his boyfriend, who had so far avoided any discussion on the subject, would *have* to accompany him there.

My friend Paul Henry, the choreographer, and I went to see Martinus together in his new home. The place was so new it still smelt of paint and freshly laid carpet. His health had deteriorated rapidly, but his spirits were high. The drugs had loosened his acerbic tongue and heightened his scathingly perceptive eye. Nobody escaped his attentions. He assaulted everyone with his marvellously bitchy swoops and swipes. We talked a lot about the Russian minimalist music he loved so much that he wanted it played at his funeral. He had decided he wanted to express his understanding of Buddhahood as a classical musician in his next lifetime.

Martinus wanted Paul and me to chant with him, so we lifted

him up from either side on to his pillows. He was a bag of bones – this tall man was now no heavier than a small frail child. As we lifted him, his full catheter bag slipped out from the bed covers and fell with a loud 'plop' on to the floor. With an absolutely straight face he produced a white napkin and with a flourish placed it decorously over the offending object. He then sat up in dignified fashion to chant.

During that hour I developed a splitting headache. Martinus drifted in and out of consciousness. When we finished he was sleeping like a happy baby. I went home to bed to nurse my migraine.

When I was a small child I drowned in everyone's attentions. I remember being passed from lap to lap around my mum's family and friends by people eager to coax me out of my shell. I was painfully shy – stuck up, my mum, like Beryl, and Jeff suggest. She laughs, 'I always had the impression when you were little that you felt you were too good for us!' Later, in my early teens, during unexpected bubbles of sociability I would join my Aunt Jen in a sing-song or mimic a TV personality.

It struck me that I embodied the contrast between my father's emotion-packed silence and my mother's effusive flirtatiousness. It must be this same dichotomy agonizing inside me, the tension of these two opposing forces, that pulls me this way and that; these two powerful modes of self-expression vie with each other to take over. One's heritage is all passed down to each successive generation in the DNA. I'm still not sure whether I am a staggeringly extroverted latent introvert, or an irritatingly intro-verted latent extrovert. You tell me. Anyhow, most of the action takes place inside – sometimes I keep it to myself, sometimes I don't. More and more often nowadays I share it.

Perhaps this inner disunity is at the root of my creative 'blocks', the reason for the stop–start nature of my efforts. Perhaps the struggle to pull the schism together, to become at one with myself, is what releases the creative flow. Perhaps I owe my creative processes entirely to my parents and their ancestors. Perhaps we all do. It's strange that I had always felt at odds with my background, like a cuckoo's egg in a sparrow's nest. Now, for the first time in my life, I felt at home with my family: that I belonged.

I was on the verge of sleep one night when Maritnus entered on the edge of my dreams. I tossed and turned so much, with such energy thrilling through me, that I woke myself up. Martinus was still there in my mind. I listened as he told me about all his concerns. He told me how tired he was, how much he felt ready to die but was held back by the thought of leaving when others were not prepared. I tried to reassure him that only he could choose the time and that if it felt right he should go with it. I suppose this 'conversation' might sound odd, but it seemed very natural to me. There was no separation between his life and mine; this was a dialogue without the encumbrance of words. The communication was direct and instant.

Suddenly I felt this extraordinary feeling of sheer wellbeing; everything was pulsating with light and energy. It was not so much a matter of going towards the light, or being in the light, but that I *was* the light, and so was the entity that I knew as Martinus; everything was the light, the energy; there was nothing else but this shining. We had no shape or form; there were no points of reference at all, only a feeling of all-encompassing oneness of inner and outer self, a total fusion. I was overwhelmed with exhilaration, with joy. The whole of life was rejoicing, as if saying 'Nam' to 'Myoho-renge-kyo'. I had felt such a responsibility towards Martinus at this most critical time in his life. It had often occurred to me that I had to be completely sure I believed all I had passed on to him about Buddhism. At this moment I had no doubts whatsoever. 'It's true! It's true! *Everything* is true! Everything IS *Nam-myoho-renge-kyo*.' Martinus knew it too. His being was vibrating with happiness. I left Martinus there at that place in time and space and drifted back into sleep. The next day I had a phone call telling me what I already knew. Martinus was dead.

Hello Angel

I WROTE A SONG FOR MARTINUS around a tune Clive Langer had written. We went straight into the studio in the middle of the night to record it. The next day Charles and Cathy sent the tape of 'Comrade In Arms' round to Geoff Travis at Rough Trade, telling him I was now ready to make my 'debut' album.

By some miraculous fluke, all the people I wanted to work on my album were free at the same time. It usually takes months, even years, to bring the right elements together, if ever. Curiously, Stephen Street had a break in his work with the Psychedelic Furs because they had run out of songs to record in the middle of their album, so I had my producer. Richard Coles had just returned from a long European tour with the Communards, so I had a keyboard player. George Michael's tour rehearsals were suddenly put back, so his bass player, the wondrous Deon Estus, was free to extend our friendship into a working relationship. Neil Conti, the drummer from my 'Are You Ready To Be Heartbroken?' and 'Comrade In Arms' sessions had a gap in his work with Prefab Sprout. Kevin Armstrong found himself unexpectedly free when his recording with Elvis Costello and Paul McCartney did not work out as planned – so I had a guitarist (and subsequently co-writer) ready and waiting. It was as if a huge void in time had been created to enable me to do this at the precise moment when I was ready.

However, on the second day in the studio Neil turned up in a fluster because he had failed to tell us he was on first call to Prefab Sprout, who were suddenly on the verge of their first big hit, 'The King Of Rock And Roll'. Now, understandably, they wanted him to drop everything and promote it. On the face of it this was disastrous. We had spent the past few weeks rehearsing and arranging the songs together as a unit, and the whole of the previous day working on Neil's drum sound.

Surprisingly, I did not panic. I felt the gods were on our side. After some deliberation I asked Steve to ring Andrew Paresi, whom I had met on the Morrissey sessions in Bath. Yes, he was free. Neil helpfully left his drum kit in the studio to save us resetting the sound.

From that moment there was no stopping us. It proved to be one of the most enjoyable creative periods of my life. We had a great family team. The balance of personalities and the chemistry between us was just right. Everyone was so precious to me.

As the basic tracks were being put down, I did guide vocals behind a glass screen in the mixing-room from where I could see and talk to everyone. Richard scribbled naughty or camp messages over the music manuscript, mostly about the comparable musical merits of myself and Maria Callas, of whom I am a great fan. He held these up to the glass while I was singing – to encourage me/put me off/shock me or bring on a fit of the giggles. How he managed to do this and play keyboards at the same time gives an indication of his unique approach to anything vaguely threatening to be called 'work'. Kevin wore a series of those 'meaningful' looks he dons for inventing chords that require rubber fingers and an ambidextrous mind, and Andrew emoted full pelt all over Neil's drumkit. Meanwhile Deon, probably the most extrovert person I know, with a heart generous enough to match the enormity of his beautiful ego, grooved around the studio like it was Wembley Stadium. The songs just tripped out one after the other – the main bulk of the work having been done in the preparation at mealtimes. This consisted mostly of discussions on how we all wanted to change the world for the better. After one particularly controversial meal break, Kevin decided that he would take up Buddhist practice and put the ideas into action.

Dinners on our sessions have become notorious. Not only for the food and wine, but for the saucy and philosophical content of the conversation. Richard suggested that I should not bother to audition musicians any more, I should check out their skills as a conversationalist, find out what newspapers they read, their political and sexual persuasion, grasp of current affairs, the extent of their open-mindedness and their taste in wines. He reasoned that so much of a musician's time is spent hanging around that it was essential they 'fitted in' – homophobics, Fascists, racists, ageists, sexists, or those with an under-developed sense of humour and wonder, need not apply. I reasoned that it was important to me that the intent of the music had a direction shared by all involved.

My very first band was called the Paramounts. In those days I called very few shots. Eve and her husband Moishe found them for me on one of the many package tours they used to promote. They had a hit record called 'Poison Ivy'. To learn my songs they were sent my first album and two hit singles. Eve booked what she told me was a rehearsal room, but was the lobby of a friend's building she had acquired for nothing. Then we were allowed to meet.

It was not a case of *my* auditioning *them*: I did not know how to audition myself. So on Eve's instructions they started to play. Eve did not know the first thing about pop music, but her sharp stilettos tapped keenly throughout. At times she jumped up, shoved me out of the way and took my place at the mike. Hands on tight-skirted hips, she urged them to go faster or slower. Then she sat down again and lit a cigarette, her Schiaparelli Pink lips tugging hungrily at its tip.

I thought the group looked great. I leant over and whispered as much in Eve's ear. They were young and their hair was long and shaggy. I sensed they would be allies. Their music was good too, though Eve failed to appreciate that. When they finished they looked over at us nervously for our reaction. We must have looked a formidable pair. Having been satisfied that the band would do as *she* told them, Eve stood up abruptly.

'You're hired,' she pronounced, and flounced to the door. She stopped in the doorway and turned. 'By the way,' she added, 'see that you get your hair cut!'

I toured with the Paramounts for the next few years. During

that time we became great buddies, though not as close as I would have liked. Eve made sure that we were always separated by the star on my dressing-room door. I yearned for company of my own age. While I slept alone in faceless luxury hotels, they stayed in cosy boarding houses. While I was driven in a sleek limousine, they crammed into a jolly transit van. I would have done anything to exchange the loneliness and isolation of my world for the warmth and camaraderie of theirs.

On the other hand, they thought my grass was greener. Gary Brooker, the keyboard player, could not understand why I messed around all day in the hotel or dressing-room, wearing paint-splattered sloppy joe and jeans, daubing canvasses with my inner landscapes. I would have preferred a friend to go out with.

'Why don't you buy a groovy suede trouser suit and a fun fur, get yourself a big expensive Cadillac and whizz around town?' suggested Robin Trower, the guitarist. Which is exactly what he did when he became a heavy rock star in America a few years later.

I started to record in French (at last a school lesson came in handy!), scoring my first hit in France with '*Pourvu Que Ca Dure*', a translation of 'Long Live Love'. I was asked to sing in Paris for three weeks at the Olympia, where incredible stars like Piaf and Brel played. They were my idols. I wore their albums thin in my Earl's Court bedsit. This was immensely unfashionable in the Sixties when British was considered best.

'Come here often?' Gary teased as we shared his piano stool for our nightly duet, 'Lemon Tree'. On the first night I had stormed the Bastille and stolen the show from Richard Anthony, the French heart-throb who was headlining the bill. He had already been upset with me during rehearsals, making me cut 'Always Something There To Remind Me', because he wanted to do his French cover version of it.

'*SANDIE CHANTE AUX PIEDS NUS!*' screamed the next mornings's headlines. *Les journaux* proclaimed excitedly that I was '*Formidable!*' '*Merveilleux!*' '*Très chouette!*' Everybody loved me, but I still went home to the hotel alone and wandered lonely as a cloud around Paris every day.

'Look, our life is not as great as you think. Why don't you try it?' challenged Barry Wilson, the drummer, after a cold dreary one-nighter up in Scotland. So I did. I clambered into their over-crowded tranny for the drive home.

This was a risky proposition on their part. I discovered later that Eve was so worried about my 'getting into trouble' and ruining her plans that all the group members on the shows she promoted were left in no doubt that it would be instant dismissal for even *thinking* about laying a finger on me. Whenever an orgy took place, if I was in the vicinity everyone quickly pulled their knickers up and flushed their drugs down the loo. If Eve found out about this escapade she would go berserk . . .

As we crossed the Highlands, the rusty old van began to belch smoke. Somewhere past Cumbria there was a loud bang and a hiss. The van shuddered to a halt. We all tumbled out into the freezing night to look under the bonnet. The general opinion was that we had run out of water. We looked around in the dark. There were no lights for miles.

'Give it some Coca-Cola!' suggested Gary, and poured a bottle into the engine. We all piled back inside and every so often someone would pop out and top it up with another drink. Just past Manchester we ran out of Coke. All the shops were shut.

The roadie took command. 'We'll have to pee in the empty bottles.' He disappeared behind the bush and took first turn. Just before Watford everybody had had a go but me. I began to panic. There was a limit to being one of the boys, and this was it . . .

In 1967 the Paramounts became Procul Harum and had their huge hit with 'A Whiter Shade Of Pale'.

The new band took time off from recording while I did the first set of vocal overdubs. For the first time Steve and I had only each other to relate to. I felt my efforts weren't good enough. My insecurity made me think that Steve did not really like my voice and that he was only working with me to please Morrissey. On his part, Steve was suffering badly over a disagreement he had just had with him. It was impossible to ignore the atmosphere when every line I sang of 'Please Help The Cause Against Loneliness', which they co-wrote, seemed to plunge the knife in deeper for Steve. The spectre of Morrissey haunted the studio. Everywhere I turned his presence was felt, like a forlorn ghost desperate to be laid to rest. I felt such tension that I was unable to sing. I thought it best to clear the air.

I spilled out my doubts about Steve's motives for working with me, and he quickly put my mind at rest. The atmosphere was considerably lighter after we had exorcized that ghost. Steve and I were free to develop our own closeness, our own working relationship, independent of our friendship with Morrissey.

We started doing some instrumental overdubs. Steve thought that 'Nothing Less Than Brilliant' needed something bright and warm added to it, like a harmonica. I had recently been to Brighton to see a Pretenders show and remembered seeing Chrissie playing one. I asked her over to the studio. To be fair she did warn me, 'I'm not a real player you know . . .'

It took quite a bit of knob-twiddling and sampling to get it right, but in the end the harmonica sounded great. I was so pleased to have Chrissie on the album, as it acknowledged how much her friendship had been a part of making it happen.

Beryl organized a group of friends from the Human Revolution to do some vocal parts with me. Then, for a giggle, we invited my mate, the dee-jay Janice Long, whose needle time had been so much part of building the independent music scene in Britain, to play castanets on the track.

With Kevin I wrote two more songs called 'Strange Bedfellows' and 'Flesh And Blood'. We recorded them and then Steve re-mixed John Porter's production of my Smiths collaboration on 'Hand In Glove'. During all the arguments between Rough Trade Records, Morrissey, and Johnny Marr, the multitrack tape of that recording had gone missing. We spent weeks trying to locate its whereabouts. In desperation I rang Johnny. It turned up mysteriously on our mixing desk one morning. I still don't know how it got there. When we played the tape, Johnny was rabbiting away in the background, chivvying Andy and Mike to greater heights. We left Johnny on the front of the mix saying, 'I want you to turn it all up now – *really* loud!!!'

For the final touches I booked into Westside Studios to finish off 'A Girl Called Johnny' with Clive Langer. When I turned up Clive was, as usual, socializing in the bar. Instead of ringing through like I normally do to tell him I had arrived, I decided for some reason to go over to the bar for a drink myself.

I recognized two people as I walked in. One was Clive. The other was, to my surprise, Johnny Marr. The two yards between us felt like two miles until we met and hugged. I was so pleased to be reunited with him before the album was over.

Johnny's cocky assertiveness was gone, I encountered a softer, gentler person. His stark, black, slicked-back hair was now a longish mop of pale brown which swung boyishly around his face. He appeared really vulnerable and raw and it was obvious he had been through a lot of soul-searching. The search was not quite over for him yet. When I invited him to play some guitar on my song he became incredibly suspicious that Morrissey had something to do with it somewhere.

'Isn't he producing it?'

'No. Clive is.'

'Hasn't he written the songs?'

'No, only one.'

'This song?'

'No. It's a Waterboys song.'

'Is he singing on it?'

It was obviously still a very sore spot. I did not want to resurrect any old ghosts for Johnny, so I did not pursue it any further. We went to our respective studios next door to each other, he to record a Sixties Bacharach number for a film track with the Pretenders, whom he had recently joined and me to record a gutsy contemporary song for my Indie album. This game of musical chairs all seemed rather ironic – me, a figure from the past trying to break new ground, and Chrissie and

Johnny from the present teaming up to go retro with the composer of my first hit.

Geoff Travis suggested I call the album *Hello Angel*, after the postcard that started it all. Soon it was time for the packaging to be designed. My confidence crumbled away. I had been so sure of the way I wanted things to sound, but I had absolutely no idea how I wanted it to look. The reality was that I was an older woman in a business overrun by deliciously pubescent bimbos and intellectually strident young women. I certainly could not compete with that. Frantically, I rang my old Buddhist mentor and friend, Kazuo Fujii.

He laughed and said, 'Sandie you can no longer be pretty . . .'

My heart sank at the vocalizing of this dreadful truth.

'. . . but you can be beautiful by having confidence in yourself and your purpose in life.'

Ah! A ray of hope!!!

I got straight to work on my confidence.

When I was eighteen I had the appearance of someone unaware of their looks or their impact on others. By the time I was twenty-five I remember how acutely aware I had become of having to live up to people's expectations, and though physically attractive (for some tastes!), my insecurities increased accordingly. I was forever being looked at and judged at face value – or so it seemed to the socially immature wife of a clothes designer surrounded by fashion *cognoscenti*. I hated it. I grew to think that was all I had of interest to offer to anyone. At thirty I had so little self-esteem that I thought I was really old and ugly, thoroughly unaccomplished and completely unlovable. In an attempt to make me feel better, Jeff asked his model friend Sue Mann to come and stay with us in Ireland and help me with my make-up. In the photos I looked pretty enough, but I felt hideous and depressed inside. I had no direction, no purpose. By that time in my life I had seen everything around me disintegrate, I was thoroughly disillusioned, and I had no hope at all for the future. So the way I looked had very little to do with what was happening on the inside. Somehow, despite all the skill of Sue and the photographer, this came through in the photos. There were no wrinkles around my eyes, but the world-weary sadness of them belied my youthful looks.

In casual snaps taken of me when I was around thirty-five I looked wonderful, as if I was really in love with life. But at forty I was uncomfortable sitting under the now unfamiliar, formal glare of the spotlight that I had so studiously avoided. My album was a strong and honest statement. The cover had to reflect that too. A casual shot would not be correct, I had to look as assertive as I sounded. I wanted to come across peace-loving but not passive; someone not just satisfied with armchair philosophizing but ready to roll their sleeves up and take action.

I chose the photographer, Peter Ashworth, and talked him through my worries, from lighting to make-up, from wrinkles to sexuality, then on to symbolism. The less I concentrated on the superficiality and the more I concentrated on what exactly I wanted to put across, the less concerned I became. The clearer I felt about what was going on inside, the clearer I saw the way it had to look on the outside.

My friend Paula Owen flew in from Milan to do my make-up, and Dawn from Charles's office and my daughter Grace came along to do wardrobe and opinionating respectively. We started off by shooting my face with no make-up or lighting effects. When I finally managed to look at the Polaroids without laughing or crying, I saw that I did not look so bad after all. However, I decided a little make-up would definitely help. So Paula began performing her miracles, while Peter concocted the dramatic lighting we had decided upon, Dawn sewed the silver CND buttons on my jacket, and Grace read Evelyn Waugh.

I was really happy with the end result. We used objects and ornaments with particular qualities – angels, harps, earlike euphoniums, prayer beads, violet and amethyst flowers, body shapes and hand movements under stark Yin and Yang lighting. I love to communicate in the profound language of symbols. This primitive forgotten tongue bypasses conscious thought and sinks deep into the realms of what Jung would call the collective unconscious, or what Buddhists have always called the karma storehouse. Everyone innately understands symbolism. I like sending arcane messages as an underscore, a sub-text to my main theme. I send some knowingly, and others quite unawares, without the censorship imposed by the hang-ups of my conscious mind. My most effective symbol was, of course – my bare feet! Nowadays I am more subtle . . .

Through this experience with the album cover my conception of beauty has changed. For me, a beautiful woman is someone with the openness to perceive and admire the beauty around her, someone who points out a ravishing sunset, or notices the care put into a gift; someone who continually seeks the best in people. This is the kind of person who is attractive to be with.

The next hurdle was publicity. I am such a pressophobic. In the past I have been unable to recognize the person that they say is me on the news stands. My inner world seemed totally at odds with my public persona. One gets stung so many times by writers/editors looking for the shocking quote or compromising picture, disregarding the humanness of the subject or the better nature of its readers, that the distrust leads to a mutual antagonism. I don't know how many times I used to pick up the paper and moan, 'I never said that!' Not big libellous things, but a niggling accumulation of tiny inconsequential tedia. I developed a fear of tabloid journalists. I have spent whole days in the past, even weeks when the news was as explosive as divorce scandals or business crashes, crawling around the house on my hands and knees to avoid the eyes of the cameras peering through the window and peeking through the letterbox, and wearing earmuffs to drown out the noise of the journalists banging on the front door.

You get used to choosing your words carefully, never giving anything away in case your quote is used out of context. It is a skill that most stars who manage to stay around acquire in order to survive. It leads to some very bland, unforthcoming, unprovocative interviews which, quite understandably, are a chore for everyone concerned. I really am no good at any type of phoniness. If I am less than honest it makes me physically ill; added to that, during my many years of disappearance from public scrutiny I got into the habit of expressing myself freely without fear or worry. I was not prepared to compromise my integrity, but I was afraid this would leave me wide open to misinterpretation. Besides, I felt very possessive towards my well-nurtured semi-anonymity. On this basis could I ever enjoy a relationship with the press? It was a big challenge.

I was fine with radio or even television interviews, especially live ones, because they cannot be edited. Also, the voice and the eyes cannot lie, so my sometimes camp humour or humane concerns would come across as intended, not as insensitive or sentimental. With the release of *Hello Angel* I jumped from the safety of my warm cloud of familiar friends into the cold air. Could I fly?

The interviews were hour-long, back-to-back, four days a week. At first I squirmed and wriggled with embarrassment like an angel on a pin. But eventually, exhausted by the effort of being a victim, I got up, dusted off my wings, and zoomed about the interviewers wherever I pleased – I even began to enjoy it. This inspired some to try their wings too – 'the temptation to put down your pen and have a good chat is overwhelming' – and left others feeling a bit dizzy – 'One leaves a Sandie Shaw interview feeling somewhat affected.'

My stomach churned in anticipation of the reviews. I need not have worried – they were ecstatic. They could not have been better had I dictated them myself. I was stunned.

Of my voice they crooned, *The control, the tone, the precise but still natural sounding diction.* Wotcha cock! And more fortissimo, *Sandie tinkles the ivories of her grand piano voice* – shove over Ms Callas!

Of my songs they waxed lyrical, they were *perfect pop narratives* – Hi Pop Pickers! My writing had added *an extra dimension to my artistic armoury* . . . Joan of Arc, come on down. One song was *an obsessive doomed search for perfect monogamy* . . . Ophelia would turn in her grave. Another was *all belted raincoats and callous innocence* . . . I could always turn my pen to detective stories.

For the gourmet the album was *succulent, a platter of salty aphorisms and sugared almonds.* – Hic! For the penny pincher it was *a bargain at the price.* For the spendthrift they advised, *buy one for your Ma and one for you.* – Watch it!

Any ageists in the house? Apparently not. I was *at 41 sexier than ever,* (tell that to my husband); I had *pulled off the priceless trick of growing up without growing old* (well, actually it did cost a few quid), and the album had achieved *the complete and utter rejuvenation of the possibly god-like Sandie* – pass the Grecian 2000!

Not surprisingly, sex reared its ugly head. I had *the touch of an angel, shimmering sensuality, naked enthusiasm, brazen thrust* . . . hang on! Is this my album or one of Nik's videos?

They thought the whole exercise was *a jangling tale of self-assertion.* Oh, YES!!! It was *vastly significant, highly accomplished, an absolute gem.* Shine on! I had *a thundering confidence* – wait till they read this book!

Of my present status they said I was *a space chanteuse, back from time travelling,* and *beholden to no known life-form or philosophy* – New Age or what?

What future did this planet have in store for the *Dagenham Diva,* this *goddess with myopia and an enigmatic smile?* (that's a classic!) Well . . . *Talk of this woman's Sixties success is no longer relevant. The Queen is dead . . . long live the Queen.*

I rest my case.

If you can take all that on board and remain level-headed – well . . .

I crossed the channel to promote *Hello Angel,* back and forth to Spain, Germany and Italy. I returned to San Remo and sang in the international rock and roll tent instead of the casino. It was not so much fun. Charles and I visited the restaurant we had discovered the previous year with Cathy, which specialized in hand-made pasta parcels stuffed with chopped artichoke hearts. Rough Trade's Italian licensee, CDG, bubbled as appreciatively as a bottle of Asti Spumante, while I sparkled on about the album on the promotional merry-go-round until my fairy wand ran out of spells and the tinsel began to fade. Unbeknown to me, my hard work was all in vain. A few weeks later CDG ran out of fizz. They were taken over by Warner's and ceased to be Rough Trade's licensees. So unfortunately *Hello Angel* was not given the chance it deserved to spread its wings in Italy.

I returned home to recharge. Then more press. Four days a week of endless phone conversations about my 'latest product'. Fortunately my enthusiasm for *Hello Angel* remained strong, and I tried to give each interviewer something different; though after a while one's head spins and the thought of a halo and a pair of wings has a more devilish ring.

I visited Germany frequently to plug the album. On one occasion I agreed to do a family TV show, providing no reference to 'Puppet On A String' was made to deflect people's attention from my new offering. The German agent gave me his assurance that this would not happen. I did the run-through of 'Nothing Less Than Brilliant' in the afternoon for the cameras, then retired to the '*MASKE*' room for my make-up.

The show was going out live. I stood behind a screen ready for my cue to walk on to camera. As I waited I could hear the compère prattling away in German. I felt sure I heard him say 'Puppet On A String'. 'No, must be my paranoia,' I thought. Suddenly the unmistakable oompah strains heralded my entrance.

The screens opened to reveal an empty space. I was already off. On millions of TV sets all over Germany I could be heard shouting offstage at the agent as I chased him around the studio, upstairs and over the scaffolding. 'How dare you deceive me! How dare you exploit me!' Then I heard the opening bars of 'Nothing Less Than Brilliant,' so I calmly returned to my spot in front of the cameras and sang my song. The audience, believing it to be part of the show, thought it highly entertaining. It must have looked very funny. Whatever, I had made my point.

When I arrived in the TV studios at Frankfurt for another album plug the following week, the atmosphere was bristling with expectancy. Would I check the script? The lighting? The running order? The canteen menu? They went out of their way to consult me on each camera shot and call-time. They loved the song I had chosen to sing, 'Comrade In Arms', and asked me to explain certain lyrics to them exactly. No reference was made to my previous German episode. The studio was right next to the American army base. I sang wearing one of my CND outfits as US jets flew overhead.

In Cologne I chatted with students and discovered the most amazing vegetarian restaurant with cordon vert cuisine, serving dishes like the Buddha's Delight – my favourite item on the menu. I spent many a night there, eating and talking Green politics, a favourite German pastime.

Hello Angel was gradually released around the world and the flow of appearances and interviews was incessant. As the independent music scene does not have the financial or organizational clout of the major international companies, you have to make up for it with a hundred times more effort publicizing your offering with underground 'street cred' publications and shows to make an accumulative impact rather than the one major swipe at sales. This can work if your product distribution is flexible and highly tuned to its marketing. It also tends to work well on home territory supported by word of mouth, but abroad it is just a tiny drop in the ocean and demands consistent time and effort from the artist. Nevertheless, it is great fun to flout the system.

I heaved a sigh of relief as the Christmas holidays beckoned. I was exhausted. In the New Year of '89 I went in to hospital for a stomach operation. The day after I checked out I performed at a CND benefit. During the second song my operation wound opened, became infected, and I was out of action for a month, during which I reflected on the previous year's activities.

A lot of my new fans wrote regularly. I read every letter and spent three weeks replying by hand in varying depths as the mood took me. I pinned on the wall or wore all the angel memorabilia they sent me: the ornaments, postcards, original artwork, tee-shirts, poems, jewellery and written intimacies, thanking each person in turn for their thoughts. In the old days my poor mum was hard-pressed to get me to sit down to write autographs.

I was booked to do another TV promotion of *Hello Angel* in

Germany. Although not fully recovered physically, I honoured the obligation. Katharine Hamnett sweetly lent me one of her green 'Clean Up Or Die' outfits, complete with leather studded jacket and G-string.

To be truthful, I did not enjoy the show. Although it was bursting with new friends, it felt like a chore. It seemed to me that the album had already served its purpose brilliantly. I had found the confidence to succeed in completing something I had set out to do – without artistic compromise, being absolutely true to myself – and had an amazing reaction. We were now trying to make *Hello Angel* out to be something other than intended: a debut, a hint of promise, a reaffirmation of life, an adventure, an opportunity to spread my wings. They would not stretch any further.

I woke up one morning and thought, 'Promoting this is turning into a full-time job. I only ever wanted to be a part-time megastar. Now I want to write my book.' With this in mind, I kissed goodbye to my beautiful Indie album, *Hello Angel*, and watched it fly away, high up in the sky away . . .

Footnote

SOME PEOPLE BELIEVE IN DESTINY OR FATE, that things don't just happen randomly. I understand it as karma – cause and effect. Nothing just happens. We cause it to happen. Everything that you are, that is happening to you in the present, is an effect of a cause you have made through thought, word or deed in the past. Everything you think, say or do today is the cause for what you will be, what will happen to you in the future. For instance, someone who continues to respond angrily or slanderously to the people and events around them is making the cause for more people and events in their environment to make them angry and unhappy. Someone who lives dominated by fear is making the cause to attract situations that perpetuate that fear. Someone who makes others suffer is making the cause to suffer themselves. But someone who strives to see the potential for change, for joy, in everything they encounter in life, and grabs it with both hands, is making the cause to be happy and fulfilled. Once you understand cause and effect – karma – you are master or mistress of your own fate.

I have not changed my basic nature. I'm still scatty, an emotional volcano, prone to occasional bouts of massive self-doubt. I still love to live in a fantasy world and have a child's outlook on life. What I *have* changed is that nowadays it all seems to work in my favour.

The kind of tapestry we weave of our life depends on the relationship we have with our pure inner selves. I think of the warp of the cloth as our spiritual understanding and the weft as the day-to-day happenings. How we deal with tragedy, success, loss or gain, depends on the extent to which we develop and reveal the depth and strength of our spiritual life. The tapestry

can be rich and warm with rewarding experiences and relationships or impoverished and restricted with lost opportunities and
bitterness.

Although I believe in angels, that we have the power to
transcend anything, I don't believe in fairy stories any more. I
don't believe there is someone out there who's going to wave a
magic wand and make everything turn out fine. I do believe
we are able to change our destiny, and that of the world,
ourselves. This is the greatest challenge, the final frontier, the
ultimate personal adventure. All it takes is wisdom, compassion,
and courage – and the all-encompassing desire to do it.

Index